CONTENTS

Workbook to Accompany
A BIOGRAPHY
OF THE ENGLISH
LANGUAGE

C.M. Millward
BOSTON UNIVERSITY

Holt, Rinehart and Winston, Inc.

Fort Worth   Chicago   San Francisco   Philadelphia
Montreal   Toronto   London   Sydney   Tokyo

Acknowledgments appear on page 267.

ISBN: 0-03-029359-6

Printed in the United States of America

0 1 2 3   085 9 8 7 6 5 4 3 2 1

Holt, Rinehart and Winston, Inc.
The Dryden Press
Saunders College Publishing

Chapter 7:   Early Modern English   *187*

Chapter 8:   Present-Day English   *234*

PREFACE

This workbook follows the organization of *A Biography of the English Language*. It can, however, be used with virtually any other textbook of the history of English because most of the exercises are either self-contained or presuppose only access to material that will appear in any college-level textbook on the subject. The exercises vary greatly in length, difficulty, and approach. Some are so simple that the instructor (although rarely the student) may find them trivial. Others will challenge the best students. All have the aim of forcing the student to think about, not only earlier stages of English, but the relationship of these earlier stages to their own language. All are based on the assumption that the hands-on approach is the most successful path to understanding the structure of any language.

Most of the exercises use actual unedited examples of the language at various stages rather than made-up ones, even though manufactured examples are easier to work with because they do not include inconvenient anomalies that complicate the illustration. The actual examples have been carefully chosen, but variant spellings and other pesky irregularities have been allowed to remain because I feel that students should see the language in its natural state, weeds and all, rather than as the product of a compulsive grammarian.

For both the Old English (OE) and Middle English (ME) chapters, eight additional supplementary illustrative texts have been included, along with glosses, for instructors to use as they see fit. Supplementary texts are not provided for the Early Modern (EMnE) or the Present-Day English (PDE) chapters because such materials are easily available elsewhere. Similarly, the chapter on PDE contains only a minimum number of exercises because entire courses are devoted to its structure.

My materials have been drawn from a wide variety of sources, ranging from unpublished medieval manuscripts to the excited commentary of a television sports announcer. Obviously, I have depended heavily on the *Oxford English Dictionary* and the publications of the Early English Text Society. I have also shamelessly ransacked the texts of authors like Anderson and Williams, Bennett and Smithers, Sisam, and Kaiser.

Many people have helped in the preparation of this workbook. I will leave nameless those whose contributions might embarrass them, but would like to acknowledge publicly the assistance (sometimes inadvertent) of Brinda Bose, Mary Campbell, Andrew Gardner, Anne Gardner, Arthur Golden, Margaret Laing, Rachael Lynch, Angus McIntosh, James Millward, Madhulika Sikka, and Hayden Williams. A particular note of thanks is due Dr. Rupert Snell of the School of Oriental and African Studies of the University of London.

I would also like to thank Michael Rosenberg, Charlie Dierker, Vicki McAlindon Horton, and Tad Gaither of Holt, Rinehart and Winston for their assistance in this project.

Finally, I owe much to my students, not just for their performance and comments on many of these exercises, but for the pleasure they have given me—from the satisfaction of seeing their skills and understanding develop, to the instantaneous delight of reading on an examination paper that "Adam Bede wrote the Anglo-Saxon Chronicle."

C.M.M.

Workbook to Accompany

A BIOGRAPHY OF THE ENGLISH LANGUAGE

CHAPTER 1

INTRODUCTION

1.1 Important Terms

1. analogical change
2. conditioned change
3. Early Modern English (EMnE)
4. external history
5. grapheme
6. graphics
7. internal history
8. lexicon
9. Middle English (ME)
10. morpheme
11. morphology
12. Old English (OE)
13. phoneme
14. phonemics
15. phonetics
16. phonology
17. Present-Day English (PDE)
18. principle of least effort
19. semantics
20. syntax
21. unconditioned change

1.2   Questions for Review and Discussion

1. Do animals have language? Provide evidence both for and against your answer.
2. Give three or more examples of the systematic nature of English other than those mentioned in the text.
3. Imagine and describe a language based solely on touch (as opposed to sound or sight). Describe how it might work and list some of its disadvantages as well as advantages it might have over sight- or sound-based language systems.
4. What is the difference between phonetics and phonemics?
5. What is the difference between a morpheme and a word in English?
6. Give two examples in which syntax alone distinguishes two English utterances (i.e., the phonemes and morphemes are the same, but the word order is different).
7. Why is redundancy essential in natural language?
8. In what ways does the written version of a language affect the spoken version?
9. List possible explanations for *why* languages change.
10. Why is the principle of least effort unsatisfactory as an explanation for all changes that occur in language?
11. What are some of the external pressures that have led to changes in American English?
12. Summarize the reasons for the terminal dates of OE, ME, and EMnE.
13. What are the primary sources of information about earlier stages of English?
14. Summarize the problems associated with using texts as a source of information about earlier stages of a language.
15. Why are translated texts less than satisfactory as a source of information about earlier stages of a language?

1.3 Onomatopoeia

Onomatopoeia, or the formation of words by imitating the natural sounds associated with the object or action being referred to, is inadequate as an explanation for the origin of all human language. Nonetheless, all languages have at least a few onomatopoeic (or echoic or imitative) words, especially for animal sounds and environmental noises. Such words are often similar across languages, as is the case, for example, with the word for the sound made by a cat: Spanish *miau,* Afrikaans *miaau,* Chinese *miao,* French *miaou,* Swedish *mjau,* and so forth. On the other hand, such words must fit the sound system of the language; if a language had no *m* sound, the speakers' cats could not "say" *miao.*

A.   Listed here are the words for several noises or things that tend to be represented by onomatopoeic words in many languages, though not every word is necessarily onomatopoeic in origin. Match the words with their meanings by writing the appropriate number of the meaning beside each set of words.

1. bark of a dog	6. snore
2. crowing of a rooster	7. sound of a bell
3. cuckoo	8. sound of a clock
4. hiccough	9. sudden loud noise
5. noise made by a horse	

____ French *hoquet*	____ French *hennir*	____ Chinese *dīngdāng*
Russian *ikota*	German *wiehern*	French *digue-din-don*
Scots Gaelic *aileag*	Irish *seitreach*	German *kling-klang*
Swahili *kwikwi*	Russian *rzhat'*	Irish *ding deang*
Swedish *hickning*	Swedish *gnägga*	Russian *din'-din'*
Turkish *hiçkirik*	Tagalog *halinghíng*	Swedish *bingbång*

____ Chinese *wāngwāng*	____ French *coucou*	____ Chinese *hānshēng*
French *ouâ-ouâ*	German *Kuckuck*	French *ronfler*
German *wauwau*	Russian *kukushka*	German *schnarchen*
Irish *amh-amh*	Spanish *cuco*	Irish *srannaim*
Russian *am-am*	Swedish *gök*	Swahili *koroma*
Swedish *vov-vov*	Turkish *guguk kuşu*	Swedish *snarka*

___ Chinese *dīdā*	___ Chinese *wō*	___ French *boum*
French *tic-tac*	French *cocorico*	German *bums*
German *tick-tack*	German *kikeriki*	Irish *plimp*
Irish *tic*	Swahili *wika*	Lao *bpa:ng*
Swahili *ta-ta-ta*	Swedish *kuckeliku*	Swahili *bomu*
Tagalog *tumik-tak*	Tagalog *tilaok*	Swedish *pang*

B. Make up new onomatopoeic words for the following sounds.

Typewriting on an old manual portable _____

A toenail clipper in use _____

A dogfight _____

A washing machine with an unbalanced load _____

Plastic bottles filled with liquid rolling around in the trunk of a car _____

1.4 Spoken and Written English

Make a brief recording (about five minutes) of the spontaneous speech of an educated person; an articulate classroom lecturer who does not actually read his or her notes would be a good choice. Transcribe this recording into written English, word for word, including *ums* and *ahs,* false starts, meandering sentences, and the like. Then compare the syntax, vocabulary, and style of this educated speech with that of educated writing. An article or a portion of a book written by the same speaker would be ideal, but use written material on a similar subject by another person if necessary.

What differences do you find between good spoken and good written English? Which is better English? Explain your answer.

1.5 Morphology: Inflectional and Derivational Suffixes

English has scores of derivational suffixes, but only a few inflectional suffixes. In the following passage, indicate in the blank following each underlined suffix whether it is inflectional (I) or derivational (D).

¹The main build<u>ing</u> ____ at NAFEC is immense, with slid<u>ing</u> ____ steel door<u>s</u> ____ seventy ____ feet high clos<u>ing</u> ____ the end<u>s</u> ____ of a room in which several big jet<u>s</u> ____ and any number of small plane<u>s</u> ____ can be hous<u>ed</u> ____ at the same time. ²The floor personne<u>l</u> ____ have work<u>ed</u> ____ on just about everything, milit<u>ary</u> ____ or civili<u>an</u>, ____ that flie<u>s</u> ____ in Americ<u>an</u> ____ sky. ³It is hard to imagine any sort of aircraft that would draw from them more than a glance. ⁴Around nine o'clock in the morn<u>ing</u>, ____ though, on that August day, when Aereon 26 came in and was lift<u>ed</u> ____ off the flatbed traile<u>r</u>, ____, men from every part of the hangar lef<u>t</u> ____ the plane<u>s</u> ____ they were work<u>ing</u> ____ on and collect<u>ed</u> ____ in a wide circle around it. ⁵They look<u>ed</u> ____ at it in silence. ⁶In time, they would be mak<u>ing</u> ____ cynic<u>al</u> ____ remark<u>s</u> ____ about the wing<u>less</u> ____ orange vehicle and it<u>s</u> ____ trial<u>s</u>, ____ but now they just stood there and took it in. ⁷The 26 was plac<u>ed</u> ____ at one side of the hangar. ⁸Two fifty-____ pound weight<u>s</u> ____ were hung from it<u>s</u> ____ nose, because it<u>s</u> ____ balance was so critic<u>al</u> ____ that, without a pilot inside it, the 26 would other<u>wise</u> ____ have cant<u>ed</u> ____ back<u>ward</u>. ____*

1. What is the difference between the *-ing* in *building* (sentence 1) and the *-ing* in *working* (sentence 4)? _____

_____

2. What is the difference between the *-s* in *doors* (1) and the *-s* in *its* (6)? _____

_____

3. What is the difference between the *-ed* in *worked* (2) and the *-ed* in *collected* (4)?

_____

4. Why are *-craft* in *aircraft* (3) and *-bed* in *flatbed* (4) not treated as suffixes? _____

_____

5. Only suffixes have been underlined in this passage, but it also contains a few derivative prefixes. List some of these. Check a dictionary if you are uncertain. _____

_____

*John McPhee, *The Deltoid Pumpkin Seed* (New York: Ballantine Books, 1973), p. 5.

1.6   The Importance of Syntax

A.   A change in word order alone often changes the meaning of an English utterance. For each of the following pairs of sentences, describe the change of meaning that results from the change in word order.

1. (a) Paula threw a shoe at Myrtle.
    (b) Myrtle threw a shoe at Paula.

2. (a) The senator has destroyed his records.
    (b) Has the senator destroyed his records?

3. (a) Mother frequently told Nigel to wash his ears.
    (b) Mother told Nigel to wash his ears frequently.

4. (a) Samson had pulled down the temple.
    (b) Samson had the temple pulled down.

5. (a) Here comes the meter-reader.
    (b) The meter-reader comes here.

6. (a) She liked whatever he bought her.
    (b) He bought her whatever she liked.

7. (a) They ate their lunch happily.
    (b) Happily they ate their lunch.

8. (a) You'd better like it.
    (b) You'd like it better.
(This one is not quite fair. Why?)

B.   Sometimes, however, word order can be altered without an obvious change in meaning. What is the effect of the change in word order in each of the following pairs of sentences?

1. (a) He ate the chicken and he threw away the spinach.
    (b) The chicken he ate and the spinach he threw away.

2. (a) I have never seen such a mess.
   (b) Never have I seen such a mess.

_____

3. (a) We'd do anything for you.
   (b) For you we'd do anything.

_____

4. (a) Paula rooms with Myrtle.
   (b) Myrtle rooms with Paula.
(Why is this different from A. 1.?)

_____

C. Sometimes a particular word order can be interpreted in two very different ways. Explain how each of the following sentences is ambiguous.

1. Samuels had his books audited. _____

_____

2. Jane called her dog a caretaker. _____

_____

3. I don't enjoy drawing rooms. _____

_____

4. Those soldiers are too young to kill. _____

_____

D. Sometimes the meaning of a given word order varies according to the lexical items used. Explain how the choice of the final word in each of these sentences affects the meaning.

1. Janet made him a good dinner.
2. Janet made him a good husband.
3. Janet made him a good wife.

_____

_____

_____

1.7 Graphics: Graphemes and Allographs

Just as phonemes have allophones, so graphemes have allographs. This is most obvious in the different typefaces found in printing. But individuals use different allographs of the same grapheme in their handwriting, too. Indeed, allographs provide one of the clues we use to identify the handwriting of a particular person.

For the five samples of handwriting reproduced here list all the major allographs you find, both within one individual's handwriting and across individuals. For example, **d** , **ð**, and **ꝺ** are the major allographs of the grapheme ⟨d⟩ in the samples. You may find no major allographic differences for some graphemes, and you may not even find any examples of some graphemes.

I am paticularly interested in studying on an assistantship basis, as I am unable to fund myself fully unless I can work as I study. I find the idea of teaching or research alongside my degree work potentially an interesting challenge and very useful to my development as a student, and as an individual. If assistantships are

in mind to use the Pricke of Conscience in several versions, rather as you have done, to illustrate variety across the country. I hope you don't mind if I crib the idea for one of my chapters. I would use a longer sketch of text (about 40 lines), and I plan to use different MSS from the ones you have, trying to fill in the spaces between them. This way I could refer to your book (if that's all right) and anyone with access to both books would then be able to achieve a more detailed picture of the linguistic spread.

What's the best way for me to pay you? Before you lay out any money yourself, let me know how you would like me to send it to you. If it's easiest, I can just write you a blank check, but then you'd have to get it changed. Would you like an international money order— that's okay.

Meg was _delighted_ with your allusion to the smashing outfit, though she would have me believe that she couldn't remember what she was wearing. But she said that you had such good taste in these matters yourself that she took what you said as a great compliment.

I just handed in to Bill a revised prospectus, or at least most of one. If he likes it, we can re-submit it within a couple of weeks. And I think I am reading to start writing. Gasp!. Enjoy

Grapheme	*Allographs*	*Grapheme*	*Allographs*
a	_____	n	_____
b	_____	o	_____
c	_____	p	_____
d	_____	q	_____
e	_____	r	_____
f	_____	s	_____
g	_____	t	_____
h	_____	u	_____
i	_____	v	_____
j	_____	w	_____
k	_____	x	_____
l	_____	y	_____
m	_____	z	_____

1. Which letters have the greatest number of allographs? _____

_____

2. For most printed typefaces, which five (or more) of the letters have identical or nearly identical forms—apart from size—in both their capital and lowercase forms? _____

_____

3. Which five (or more) letters are most different in their capital and lowercase forms in printed fonts? _____

1.8 The Systematic Nature of Language

All languages are systematic; otherwise we would not be able to say anything new in them. All natural languages also have irregularities in their systems that must be learned item by item. Still, more often than not, we can predict the correct form of something we have never heard or seen because we have learned the rules of the system.

I. Morphological systems

1. Listed below are the demonstrative adjectives/pronouns of Turkish. By examining the complete forms given, fill in the blanks with the correct endings of the remaining forms. There are no irregularities.

	"this"		"that"		"that yonder"	
	Singular	*Plural*	*Singular*	*Plural*	*Singular*	*Plural*
Subject case	bu	bunlar	şu	şunlar	o	onlar
Possessive case	bunun	_____	şunun	şunlarin	onun	onlarin
Dative case	buna	bunlara	_____	şunlara	_____	onlara
Objective case	_____	bunlari	şunu	şunlari	onu	_____
Locative case	bunda	bunlarda	_____	_____	onda	onlarda
Ablative case	bundan	bunlardan	şundan	şunlardan	_____	_____

2. What is the plural ending (affix), regardless of case? _____

3. Which is attached to the base word first in Turkish, the plural affix or the case affix?

_____

4. Which is attached first in English, the possessive case ending or the plural ending? (Big hint: Think of the words *child* and *alumnus*.) _____

II. Syntactic Systems

Listed here are several sentences in Scots Gaelic, together with their English translations. The translations are English equivalents of the Gaelic sentences, *not* word-for-word glosses of them.

1. Tha each agam.   I have a horse.
2. Tha tigh agad.   You have a house.
3. Tha peann aige.   He has a pen.
4. Tha ad aice.   She has a hat.

5. Tha an cu agad.   You have the dog.
6. Tha an sgian agad.   You have the knife.
7. Tha am bàta aige.   He has the boat.
8. Tha an sgian aig a'ghille.   The boy has the knife.

9.	Cha'n eil sgian agam.	I don't have a knife.
10.	Cha'n eil ad agam.	I don't have a hat.
11.	Cha'n eil sgian aige.	He doesn't have a knife.
12.	Am bheil ad agad?	Do you have a hat?
13.	Nach eil sgian agam?	Don't I have a knife?
14.	Nach eil tigh aige?	Doesn't he have a house?
15.	Nach eil an leabhar aice?	Doesn't she have the book?

1. Translate the following Scots Gaelic sentences into English.

Tha peann agad.   _____

Tha leabhar aice.   _____

Tha an tigh agam.   _____

Cha'n eil am bàta agad.   _____

Am bheil sgian aige?   _____

2. Translate the following English sentences into Scots Gaelic.

He has a house.   _____

I have the book.   _____

You don't have a horse.   _____

Does she have a book?   _____

Don't you have the boat?   _____

1.9   Types of Linguistic Change

The following passage is from an early fifteenth-century version of *Mandeville's Travels*, a work written originally in French and translated several times into English. Following the ME text is a translation into modern English. Using the translation as a rough guide, list changes in graphics, morphology, syntax, lexicon, and semantics that have occurred in English since the ME manuscript was written. (Remember that the translation into modern English is only one possible translation; just because it does not follow the ME exactly does not mean that the ME would not be possible in modern English. In answering the questions, ask yourself, "Could or would I say this today?"

> Ethiope is departed in two princypall parties; and þat is in the Est partie, and in the Meridionall partie, the whiche partie meridionall is clept Moretane. And the folk of þat contree ben blake ynow, and more blake þan in the toþer partie; and þei ben clept Mowres. In þat partie is a well, þat in the day it is so cold þat no man may drynke þereoffe; and in the nyght it is so hoot þat no man may suffre hys hond þerein. And beʒonde þat partie, toward the South, to passe by the See Occean, is a gret lond and a gret contrey. But men may not duell þere, for the feruent brennynge of the sonne, so is it passynge hoot in þat contrey. . . .
>
> In Ethiope, whan the children ben ʒonge and lytill, þei ben all ʒalowe; and whan þat þei wexen of age, þat ʒalownesse turneth to ben all blak. In Ethiope is the cytee of Saba, and the lond of the whiche on of the þre Kynges, þat presented oure Lord in Bethleem, was kyng offe.*

Translation

Ethiopia is divided into two principal regions: into an eastern region and into a southern region, the southern region being called Mauretania. The people of that country are extremely black, blacker than in the other region, and they are called Moors. In that region there is a well which is so cold during the day that no one can drink from it, and at night it is so hot that no one can stand to put his hand in it. Beyond that region, toward the south, going along the Indian Ocean, is a big land and big country. But people cannot live there because of the hot burning of the sun, so exceedingly hot is it in that country.

In Ethiopia, when the children are young and little, they are all yellow; when they grow up, that yellowness turns all black. In Ethiopia is the city of Saba, and the land which one of the three kings who gave gifts to our Lord in Bethlehem was king of.

Graphic differences from PDE _____

_____

Morphological differences from PDE _____

_____

Syntactic differences from PDE _____

_____

_____

_____

*Adapted from the British Library Ms. Cotton Titus C xvi manuscript transcription in Kenneth Sisam, ed., *Fourteenth Century Verse & Prose* (Oxford: Clarendon Press, 1970), pp. 96, 97. Translation by C. M. Millward.

Lexical differences (list only words no longer used in PDE) _____

_____

Semantic differences (list words still existing today but used in a different meaning or

context) _____

_____

_____

Other observations? _____

_____

_____

1.10　Semantic Change

Semantic change is much less highly structured and frequently more subtle than phonological, morphological, or syntactic change. The italicized words in the following quotations from Shakespeare make perfectly good grammatical sense to the modern reader, and some of them seem to be semantically appropriate. Yet, in each instance, Shakespeare's meaning was distinctly different from the meaning of the words today. With the help of a good annotated edition of Shakespeare and/or the *Oxford English Dictionary*, determine the meaning of each of the words for Shakespeare.

1. Malvolio: Maria once told me she did *affect* me (*Twelfth Night* II.5.24) _____

2. Queen Elizabeth: I would to God all strifes were well *compounded* (*Richard III* II.1.75)

3. Edgar: But mice and rats, and such small *deer,*
   　　　　Have been Tom's food for seven long year. (*King Lear* III.4.137–38)

4. Sentry: Hark, the drums *demurely* wake the sleepers. (*Antony and Cleopatra* IV.9.34)

5. Angelo: When men were *fond,* I smil'd and wond'red how. (*Measure for Measure* II.2.186)

6. Arthemidorus: If thou beest not immortal, look about you. *Security* gives way to conspiracy. The mighty gods defend thee! (*Julius Caesar* II.3.6–8) _____

7. First Captain:　Great Jupiter be prais'd! Lucius is taken.
   　　　　　　　'Tis thought the old man and his sons were angels.
   Second Captain: There was a fourth man, in a *silly* habit,
   　　　　　　　That gave th'affront with them. (*Cymbeline* V.3.86)

8. Polonius: Th'ambassadors from Norway, my good lord,
   　　　　Are joyfully return'd.
   King:　Thou *still* hast been the father of good news. (*Hamlet* II.2.40–42)

9. Viola: What *thriftless* sighs shall poor Olivia breathe! (*Twelfth Night* II.2.39)

10. Canterbury: If we, with thrice such powers left at home,
   　　　　　　Cannot defend our own doors from the dog,
   　　　　　　Let us be *worried,* and our nation lose
   　　　　　　The name of hardiness and policy. (*Henry V* I.2.217–20)

1.11 Dating Texts

Although it takes long experience to date earlier English texts with precision, most native speakers have a good intuition about the relative dates of texts. The following are excerpts from English texts dating from the eighth to the twentieth century. The dates (sometimes approximate) are 750, 1000, 1154, 1250, 1300, 1395, 1490, 1582, 1651, 1754, 1818, 1880, and 1933. Write the appropriate date on the line before each text.

1. _____ After dyuerse werkes made, translated and achieued, hauyng noo werke in hande, I sittyng in my studye where as laye many dyuerse paunflettis and bookys, happened that to my hande cam a lytyl booke in frenshe, which late was translated oute of latyn . . .

2. _____ Cethegrande is a fis, ðe moste ðat in water is, ðat tu wuldest seien get, gef ðu it soge wen it flet, ðat it were a neilond ðat sete one ðe se sond. ðis fis ðat is vnride, ðanne him hungreð he gapeð wide.

3. _____ Forsothe Adam knewe Eue his wijf, which conseyuede, and childide Cayn, and seide, Y haue gete a man bi God. And efte sche childide his brother Abel. Forsothe Abel was a kepere of scheep, and Cayn was an erthe tilyere.

4. _____The generall use of Speech, is to transferre our Mentall Discourse, into Verbal; or the Trayne of our Thoughts, into a Trayne of Words; and that for two commodities; whereof one is, the Registring of the Consequences of our Thoughts; which being apt to slip out of our memory, and put us to a new labour, may again be recalled, by such words as they were marked by.

5. _____ Herkneth to me, gode men, wiues, maydnes, and alle men, of a tale þat ich you wil telle, Wo-so it wile here and þerto duelle. Þe tale is of Hauelok imaked; wil he was litel, he yede ful naked.

6. _____ I had long lamented that we had no lawful standard of our language set up, for those to repair to, who might chuse to speak and write grammatically and correctly: and I have as long wished that either some one person of distinguished abilities would undertake the work singly, or that a certain number of gentlemen would form themselves, or be formed by the government, into a society for that purpose.

7. _____ It is because it is learned early and piecemeal, in constant association with the color and the requirements of actual contexts, that language in spite of its quasi-mathematical form is rarely a purely referential organization. It tends to be so only in scientific discourse, and even there it may be seriously doubted whether the ideal of pure reference is ever attained by language.

8. _____ As for the antiquitie of our speche, whether it be measured by the ancient *Almane*, whence it cummeth originallie, or even but by the latest terms which it boroweth daielie from foren tungs, either of pure necessitie in new matters, or of mere brauerie, to garnish it self withall, it cannot be young.

9. _____ On þis gær wærd þe king Stephne ded & bebyried þer his wif & his sune wæron bebyried æt Fauresfeld; þæt ministre hi makeden. Þa þe king was ded, þa was þe eorl beionde sæ; & ne durste nan man don oþer bute god for þe micel eie of him.

10. _____ Peremptory and unreasoned pronouncements as to what is bad English are not the least of the minor pests which vex our enlightened age; and the bulk of them, as the better-informed are well aware, may be traced to persons who have given only very slight attention to verbal criticism. The effective disseminators of these pronouncements are, indeed, far from numerous.

11. _____ Þær wæs madma fela of feorwegum frætwa gelæded; ne hyrde ic cymlicor ceol gegyrwan hildewæpnum ond heaðowædum billum ond byrnum; him on bearme læg madma mænigo, þa him mid scoldon on flodes æht feor gewitan.

12. _____ Gregorius se halga papa, Engliscre ðeode apostol, on ðisum andwerdum dæge, æfter menigfealdum gedeorfum and halgum gecnyrdnyssum, Godes rice gesæliglice astah. He is rihtlice Engliscre ðeode apostol, for ðan ðe he þurh his ræd and sande us fram deofles biggengum ætbræd . . .

13. _____ We have, here, a pretty good proof, that a knowledge of the Greek and Latin is not sufficient to prevent men from writing bad English. Here is a *profound scholar*, a teacher of rhetoric, discussing the comparative merits of Greek and Latin writers, and disputing with a French critic: here he is, writing English in a manner more incorrect than you will, I hope, be liable to write it at the end of your reading of this little book.

1.12   Using Dictionaries Effectively

I. Desk Dictionaries

Desk dictionaries contain a vast amount of information organized in a highly condensed fashion. Unfortunately, many people do not know how to make the best use of their dictionaries, and there are numerous misconceptions about the significance of such things as order of entries. Few people even realize how different one good dictionary can be from another.

   In this exercise, you are to compare your desk dictionary (*not* a paperback!) with another one. If your dictionary is over ten years old, you should buy a new one (but keep the old one for comparison). Among the good American desk dictionaries are *Funk & Wagnalls Standard College Dictionary, Webster's New World Dictionary of the American Language, The Random House College Dictionary, Webster's Ninth New Collegiate Dictionary,* and *The American Heritage Dictionary.* Among the good British dictionaries are those published by Collins, Oxford, and Chambers. You can find copies of most or all of these dictionaries in the reference room of your library.

1. Name of your dictionary (Dictionary A) _Webster's New World Dictionary_
Name of the other dictionary (Dictionary B) _The American Heritage Dict. / Funk Wagnall's New Standard Dictionary_

Date of printing of Dictionary A _1988_
Date of printing of Dictionary B _1969_

2. Where is the list of abbreviations used in the dictionary? Does it appear in more than one place? _In Dictionary it was only on page 1565 In B. it was on page X._

3. Where is the pronunciation key? _A. was on page XII In B it was on XXXV to XXXVII_

Where is the pronunciation key explained in detail? _Same as above._

4. Look up the words *usable* and *tsar*. Where does the dictionary put acceptable spelling variants? _Dictionary A gave pronunciations between spellings Dictionary B. gave one spelling after another_

If the variants appear one after the other in the main entry, is the first variant the preferred one? If not, what determines position? _Yes it seems to be so._

5. Look up the words *jack-in-the-pulpit, jackknife, jack rabbit,* and *jack-tar.* How is syllable division indicated? How is hyphenation indicated? If you had looked up *jack rabbit* and then needed to hyphenate *rabbit,* how would you find out the proper place to put the hyphen? _Syllables are indicated by dots in B and slashes in A._

6. Look up the term *Turkish towel*. How do the dictionaries indicate capitalization? Is *Turkish towel* preferred over *turkish towel*? _Both had the former spelling._

7. Look up the word *mercenary*. How is major stress on a word indicated? How is secondary stress indicated? _In A. by different size stress symbols. In B by a // and /'/_

Look up the word *magazine*. What is the difference between the two pronunciations listed? What determines the order in which the variant pronunciations appear? _The stress is moved from the beginning to the end._

8. Look up the word *coral*. Where in the entry is the etymology listed? How does the dictionary distinguish between immediate source and ultimate etymology? How does the dictionary distinguish between source words and cognate words? _The etymology follows the pronunciation. Source words come first and then the cognate_

9. Look up the words *joy* and *joie de vivre*. How does the dictionary distinguish between loanwords and unassimilated foreign words? _It identifies the second as a French word._

10. How is the order of the definitions under each entry determined? By preferred meaning first? Historically earliest meaning first? _They give the preferred meaning first_

11. Look up the word *level*. Are the different parts of speech (adjective, noun, verb) all under the same main entry? _In both yes._

Within the entry, where are inflected forms given (e.g., *leveled*)? _After the definitions._

Where are idioms involving the word located (e.g., *level best*)? _Before the inflected forms._

12. Find the discussion of usage labels in the introductory material. Which labels are used? _It is given in Guide in A. Usage labels appear at end of entry_

13. Look up the word *doubt*. How does the dictionary handle words with many closely related synonyms? _It seperates doubt from doubtful_

14. No native speaker planning to leave her apartment simply because she is moving to another city would be likely to write to her landlord, "I will *evacuate* the apartment by August 25." Why? Look up the words *evacuate* and *vacate* as transitive verbs in the dictionaries. Which one would best help a nonnative speaker avoid this error in usage?

Explain. _____

_____

_____

_____

If neither is satisfactory, rewrite the definition of *evacuate* to distinguish its implications

from those of *vacate*. _____

_____

15. You would be unlikely to say, "Though she's not a true beauty, she has a lovely *grin*." Look up *grin* (noun) and *grin* (verb) in the two dictionaries. Is either definition

adequate to explain why the sentence is unacceptable? _____

Look up the word *grin* in the *Oxford English Dictionary*. Comment. _____

_____

_____

16. Write a paragraph explaining in full the following dictionary entry from the *Random House College Dictionary*, revised edition, 1975.

> **staff**[1] (staf, stäf), *n.*, *pl.* **staves** (stāvz) or **staffs** for 1–3, 8, 9; **staffs** for 4–7; *adj.*, *v.*—*n.* **1.** a stick, pole, or rod for aid in walking or climbing, for use as a weapon, etc. **2.** a rod or wand serving as an ensign of office or authority. **3.** a pole on which a flag is hung or displayed. **4.** a group of assistants to an executive. **5.** a group of persons charged with carrying out the work of an establishment or executing some undertaking. **6.** *Mil.* **a.** a body of officers without command authority, appointed to assist a commanding officer. **b.** the parts of any military force concerned with administrative matters, planning, etc., rather than with participation in combat. **7.** the members of an organization that serve only in auxiliary or advisory capacity on a given project. **8.** Also called **stave**. *Music.* a set of five horizontal lines, together with the corresponding four spaces between them, on which music is written. **9.** *Archaic.* the shaft of a spear or lance. —*adj.* **10.** of or pertaining to a military or organizational staff; *a staff member.* **11.** (of certain professional persons) working full-time on the staff of a corporation, newspaper or magazine company, etc., rather than self-employed or practicing privately: *a staff writer.* —*v.t.* **12.** to provide with a staff of workers. [ME *staf*, OE *stæf*; c. D *staf*, Icel *stafr*, G *Stab* staff, Skt *stabh-* support]

II. *The Oxford English Dictionary*

The *Oxford English Dictionary*, or *OED* as it is frequently called, is the most complete historical dictionary ever made of any language. The first volumes of its first edition began appearing in the 1880s; the final volume, a "catch-up" supplement to the rest of the volumes appeared nearly half a century later. Another four-volume updated supplement was published between 1972 and 1986; the integration of the original edition and the four-volume supplement comprises the twenty-volume second edition.

Your library will probably have copies of both the first and the second editions. If it does not have the second edition as such, it will have the first edition and the four-volume supplement to the first edition.

A.   Read the introductory material in the first volume and note the location of the list of abbreviations and the pronunciation key.

1. Why did the publishing firm of Macmillan want a new dictionary? _____
_____

2. When was the contract between the Oxford University Press and the Philological Society signed? _____
_____

3. How many of the 15,487 pages of the first edition did Sir James Murray edit?
_____

4. What is the relevance of the term *Scriptorium* to the preparation of the *OED*?
_____

5. In what year did the first volume of the *OED* appear? _____ The last volume of the first edition? _____

B.   Find the following words in the *OED* and answer the questions. If the edition is not specified, the word will be in both the first and the second editions. If the second edition is specified, you can use either the second edition as such or the four-volume supplement to the first edition.

1. **autopsy.** What is the immediate source of the word? _____
What is the ultimate source? _____
What does the term mean in its ultimate source? _____
2. **contrary** (verb). What does the † in front of the main entry mean? _____
_____

How was the word sometimes spelled in the fourteenth and fifteenth centuries? _____
_____

When is the *OED*'s last recorded use of the word as a verb? _____
When is its next-to-last recorded use? _____
3. **courgette** (2d ed.). What language is the word from? _____
What is the equivalent of a vegetable marrow in American English? _____
(If you give up trying to find the American equivalent of *courgette*, look up *zucchini* in the second edition of the *OED*.)
4. **curtain-lecture.** What does the term mean? _____
_____

Why the word *curtain*? (If you don't know, look up the word *curtain*.) _____
_____

Though it is not marked as such, this expression could be considered obsolete today. Why? _____

What expression has partly replaced the term? _____

5. **demimonde.** From what language did English borrow this word? _____

What does the ‖ in front of the word signify? _____

Who invented the term? _____

6. **fash** (verb[1]). What is the origin of the word? _____

What does it mean? _____

What regional restrictions are there on the word? _____

Which came first, noun[1] or verb[1]? _____

7. **fizzle.** Which came first, the noun or the verb? _____
Has the usual meaning of the word ameliorated or degenerated since its introduction into

English? _____

8. **galleon.** What is the immediate source of the word in English? _____

What is the ultimate source? _____

What does the entry "6–9 **galeon**" mean? _____

9. **hengest.** What does the † in front of the entry mean? _____

In what modern Germanic language(s) does the word survive? _____
In what work and at what date was its last appearance in English? (You will need to check

the list of books quoted at the end of the last volume.) _____

_____

What various meanings has the word had in different languages and different periods?

_____

How has it been used as a proper noun? _____

_____

10. **lilac.** What is the immediate source of the word in English? _____

What is the apparent ultimate source? _____

Which meaning came first, the name of the flower or the name of the color? _____

_____

What other spelling did the word sometimes have in the seventeenth century? _____

_____

11. **migraine.** Look the word up in both the first edition and the second edition. What

change is made in the second edition? _____

_____

Is the pronunciation listed the one you are familiar with? _____
Look up the pronunciation of the word in your desk dictionary. Explain the difference.

_____

What other word for the same phenomenon is the reader referred to in the *OED*? _____

_____

12. **point** (verb[1]). What did Chaucer mean by this word? _____

Is this meaning still current? _____

What specialized meaning does the word have in bricklaying? _____

_____

What do the square brackets around the citations for 1375 and 1391 signify?

_____

13. **rug** (noun[2]). What was the earliest meaning in which the word was used in English?

_____

Is this meaning current today? _____ What is the origin of the word? _____

_____

14. **secret** (adjective and noun). What is the Spanish cognate of this word? _____

_____

Is its earliest meaning in English current today? _____

What did Shakepeare mean by *secret* when he wrote, "How now you secret, black, &

midnight Hags? What is't you do?" _____

Is this meaning current today? _____

15. **snuck** (2d ed.). Where in the English-speaking world did this form originate?

_____

How long has it been around? _____

From all the citations given, would you say the acceptability of *snuck* (vs. *sneaked*) has

increased or decreased in the century or so of its citations recorded here? _____

_____

16. **strudel** (2d ed.). How do the two pronunciations listed differ? _____

_____

From what language did English borrow the word? _____

What is the literal meaning of the word in that language? _____

17. **tornado.** From what language did English borrow the word? _____

What major change in pronunciation (and spelling) occurred when the word was used in

English? _____

What is the earliest recorded date of its use in English? _____

Suggest why English had not needed the word prior to this time. _____

_____

18. **twat** (1st and 2d eds.). Why is the word not defined? _____

Is the word obsolete? _____

What usage label is given the word? _____

19. **ukulele** (2d ed.). The word is not in the first edition of the *OED*. Why? _____

_____

What does the word mean in Hawaiian? _____

20. **wallop** (noun). Of what word is *wallop* a doublet? _____

What was its earliest meaning in English? _____

Of the four meanings listed (1–4), which ones are in general use today? _____

_____

21. **wiseacre.** When is the first recorded use of this word in English? _____

_____

From where did English get the word? _____

What unexplained change has occurred in its pronunciation and spelling? _____

_____

22. **wonder** (noun). What is the origin of this word? _____

What is its earliest citation in English? _____

What is the cognate Swedish word? _____

CHAPTER 2
PHONOLOGY

2.1 Important Terms

1. affricate
2. allophone
3. alveolar
4. alveolar ridge
5. apex
6. articulator
7. aspiration
8. bilabial
9. blade
10. consonant
11. dental
12. diphthong
13. dorsum
14. epiglottis
15. fricative
16. front, central, back vowels
17. glottal stop
18. glottis
19. hard palate
20. high, mid, low vowels
21. interdental
22. labial
23. labiodental
24. larynx
25. lateral
26. lax
27. liquid
28. nasal
29. palatal
30. pharynx
31. phoneme
32. plosive
33. point of articulation
34. primary stress
35. prosody
36. reduced stress
37. resonant
38. retroflex
39. schwa
40. secondary stress
41. semivowel
42. spirant
43. stop
44. tense
45. trachea
46. uvula
47. uvular trill
48. velar
49. velum
50. vocal cords
51. voiced
52. voiceless
53. vowel

2.2   Questions for Review and Discussion

1. What is the difference between a phoneme and an allophone?
2. What is the meaning of the expression "one man's phoneme is another man's allophone"?
3. What distinguishes nasals from stops?
4. What distinguishes voiced from voiceless sounds?
5. What distinguishes fricatives from affricates?
6. What distinguishes /l/ from /r/?
7. What features do /ɛ/ and /ɔ/ share?
8. What features do /i/ and /ɪ/ share?
9. What features do /e/ and /ɛ/ share?
10. We smile when we hear a nonnative speaker say something that sounds like, "He crossed the ocean on a *sheep*." Probably the speaker's native language has no phonemic distinction between /i/ and /ɪ/. List some other pronunciation errors or characteristics of foreign accents in English, and suggest in what way the phonemic system of the native language probably differs from that of English.

2.3   Reading Transcription

First read the following poem aloud.* Then transliterate it into standard English spelling.
In some instances, the pronunciation represented here may differ slightly from your own.

/əv ɔl ðə kaɪnz əv lɛkčərər   _____

ðə lɛkčərər aɪ most ditɛst   _____

ɪz hi hu fɪnɪšɪz ə peǰ   _____

æn plesɪz ɪt bəhaɪn ðə rɛst   _____

aɪ məč prəfər ðə lɛkčərər   _____

hu teks ðə peǰɪz æz i fɪnɪšɪz   _____

æn puts ðəm ɔn ə maʊntɪŋ paɪl   _____

æz ði ɔrɪǰɪnəl paɪl dəmɪnɪšɪz   _____

bət bɛst əv ɔl ðə lɛkčərər   _____

hu gɛts ɪz pepərz ɪn kərz kənfjužən   _____

æn primətjurli lɛts əskep   _____

ðə trəmpɪt-frez "ænd ɪn kənklužən"/   _____

*from Morris Bishop, *A Bowl of Bishop*. (New York: Dial Press, 1954)

2.4   Transcribing Vowels

On the lines to the right of each word, write the phonemic symbol for the underlined vowel or diphthong.

free	____	bus	____	sauce	____
stick	____	car	____	hide	____
late	____	blue	____	voice	____
met	____	hood	____	cloud	____
pack	____	Joe	____		

2.5 Transcribing Consonants

On the lines to the right of each word, write the phonemic symbol for the underlined consonant(s).

ha<u>pp</u>y	___	my<u>th</u>	___	<u>h</u>air	___
<u>b</u>ring	___	brea<u>the</u>	___	ha<u>mm</u>er	___
<u>t</u>op	___	di<u>c</u>e	___	pla<u>n</u>	___
sen<u>d</u>	___	rai<u>s</u>e	___	thon<u>g</u>	___
lo<u>ck</u>	___	ca<u>sh</u>ew	___	ye<u>ll</u>ow	___
ba<u>gg</u>age	___	ca<u>s</u>ual	___	<u>wr</u>ist	___
wi<u>fe</u>	___	ran<u>ch</u>	___	<u>w</u>ater	___
c<u>r</u>ave	___	en<u>g</u>ine	___	<u>y</u>oung	___

2.6   Multiple Spellings for One Vowel Phoneme

Put the following words into phonemic transcription.

sit	_____	pretty	_____	build	_____
cyst	_____	weird	_____	give	_____
hear	_____	sieve	_____	marriage	_____
peer	_____	women	_____	sphere	_____
mere	_____	busy	_____	been	_____
leopard	_____	friend	_____	health	_____
cabin	_____	plaid	_____	laugh	_____
said	_____	flesh	_____	stare	_____
cup	_____	cousin	_____	money	_____
dark	_____	sergeant	_____	reservoir	_____
does	_____	fudge	_____	myrtle	_____
scream	_____	cheese	_____	theme	_____
good	_____	sugar	_____	would	_____
grief	_____	hungry	_____	me	_____
brawl	_____	naughty	_____	water	_____
people	_____	suite	_____	valley	_____
moth	_____	broad	_____	bought	_____
favor	_____	praise	_____	eight	_____
fluid	_____	true	_____	knew	_____
oboe	_____	load	_____	grow	_____
play	_____	age	_____	prey	_____
group	_____	spook	_____	do	_____
comb	_____	sew	_____	poultry	_____
time	_____	height	_____	rhyme	_____
boil	_____	enjoy	_____	Freud	_____
owl	_____	noun	_____	umlaut	_____
buy	_____	aisle	_____	dye	_____

2.7   Multiple Spellings for One Consonant Phoneme

clap	_____	chorus	_____	quiet	_____
goose	_____	egg	_____	ghost	_____
steak	_____	khaki	_____	oblique	_____
turn	_____	Thompson	_____	mixed	_____
reef	_____	rough	_____	lymph	_____
vest	_____	of	_____	Stephen	_____
cease	_____	fuss	_____	chance	_____
zeal	_____	fizzle	_____	busy	_____
scene	_____	blitz	_____	Xerox	_____
shop	_____	issue	_____	Chicago	_____
usual	_____	division	_____	cashmere	_____
spacious	_____	partial	_____	suspension	_____
chain	_____	question	_____	virtue	_____
job	_____	gem	_____	dodge	_____
hatch	_____	cello	_____	cordial	_____
worry	_____	quote	_____	wring	_____
sink	_____	anger	_____	anxiety	_____

2.8 Multiple Vowel Phonemes for One Spelling

Put the following words into phonemic transcription.

bit	_____	verb	_____	scarf	_____
sign	_____	we	_____	chalk	_____
police	_____	had	_____	judge	_____
pretty	_____	was	_____	flu	_____
tell	_____	hate	_____	bull	_____
mother	_____	gym	_____	head	_____
do	_____	myrrh	_____	heard	_____
go	_____	city	_____	meat	_____
mob	_____	try	_____	blow	_____
soft	_____	rear	_____	how	_____
double	_____	foul	_____	weird	_____
soup	_____	dried	_____	their	_____
soul	_____	sieve	_____	vein	_____
should	_____	thief	_____	conceit	_____
course	_____	friend	_____	stein	_____
again	_____	beauty	_____	been	_____
plaid	_____	chauffeur	_____	free	_____
maid	_____	exhaust	_____	matinee	_____
Caesar	_____	plateau	_____	does	_____
Gaelic	_____	laugh	_____	shoes	_____

2.9   Multiple Consonant Phonemes for One Spelling

Put the following words into phonemic transcription.

goose _____	noose _____	chemistry _____
beige _____	busy _____	chaperon _____
genius _____	sure _____	chip _____
gnaw _____	lesion _____	schism _____
ghetto _____	Thailand _____	extra _____
cough _____	though _____	xylophone _____
sight _____	thought _____	examine _____
carry _____		
cedar _____		
social _____		
cello _____		
czar _____		

2.10 Connected Speech

Put the following sentences into phonemic transcription.

1. Reputation is commonly measured by the acre. _____

_____

2. One always has strength enough to bear the misfortunes of one's friends.

_____

_____

3. I have lived too near a wood to be frightened of owls. _____

_____

4. If the beard were all, the goat might preach. _____

_____

5. Many would be cowards if they had courage enough. _____

_____

6. In settling an island, the first building erected by a Spaniard will be a church; by a Frenchman, a fort; by a Dutchman, a warehouse; and by an Englishman, an alehouse.

_____

_____

_____

_____

2.11   Morphophonemic Alternations

Variations in morphemes according to underlying phonological patterns are often called *morphophonemic alternations*. For example, the possessive morpheme in English appears as /s/ (as in *Pete's*), /z/ (as in *John's*), and /ɪz/ (as in *Tess's*), depending on the final phoneme of the word to which the possessive marker is attached. The following words illustrate morphophonemic variation of noun plurals, third-person singular indicative present of verbs, and past tenses and past participles of verbs. The sentences illustrate some still different kinds of alternation.

Put the following into phonemic transcription.

amazes	_____	garages	_____	slaps	_____
beads	_____	pales	_____	slabs	_____
beats	_____	pigs	_____	slashes	_____
brings	_____	picks	_____	sighs	_____
clings	_____	pours	_____	pianos	_____
journeys	_____	sages	_____	wreaths	_____
maims	_____	safes	_____	writhes	_____
misses	_____	saves	_____	wretches	_____
booed	_____	hooded	_____	razed	_____
banded	_____	raced	_____	sewed	_____
dried	_____	raged	_____	rowed	_____
deemed	_____	raked	_____	flayed	_____
delayed	_____	rained	_____	vaulted	_____
failed	_____	rated	_____	wronged	_____

The priest blessed the fleet. _____

It was a blessed event. _____

He is long-legged. _____

He legged along. _____

You have to go. _____

You have two goats. _____

I used to box. _____

I used two boxes. _____

2.12   Articulatory Descriptions of Phonemes

A.   Identify the following phonemes by writing the appropriate phonemic symbol in the blank beside its articulatory description.

0. voiced alveolar stop   /d/

1. bilabial nasal   _____

2. lax high back vowel   _____

3. mid central vowel   _____

4. voiceless alveopalatal affricate   _____

5. voiceless velar fricative   _____

6. low front vowel   _____

7. alveopalatal semivowel   _____

8. voiced interdental fricative   _____

9. mid back tense vowel   _____

10. alveolar lateral   _____

B.   Give the articulatory description of the following English phonemes.

0. /n/   alveolar nasal _____

1. /p/   _____

2. /ɛ/   _____

3. /z/   _____

4. /r/   _____

5. /ɑ/   _____

6. /w/   _____

7. /ž/   _____

8. /e/   _____

9. /k/   _____

10. /f/   _____

2.13   Minimal Pairs

A *minimal pair* consists of two words or phrases that differ by only one phoneme. For example, *bag* /bæg/ and *bug* /bəg/; *height* /hait/ and *mite* /mait/; and *stiff* /stɪf/ and *stick* /stɪk/ are all minimal pairs. As in children's games where you can change one letter of a written word at a time to form new words, you can form "chains" of minimal pairs: /ǰəg/ - /ǰæg/ - /ǰæk/ - /bæk/ - /bæg/ - /bɪg/ - /bɪn - /tɪn/ - /ton/ - /tod/ - /rod/ - /rud/ - /rul/ - /ful/ - /fɪl/ - /fɪb/ - /rɪb/ - /rɑb/ - /mɑb/ - /mɑp/ . . .

1. Construct such a chain of at least twenty phonemically minimal pairs. _____

_____

_____

_____

_____

2. Can you find a minimal pair in which /ŋ/ and /h/ are the two different phonemes?

Explain. _____

_____

_____

2.14 Pronunciation Guides in Dictionaries

Look up the recommended pronunciation of the words in the left-hand column in at least three different standard collegiate dictionaries, one of which is an edition of a Merriam-Webster dictionary (e.g., *Webster's Eighth* or *Ninth Collegiate Dictionary*). Enter each dictionary's recommended pronunciation in the chart. Enter your own pronunciation of the words in the right-hand column, using the transcription system of your text.

Word	Merriam-Webster	Dictionary 2	Dictionary 3	Dictionary 4	*Your own pronunciation*
beet					
bit					
bait					
bet					
bat					
but					
bot					
boot					
put					
boat					
bought					
bite					
bout					
boy					
beer					
bear					
bar					
burr					
boor					
bore					
buyer					
bower					
boyar*					

*Use the second pronunciation if two are listed.

1. Is the transcription system used in most collegiate dictionaries phonetic or phonemic?

_____

2. Note how the dictionaries other than Merriam-Webster's treat the pronunciation of *but*.
What is the difference between *u* and *ə*? _____

Does this fit with your intuition about your own speech? _____

Do you distinguish the sounds of the first (stressed) and second (unstressed) vowels in the
word *yucca*? _____

3. In many, if not most dialects of English, the distinction between /i/ and
/ɪ/, /e/ and /ɛ/, /æ/ and /ɑ/, and /u/ and /ʊ/ is neutralized before /r/. Comment on how
consistently the dictionaries handle this phenomenon. _____

_____

_____

4. Which of the pronunciation keys is hardest to follow? _____
Which one is most accurate phonemically? _____

5. What problems might nonnative speakers of English encounter in using the pronunciation guides of these dictionaries? _____

_____

_____

CHAPTER 3

WRITING

3.1 Important Terms

1. alphabet
2. cuneiform
3. Cyrillic
4. futhorc
5. grapheme
6. ideogram
7. logogram
8. petroglyph
9. pictogram
10. rune

Alphabet: A writing system consisting of symbols that represent individual sounds (phonemes)

Cuneiform: A syllabic writing system consisting of wedge-shaped signs used by various Middle Eastern cultures from the fourth to the 1st millenium BC

Cyrillic: official alphabet of Greek Orthodox Church.

Futhorc: The Runic alphabet. The name futhorc is formed from the 1st 6 symbols of the alphabet. The sounds [F u Θ o r k]

Grapheme: A single unit in a writing system; loosely, a letter of an alphabet

Ideogram: A graphic symbol that represents an idea or meaning without expressing a specific word.

Logogram: A written symbol that stands for an entire word.

Petroglyph: A carving or drawing on rock.

Pictogram: A written symbol representing a specific object; A picture of that object.

44

3.2   Questions for Review and Discussion

1. For what purposes was writing apparently first developed? *Preservation Solidify, Buisaress*
2. Under what circumstances is writing a more suitable means of communication than speech?
3. What is the difference between a pictogram and an ideogram?
4. What is the difference between a syllabary and an alphabet?
5. What is the difference between a logogram and a grapheme?
6. Name several ideograms familiar to native speakers of English.
7. Would a syllabic writing system be more or less suitable than an alphabet for writing English? Why or why not?
8. What phonological characteristics of a language make it *best* suited for a syllabic writing system?
9. What are the advantages of a logographic writing system? The disadvantages?
10. Cumbersome as it is, the Chinese logographic writing system is perhaps the best system for writing Chinese today. Suggest reasons why.
11. What are the advantages of an alphabetic writing system? The disadvantages?

Literacy = Politics   (Book : Key to Rememberance)

Ideogram — expresses ideas —
Syllable — has a vovel or dipthong + consonant
Morpheme — has a meaning

Syllabry: each symbol stands for a syllable
Alphabet: a letter is assigned to specific sound.
~Arbitrary — has cursivity

3.3 Pictograms and Ideograms

Many of the graphemes used in the various writing systems of the world today were once pictographic, though they have been so altered and simplified over the millennia that their pictographic origins are no longer obvious. For example, the Latin letter *a* is derived from the Semitic *aleph* 'ox', and we can still see the head of an ox if we invert the capital form of the letter: ∀ . Pictograms are still widely used today, especially for brevity and in situations where speakers of different languages are to be addressed; road signs such as Ⓝ are obvious examples.

   Many other familiar ideograms are also pictographic in origin, but the association between picture and meaning may be obscured. For example, ↗ is a symbol for November because Sagittarius, the archer, is the astrological sign for November; the arrow, of course, represents the archer.

   Explain how each of the following ideograms is ultimately pictographic.

1. ♉   (sign for April-May) _____

2. ⟍   (music: *diminuendo, decrescendo*) _____

3. ✝   (biology: hybrid) _____

4. ♆   (astronomy or astrology: Neptune) _____

5. ↑   (chemistry: gas) _____

6. ✝   (preceding a date = "died") _____

7. ♈   (vernal equinox) _____

8. ♒   (sign for January) _____

3.4 Ideograms: Chinese

In the Chinese writing system, many characters contain both a semantic and a phonetic element. Frequently, the semantic element is represented by a **radical** that is itself an independent word. For example, the radical 田 *tián* 'field' appears in words such as 畴 *chóu* 'farmland' and 畜 *chù* 'livestock'.

For the following items, guess the meaning of each semantic radical by examining the meanings of the characters that contain it. Write this core meaning in the blank beside the radical.

1. 女 *nü* _____

奴 *nú* 'slave'; 奶 *nǎi* 'breasts'; 她 *tā* 'she'; 妍 *yán* 'beautiful'; 姊 *zǐ* 'elder sister'; 姻 *yīn* 'marriage'; 妖 *yāo* 'evil spirit'; 妈 *mā* 'mother'

2. 目 *mù* _____

盹 *dǔn* 'doze'; 眨 *zhǎ* 'blink'; 看 *kàn* 'see'; 眉 *méi* 'eyebrow'; 眺 *tiào* 'look into the distance'; 眸 *móu* 'pupil (of eye)'; 睇 *dì* 'look askance'; 瞄 *miáo* 'take aim'

3. 火 *huǒ* _____

灯 *dēng* 'lamp, lantern'; 灼 *zhuó* 'burn, scorch'; 炎 *yán* 'inflammation'; 炜 *wěi* 'bright'; 炝 *qiàng* 'boil'; 炽 *chì* 'ablaze'; 炮 *pào* 'cannon'; 烟 *yān* 'smoke, tobacco'

4. 虫 *chóng* _____

虻 *méng* 'horsefly'; 蚁 *yǐ* 'ant'; 蚤 *zǎo* 'flea'; 蚌 *bàng* 'clam'; 蛀 *zhù* 'moth'; 蛇 *shé* 'snake'; 蛟 *jiāo* 'flood dragon'; 蛙 *wā* 'frog'; 蛛 *zhū* 'spider'

5. 石 *shí* _____

矿 *kuàng* 'ore, mineral deposit'; 矽 *xī* 'silicon'; 研 *yán* 'pestle, grind'; 砺 *lì* 'whetstone'; 砾 *lì* 'gravel'; 硬 *yìng* 'hard'; 碣 *jié* 'stone tablet'; 礁 *jiāo* 'reef'

6. 山 *shān* _____

岌 *jí* 'lofty, towering'; 岗 *gǎng* 'hillock'; 岩 *yán* 'cliff'; 岬 *jiǎ* 'promontory'; 岭 *lǐng* 'mountain range'; 峙 *zhì* 'stand erect'; 峰 *fēng* 'peak'; 巅 *diān* 'summit'

7. 气 *qì* _____

氕 *piē* 'protium'; 氖 *nǎi* 'neon'; 氙 *xiān* 'xenon'; 氛 *fēn* 'atmosphere'; 氡 *dōng* 'radon'; 氢 *qīng* 'hydrogen'; 氟 *fú* 'fluorine'; 氧 *yǎng* 'oxygen'

8. 弓 *gōng* _____

引 *yǐn* 'draw, stretch'; 弛 *chí* 'relax, slacken'; 张 *zhāng* 'stretch, spread'; 弦 *xián* 'bowstring spring'; 弧 *hú* 'arc'; 弩 *nǔ* 'crossbow'; 弹 *dàn* 'bullet, bomb'; 弹 *tán* 'to shoot, pluck'

9. 歹 *dǎi* _____

死 *sǐ* 'die, death'; 歼 *jiān* 'annihilate'; 殁 *mò* 'die'; 残 *cán* 'savage, furious'; 殃 *yāng* 'disaster'; 殆 *dài* 'danger'; 殒 *yǔn* 'perish'; 殨 *huì* 'festering'

10. 车 *chē* _____

轧 *yà* 'run over'; 轨 *guǐ* 'path, track'; 转 *zhuàn* 'turn, revolve'; 轮 *lún* 'wheel'; 轴 *zhóu* 'shaft, axle'; 轸 *zhěn* 'carriage'; 轿 *jiào* 'sedan chair'; 挽 *wǎn* 'pull, draw'; 辋 *wǎng* 'rim of a wheel'

3.5 Syllabaries: Japanese

Modern Japanese uses three writing systems: (1) the *kanji*, based on and usually identical to Chinese logograms; (2) the *hiragana*, a syllabary used for native words other than nouns, verbs, and adjectives; for inflectional endings for all words written in *kanji*; and for some nouns, verbs, and adjectives for which the formerly used *kanji* have become obsolete; and (3) the *katakana*, a second syllabary used for foreign loanwords and foreign proper names, onomatopoeic words, names of plants and animals used in a scientific context, and a few other special contexts. (In contemporary Japan, there is a fourth de facto system: romanization, or the Latin alphabet, although it is not officially recognized.)

The *hiragana* and the *katakana* are presented in the following chart, together with their syllabic equivalents. The only additional information you need to know for this exercise is that the voiced sounds [g z d] are indicated in both kanas by two short diagonal strokes at the upper right corner of the symbol for the corresponding voiceless sound [k s t]. Thus, for example, in *hiragana*, く is [ku], and ぐ is [gu]. Similarly, in *katakana*, テ is [te], and デ is [de]. In both kanas, all syllables beginning with [p] are formed like syllables beginning with [h], but with the addition of a small circle at the upper right corner. For example, in *hiragana*, ひ is [hi], and ぴ is [pi]; in *katakana*, ホ is [ho], and ポ is [po]. In both kanas, [b] is treated as the voiced version of [h]; for example, ヒ is [hi] and ビ is [bi] in *katakana*. In *katakana*, long vowels in loanwords are indicated by a following horizontal stroke: ー , as in コーヒー ([kōhī] 'coffee').

The
Katakana

	ア a	イ i	ウ u	エ e	オ o
k	カ ka	キ ki	ク ku	ケ ke	コ ko
s	サ sa	シ shi/si	ス su	セ se	ソ so
t	タ ta	チ chi/ti	ツ tsu/tu	テ te	ト to
n	ナ na	ニ ni	ヌ nu	ネ ne	ノ no
h	ハ ha(wa)	ヒ hi	フ fu/hu	ヘ he(e)	ホ ho
m	マ ma	ミ mi	ム mu	メ me	モ mo
y	ヤ ya	—	ユ yu	—	ヨ yo
r	ラ ra	リ ri	ル ru	レ re	ロ ro
w	ワ wa	—	—	—	ヲ o
					ン n

The
Hiragana

	あ a	い i	う u	え e	お o
k	か ka	き ki	く ku	け ke	こ ko
s	さ sa	し shi/si	す su	せ se	そ so
t	た ta	ち chi/ti	つ tsu/tu	て te	と to
n	な na	に ni	ぬ nu	ね ne	の no
h	は ha(wa)	ひ hi	ふ fu/hu	へ he(e)	ほ ho
m	ま ma	み mi	む mu	め me	も mo
y	や ya	—	ゆ yu	—	よ yo
r	ら ra	り ri	る ru	れ re	ろ ro
w	わ wa	—	—	—	を o
					ん n

1. Transliterate the following Japanese words from *hiragana*.

よく   _____ 'well, often'

できる   _____ 'can, be able'

うれしい _____ 'happy'

あそこ   _____ 'there'

2. Write the following Japanese words in *hiragana*.

e ('to') _____

kono ('this, these') _____

isu ('chair') _____

hashi ('chopsticks') _____

3. The following words, written in *katakana*, mean *beer, Beethoven, bus, cream, knife, taxi, table,* and *whiskey* in Japanese. Match the *katakana* with the meaning by writing the correct meaning to the right.

タクシ   _____

バス   _____

ナイフ   _____

ビール   _____

テーブル   _____

ウイスキー   _____

クリーム   _____

ベートーベン   _____

4. Write the following words in *katakana*.

tabako ('tobacco') _____

Amerika _____

tenisu ('tennis') _____

Toyota _____

3.6   A Syllabary for English?

Invent a syllabary for English to write the following words.

1. pie _____	12. spy _____	23. strength _____
2. buy _____	13. spry _____	24. shopped _____
3. tie _____	14. sky _____	25. rubbed _____
4. die _____	15. sly _____	26. haunted _____
5. guy _____	16. snow _____	27. sill _____
6. vie _____	17. slow _____	28. silly _____
7. sigh _____	18. shrill _____	29. slowly _____
8. try _____	19. spill _____	30. usual _____
9. thigh _____	20. still _____	31. major _____
10. thy _____	21. expend _____	32. decide _____
11. shy _____	22. stronger _____	33. cheap _____

A. How many *different* characters did you need for the words in the list? _____

_____

B. What problems did you encounter in devising your syllabary? _____

_____

_____

C. Would there be any advantages to a syllabic writing system for English? Why
or why not? _____

_____

D. What would the major disadvantage be? _____

_____

3.7 Syllabary or Alphabet? Devanagari

Hindi, the most widely used of the modern Indic languages, is the native language of about 40 percent of the population of India. Its writing system is the Devanagari (or Nagari) script. Hindi has a complex phonological system with forty consonant phonemes and eleven vowels. For simplicity's sake, we will limit our illustration of the script to eleven consonants and seven vowels.

Consonants

क	/k/		प	/p/
ग	/g/		ब	/b/
त	/t/		म	/m/
द	/d/		र	/r/
न	/n/		ल	/l/
स	/s/			

Vowels

अ	/a/		उ	/u/
आ	/ā/		ऊ	/ū/
इ	/i/		ओ	/o/
ई	/ī/			

A few complete words written in the Devanagari script follow:

अब	/ab/ 'now'		बीस	/bīs/ 'twenty'
आग	/āg/ 'fire'		पानी	/pānī/ 'water'
इतना	/itnā/ 'this much'		दाल	/dāl/ 'lentil'
उनतीस	/untīs/ 'twenty-nine'		सन	/san/ 'year, era'
कब	/kab/ 'when?'		सिर	/sir/ 'head'
कम	/kam/ 'little, less'		रोग	/rog/ 'illness'
कि	/ki/ 'that'		रूप	/rūp/ 'form'
तू	/tū/ 'you' (intimate)		लाल	/lāl/ 'red'
बस	/bas/ 'bus'			

1. Does the script go from left to right or right to left? _____

2. How is /a/ written after a consonant? _____

3. What is unique about the writing of /i/ when it appears (in speech) after a consonant?

_____

4. Transliterate the following words written in Devanagari.

a.	तब	'then' _____	f.	लोग	'people' _____
b.	सो	'so' _____	g.	गीत	'song' _____
c.	बुरा	'bad' _____	h.	सूती	'made of cotton' _____
d.	पति	'husband' _____	i.	उदास	'sad' _____
e.	मन	'mind' _____	j.	कुली	'porter' _____

5. Write the following Hindi words in the Devanagari script.

    a. /pīlā/ 'yellow'   _____

    b. /din/ 'day'   _____

    c. /nal/ 'pipe, tap'   _____

    d. /sās/ 'mother-in-law'   _____

    e. /gap/ 'gossip'   _____

6. In what way(s) is the Devanagari script like a syllabary? _____

_____

_____

7. In what ways is it like an alphabet? _____

_____

3.8   Related Alphabets

Though they have diverged over the centuries, the Greek, Latin, and Cyrillic (Russian) alphabets are closely related—both the Latin and Cyrillic alphabets are derived from the Greek. Using the table of alphabets to be found in any good desk dictionary, transliterate the following words into the Latin alphabet. Then give an English version of the words, all of which exist in English, though the usual English spelling may vary slightly from the transliteration.

Greek Word	Transliteration	English Spelling
ἀκμή	akmē	acme
ἀκροβᾰτέω		
καταστροφή		
κόσμος		
κρῐτήριον		
κῠβερνήτης		
σύνταξις		
φαρμᾰκεία		
ψῡχή		

Russian Word	Transliteration	English Spelling
борзой	borzoĭ	borzoi
Большевизм		
борщ		
водка		
гласность		
Правда		
самовар		
спутник		
тундра		

3.9   Other European Alphabets

Although both the Latin and the Cyrillic alphabets are clearly based on the Greek alphabet, other alphabets not obviously connected with the Greek alphabet were used for writing Indo-European languages in the past.

A.   The Ogham alphabet was used for writing Old Irish, probably as early as the fourth century A.D. Though it was abandoned for the Latin alphabet after Christianity came to Ireland, the Ogham alphabet was still learned and occasionally used (for example, in marginal notes) throughout the Middle Ages. All the characters ("letters") were written along a vertical line. Consonants were formed by one to five horizontal or diagonal strokes written to one side of or across this vertical line. Vowels consisted of one to five short strokes written on the vertical line. The symbol for *f* was also used for *v* and *w*. There was no symbol for *p* because Old Irish had no /p/ phoneme.

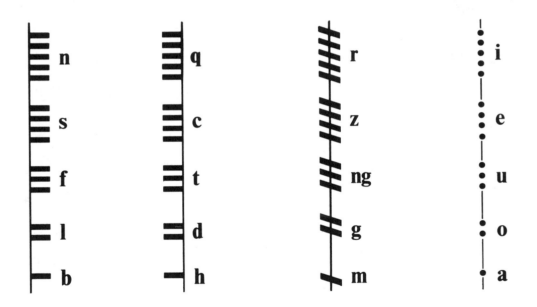

Transliterate the following into the Latin alphabet. (Although Ogham usually went from bottom to top or from right to left, this sample is written top to bottom.)

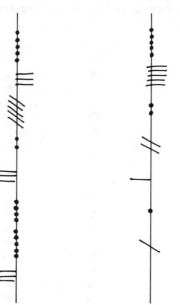

1. What are the advantages, if any, of the Ogham alphabet over the Latin alphabet? __

_____

2. What are the disadvantages, if any? _____

_____

3. Old Irish had neither /h/ nor /z/ in its phonemic system. Can you suggest a reason why symbols for these sounds were included in the Ogham alphabet?

_____

_____

B. The Glagolitic alphabet was an early Slavonic alphabet. There is some dispute over which came first, the Glagolitic or the Cyrillic alphabet, but, in any case, the Cyrillic eventually replaced the Glagolitic for writing Russian and the Slavic languages of other peoples following the Russian Orthodox Church.

Glagolitic	Transliteration	Glagolitic	Transliteration
✛	a	Ⰲ	t
Ⰱ	b	Ⰴ	u
Ⰲ	v	Ⰶ	f
Ⰳ	g	Ⱆ	x/ch
Ⰴ	d	Ⱁ	o
Ⰶ	z	Ⱋ	št
Ⰷ	ǰ	Ⱌ	ts
Ⰸ	z	Ⱍ	č
Ⰹ Ⰺ	i	Ⱎ	š
Ⰻ	i	Ⱏ	ŭ
Ⰼ	g'	ⰟⰉ	y
Ⰽ	k	Ⱐ	ĭ
Ⰾ	l	Ⰰ	æ
Ⰿ	m	Ⱓ	ju
Ⱀ	n	Ⱑ	ja
Ⱁ	o	Ⱔ	ę̄
Ⱂ	p	Ⱗ	ʒ
Ⱃ	r	Ⱘ	ję̄
Ⱄ	s	Ⱙ	jǫ̃
		Ⱚ	υ

Transliterate the following and then transliterate your transliteration into traditional English spelling.

✛Ⰹ ⰁⰑⰲ Ⰹⰲ Ⰹⱃ ⰃⰎⰰⰃⱁⰾⰹⱅⰹⰽ

_____

_____

Suggest reasons why the Cyrillic alphabet replaced the Glagolitic alphabet.

_____

_____

3.10   A Millennium of English Handwriting

Even though English has been written with the Latin alphabet since the seventh century A.D., the traditional ways of forming some of the graphemes (letters) have altered over the years. In other words, like other aspects of language, handwriting has changed. The following illustrations are of English handwriting from late OE (c. 1050), late ME (c. 1445), and late EMnE (1783).

Ælfric's *Exodus*

Gloss

þu lac þa ablendað gleawne. & awendað rihtwisra word. Ne beo þu elþeodigū grā. forþā ðe ge wæron elþeodige on egypta lande. Saw VI gear þin land & gadera his wæstmas & læt hit restan on þā seofoðan þ ðearfon eton þær of & wildeor. do þu on þ[i]nū wingearde & on þinū elebeamon. wyrc ·v[i]· dagas & geswic on þā ·vii· foðan þ þin oxa & þin assan hi gereston & þ þynre wylne sunu sy gehyrt & se utan cymena . . .

Reginald Pecock's "The Reule of Crysten Religioun"

Gloss

Eche creature in mankynde is maad of a body and of a resonable soule. The firste ptie of þis trouwþe, þat is to seie, þᵗ ech of vs haþ in beyng a body: we may knowe bi open assay or expience, fforwhi we mowe se it, touche it, and se it worche hise effectis: riȝt as we mowe knowe oþere bodies deptid from vs, þat þei verrily ben in kynde, and þᵗfore of þis partie is no dout . . .

Edward Gibbon: Notes for *Decline and Fall of the Roman Empire*

Gloss

The pleasing and even Philosophical fiction of the seven sleepers who in the year 250 retired into a cave near Ephesus to escape the persecution of Decius, and who awoke one hundred and eighty seven years afterwards (see Asseman. Bib. Orient. Tom i p 338) has been received with universal applause. It is remarkable enough that this prodigy should be related by James Sarugi who was born only fifteen years after it is supposed to have happened; and who died Bishop of Batnæ in the year 521.

Grapheme	Ælfric	Pecock	Gibbon
a			
b			
c			
d			
e			
f			
g			
h			
i			
j			
k			
l			
m			
n			
o			
p			
q			
r			
s			
t			
u			
v			
w			
x			
y			
z			
æ			
þ			
ð			
ʒ			
&			

1. Can you guess what a macron (line) over a vowel represents in the Ælfric manuscript?

   _____

2. What other abbreviations appear in the three texts? _____

   _____

3. Pecock uses two different forms of *s*. What are they? _____
   Is their distribution arbitrary? _____

   _____

4. Explain the formation of double *s* in the Gibbon manuscript (see the word *Asseman*).

   _____

5. How does Gibbon form a capital *I*? _____ A capital *J*? _____

   _____

6. Which letters show little basic variation over the centuries? _____

   _____

7. Which letters show the most variation over the centuries? _____

   _____

CHAPTER 4

LANGUAGE FAMILIES AND INDO-EUROPEAN

4.1 Important Terms

1. ablative
2. ablaut
3. accusative
4. active voice
5. agglutinative language
6. Albanian
7. Anatolian
8. aorist
9. apophony
10. Armenian
11. aspect
12. Balto-Slavic
13. Franz Bopp
14. Britannic
15. case
16. Celtic
17. centum languages
18. Classical Latin
19. cognate languages
20. Common Germanic
21. Common Indo-European
22. dative
23. definite (weak) adjective
24. demotic
25. dental preterite
26. dialect
27. East Germanic
28. family tree
29. First Grammarian
30. First Sound (Consonant) Shift
31. futhorc
32. future
33. gender
34. genitive
35. Germanic
36. Glagolitic alphabet
37. Goidelic
38. Gothic
39. Jakob Grimm
40. Grimm's Law
41. Hellenic
42. High German
43. Hittite
44. Bedřich Hrozný
45. imperative
46. imperfect
47. indefinite (strong) adjective
48. indicative
49. Indo-European
50. Indo-Iranian
51. inflectional language
52. injunctive
53. instrumental
54. isolating language
55. Italic
56. Sir William Jones
57. koine
58. Kurgan culture
59. labiovelar
60. language family
61. Linear B
62. loanword
63. locative
64. Low German
65. middle voice
66. mood
67. native word
68. nominative
69. North Germanic
70. number
71. Ogham
72. Old Norse
73. optative
74. passive voice
75. perfect
76. person
77. pluperfect
78. present
79. preterite
80. prosody
81. Rasmus Rask
82. Romance language
83. Sanskrit
84. satem languages
85. J. J. Scaliger
86. Friedrich von Schlegel
87. Johannes Schmidt
88. Second Sound (Consonant) Shift
89. *Stammbaum* theory
90. subjunctive
91. Tocharian
92. Bishop Ulfilas
93. Michael Ventris
94. Karl Verner
95. Verner's Law
96. vocative
97. voice
98. vowel gradation
99. Vulgar Latin
100. *Wellentheorie*
101. West Germanic

Non-Indo-European Language Families

1. Afro-Asiatic
2. Algonquian
3. Altaic
4. Arawak
5. Athabaskan
6. Australian
7. Austronesian
8. Austro-Tai
9. Carib
10. Caucasian
11. Eskimo-Aleut
12. Etruscan
13. Finno-Ugric
14. Hamito-Semitic
15. Iroquois
16. Khoisan
17. Malayo-Polynesian
18. Mayan
19. Mon-Khmer
20. Muskogean
21. Niger-Congo
22. Papuan
23. Quechua
24. Sino-Tibetan
25. Siouan
26. Tai
27. Tupi-Guarani
28. Uralic
29. Uto-Aztecan

4.2 Questions for Review and Discussion

1. What are some of the reasons why words with the same meaning may have the same or similar phonological form in different languages?
2. When seeking to determine the relationship between two languages, what kinds of shared vocabulary items provide the best evidence for relatedness?
3. What are some of the important language families of the world apart from Indo-European?
4. Explain the difference between the *Stammbaum* theory and the *Wellentheorie* of similarities among languages.
5. What do Basque and Etruscan have in common?
6. Is PDE best classified as an inflecting, agglutinative, or isolating language?
7. What are the principal subdivisions of Indo-European?
8. What are some of the features common to most or all Indo-European languages?
9. What evidence is used to determine the original home of the Indo-Europeans?
10. When did Indo-European start to split into separate groups?
11. For which Indo-European languages do we have the oldest surviving written records?
12. Why is Hittite of particular interest to Indo-European scholars? Tocharian? Lithuanian?
13. What delayed recognition of Indo-European as a language family?
14. Why is Sir William Jones important to historical linguistics?
15. Where does Indo-European ablaut survive in PDE?
16. What is the difference between aspect and tense?
17. Apart from a marginally surviving subjunctive inflection, how does PDE express mood?
18. What major characteristics distinguish Germanic languages from other Indo-European languages?
19. Why is Gothic of particular interest to Germanic scholars?
20. What do the terms "High" German and "Low" German refer to?
21. Where did Germanic acquire its Common Germanic vocabulary not shared by other Indo-European languages?
22. Describe the operation of the First Consonant Shift (Grimm's Law and Verner's Law).

4.3 Lexical Similarities Between Languages

Almost any two languages in the world will have some words similar in both meaning and sound. Among the different reasons for such similarities are

  (a) Onomatopoeia: the words echo the actual sound (English *miaow-miaow*; Chinese *miao*)
  (b) Coincidence (English *me*; Swahili *mimi*)
  (c) Borrowing, either from one language to the other or both from a third language (English *mirror*; French *miroir*)
  (d) Common origin: both languages descend from a common parent language (English *mild*; German *mild*)

Indicate the most likely explanation for the similar pairs listed below by placing the appropriate letter (a), (b), (c), or (d) in the blank to the right. Use your intuition, knowledge of history and geography, and any dictionaries you like, to help you decide.

 1. English *discretion*; Czech *diskrétnost*   _____

 2. Russian *meh*; Ibo *nmáa* 'noise made by a goat'   _____

 3. Spanish *domar*; Italian *domare* 'to tame'   _____

 4. English *seven*; Hebrew *ševa*   _____

 5. English *crab*; Icelandic *krabbi*   _____

 6. Hieroglyphic Egyptian *bu*; Chinese *bu* 'not'   _____

 7. Hungarian *garázs*; Turkish *garaj* 'garage'   _____

 8. English *chuckle*; Swahili *chekelea*   _____

 9. Japanese *sansui*; Chinese *shanshui* 'landscape'   _____

10. English *bang*; Tagalog *banggâ*   _____

11. Hindi *do*; Persian *do* 'two'   _____

4.4 Cognate Languages

The accompanying chart lists fourteen words from seventeen different languages. Of these seventeen languages, twelve are Indo-European and represent three different subdivisions of Indo-European. The remaining five languages represent three different sets of related, non-Indo-European languages. Inspect the list and sort the languages into six groups, three Indo-European and three non-Indo-European. Remember that some forms will not be cognate, even between closely related languages; further, the more distantly related two languages are, the more differences between them will be found.

1. Write the numbers of the languages in each group on the lines provided.

Group I, Indo-European (four languages) _2,_____

Group II, Indo-European (four languages) _3,_____

Group III, Indo-European (four languages) _5,_____

Group IV, non-Indo-European (two languages) _1,_____

Group V, non-Indo-European (two languages) _4,_____

Group VI, non-Indo-European (one language) _____

2. From your knowledge that English is a Germanic language, identify which of the groups above is Germanic. _____

3. Can you identify any of the other groups? _____

_____

_____

4. In which *group* do the member languages seem to be *least* closely related? _____

_____

5. How do you explain the fact that the word for "tobacco" is obviously from the same root in many different, unrelated languages, yet is sometimes from different roots in two related languages? _____

_____

_____

Language	"hand"	"fish"	"eye"	"water"	"under"	"tobacco"	"wind"
1	yad	samak	ayn	ma	taht	tabgh	rih
2	ruka	ryba	oko	voda	pod	tabák	vítr
3	hand	vis	oog	water	onder	tabak	wind
4	käsi	kala	silmä	vesi	alla	tupakka	tuuli
5	main	poisson	œil	eau	sous	tabac	vent
6	Hand	Fisch	Auge	Wasser	unter	Tabak	Wind
7	yad	dag	ayin	mayim	tachat	tabak	ruach
8	kéz	hal	szem	víz	alatt	dohány	szél
9	tangan	ikan	mata	air	bawah	tempakau	angin
10	mano	pesce	occhio	acqua	sotto	tabacco	vento
11	hånd	fisk	øye	vann	under	tobakk	vind
12	ręka	ryba	oko	woda	pod	tytoń	wiatr
13	mînă	peşte	ochi	apă	sub	tutun	vint
14	ruká	riba	glas	vadá	pod	tabák	vyéter
15	ruka	riba	oko	voda	ispod	duhan	vjetar
16	mano	pescado	ojo	agua	bajo	tabaco	viento
17	hand	fisch	oig	vasser	unter	tabik	vind

Language	"red"	"death"	"elbow"	"fire"	"liver"	"oak"	"three"
1	ahmar	mawt	mirfaq	nar	kabid	ballout	tsalatsa
2	červeny	smrt	loket	oheň	játra	dub	tři
3	rood	dood	elleboog	vuur	lever	eik	drie
4	punainem	kuolema	kynärpää	tuli	maksa	tammi	kolme
5	rouge	mort	coude	feu	foie	chêne	trois
6	rot	Tod	Ellenbogen	Feuer	Leber	Eiche	drei
7	adom	mavet	marpek	esch	kaved	alon	schloschah
8	piros	halál	könyök	tüz	máj	tölgy	három
9	mérah	mati	siku	api	hati	ék	tiga
10	rosso	morte	gomito	fuoco	fegato	quercia	tre
11	rød	død	albue	ild	lever	eik	tre
12	czerwony	śmierć	łokieć	ogień	wątroba	dąb	trzy
13	roşu	moarte	cot	foc	ficat	stejar	trei
14	krásni	smyert	lókat	agón	pyéchen	dup	tri
15	crven	smrt	lakat	vatra	jetra	hrast	tri
16	rojo	muerte	codo	fuego	hígado	roble	tres
17	roit	toit	elen boigen	sreife	leber	demb	drei

4.5   The Spread of the Indo-Europeans

The accompanying map indicates by arrows the general direction of the spread of the ten branches of Indo-European from its presumed original homeland in eastern Europe/western Asia in the area north of the Black and Caspian Seas. (The arrows do *not* reflect the fact that these migrations extended over several millenia, nor do they necessarily reflect the exact path taken by the migrating peoples.)

By consulting your text (and an atlas if necessary), match the branches with the numbers indicated by the arrows.

____ A. Albanian   ____ F. Germanic
____ B. Anatolian   ____ G. Hellenic
____ C. Armenian   ____ H. Indo-Iranian
____ D. Balto-Slavic   ____ I. Italic
____ E. Celtic   ____ J. Tocharian

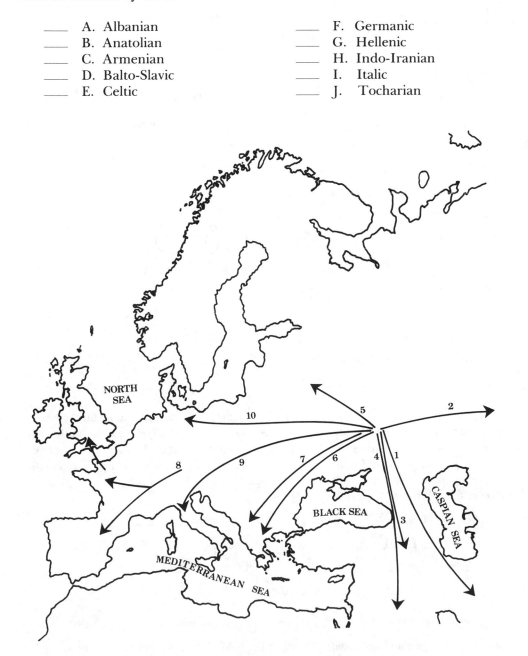

4.6   Applying Grimm's and Verner's Laws

1. Give the PDE reflex (descendant) of the following reconstructed Indo-European (IE) roots. Every example includes at least one application of Grimm's Law or Verner's Law, or both. Because the development of vowels from IE to PDE is extremely complex, you will have to ignore the vowels for this exercise. Concentrate on consonant correspondences. The part-of-speech category may have changed, and the meaning may be slightly different.

IE Root	PDE Reflex
*bhreg- 'break'	break
*dom-o- 'to constrain'	
*gwou- 'cattle'	cow
*kerd- 'cardiac'	heart
*mn-ti- 'to think'	mind
*gn-ti- 'origin, race' — hereditary	
*pū-lo- 'to rot, decay'	fallow
*reug- 'to vomit, belch, smoke'	
*roup- 'to snatch'	grab (sear)
*saus- 'dry' — roast —	stab
*steip- 'to stick, compress'	sweet
*swād- 'pleasant'	sweat
*swod- 'to exude'	knot
*nod- 'to tie, bind'	
*pleus- 'feather, animal coat'	
*yeug- 'to join'	

2. Grimm's and Verner's Laws can be applied in reverse, so to speak, to identify cognates of English words in Indo-European languages which did not undergo these sound changes. For example, given native English *fallow*, we would expect its Latin cognate to begin with [p]. And, indeed, English *fallow* is cognate with the Latin loan *pallor*. For the following native English words, supply a cognate loan in English from French, Latin, or Greek that illustrates the original IE stops.

fire	pyre	mother	mater
fish	pices	three	tres
foot	pod - pedis	tooth	dentis
horn	cornu - cornet		

3. If we know that *grain* in Indo-European is *grə-no-, why are we certain that *grain* is a borrowed word and not a native word in English? (Because g > k)

4. Given that the Latin loans *stolid* and *stance* are cognate with native English *still* and *stand*, respectively, why did Grimm's Law not apply to the second consonant [t]? <u>Voiceless stops in IE are preserved in Germanic when following another voiceless stop or /s/</u>

4.7 Semantic Shift from IE to PDE

The items in the first column are probable IE roots and their basic meaning. The items in the second column are PDE derivatives, direct or indirect, from these IE roots. In each instance, the PDE meaning deviates in some way from the IE meaning. Trace the probable path or nature of the shift in meaning.

IE	PDE	Nature of Shift in Meaning
0. *bhāghu- 'elbow, shoulder'	bough	*From a joint in a human to a joint in a tree.*
1. *agro- 'field'	acre	
2. *bhāgo- 'beech tree'	book	
3. *bhē- 'to warm'	bath	
4. *bhedh- 'to dig'	bed	
5. *ghasto- 'rod, staff'	yard	
6. *ghow-ē- 'to honor, worship'	gawk	
7. *kenəko- 'yellow, golden'	honey	
8. *kēwero- 'north, north wind'	shower	
9. *kleng- 'to bend, turn'	link	
10. *meigh- 'to urinate'	mist	
11. *molko- 'skin bag'	mail	
12. *preu- 'to hop'	frog	
13. *rebh- 'to roof over'	rib	

14. *skep- 'to cut, scrape'   shape   _____

_____

15. *splei- 'to splice, split'   flint   _____

_____

16. *terkw- 'to turn'   queer   _____

_____

17. *teuə- 'to swell'   thigh   _____

_____

18. *weidh- 'to separate'   widow   _____

_____

19. *weik- 'to bend, wind'   wicker   _____

_____

20. *wespero- 'evening, night'   west   _____

_____

4.8   Cognate Words in Germanic Languages

The parallel passages here are from Matthew 9:1–8.* The Gothic was translated from Greek in the fourth century A.D. and is heavily influenced by Greek syntax. The Old English and the Old Norse are based primarily on the Latin Vulgate; the Old English translation was made in the late tenth century, and the Old Norse text even later. Nonetheless, despite the disparity in dates and translation history, the texts show clearly that the three languages are all related, though differing spelling traditions tend to obscure some of the similarities. The gloss is for the Old English text; it will often not correspond exactly to the Gothic and Old Norse texts.

Gothic   Jah atsteigands in skip   ufarlaiþ   jah qam
Old Norse   Ok er Jesus stē ā skip,   fōr hann yfer um aptr, ok kom
Old English þā āstāh hē on scyp,   and ofer-seglode   and cōm
            Then climbed he on ship and over-sailed   and came

Goth in seinai baurg.   þanuh atberun   du imma   usliþan
ON   ī sīna borg.   Ok siā, at þeir førþo til hans iktsiūkan mann,
OE   on his ceastre.   þā brōhton hig   hym   ænne laman
     into his city.   *Then brought they*   *him*   *a cripple*

Goth ana ligra ligandan. Jah gasaiƕands Jesus galaubein   ize qaþ
ON   sā er ī sæng lā.   En sem Jesus leit   þeira trū,   sagþe hann
OE   on bedde licgende;   þā geseah sē Hǣlend   hyra gelēafan and cwæþ
     in bed lying.   *Then saw the Savior* *their faith* *and said*

Goth du þamma usliþin: þrafstei þuk, barnilo
ON   til hins iktsiūkan:
OE   tō þām laman,   Lā, bearn, gelȳfe;
     to the cripple,   *Lo, child, believe;*

Goth afletanda þus frawaurhteis þeinos. þaruh sumai þize bokarje qeþun
ON   þīnar synder ero þēr fyrergefnar.   Ok, siā, at nokkorer af skriptlærþom sǫgþo
OE   þē bēoþ þīne synna forgyfene.   þā cwǣden hig sume þā bōceras
     (to) you are your sins forgiven. *Then said they some (of) the scholars*

Goth in sis silbam: sa wajamereiþ.   Jah witands Jesus
ON   meþ siǫlfom sēr, siā guþlestar.   Ok sem Jesus sā
OE   him betwȳnan,   þes spycþ bysmorsprǣce.   þā sē Hǣlend geseah
     them between, *this (one) speaks blasphemy.* *When the Savior saw*

Goth þos mitonins ize qaþ: Duƕe jus mitoþ ubila
ON   þeira hugsaner, sagþe hann: huar fyrer hugseþ ēr suā vǫndt
OE   hyra geþanc,   þā cwæþ hē: Tō hwī þence gē yfel
     their thought, *then said he:* *Why think you* *evil*

Goth in hairtam izwaraim? ƕaþar ist raihtis azetizo qiþan:
ON   ī yþrom hiǫrtom?   Huārt er auþveldara   at segia:
OE   on ēowrum heortum?   Hwæt is ēaþlīcere   tō cweþenna,
     in your hearts?   *Indeed is easier*   *to say,*

*Specimen texts from E. Prokosch, *A Comparative Germanic Grammar* (Baltimore: Linguistic Society of America, 1939; repr. 1960), pp. 295, 296.

Goth afletanda þus frawaurhteis, þau qiþan: urreis jah gagg?
ON þēr ero þīnar synder fyrergefnar eþa at segia: statt upp ok gakk?
OE þē bēoþ forgyfene þīne synna, oþþe tō cweþanne, Ārīs and gā?
  (to) you are forgiven your sins *than to say,* *Arise and go?*

Goth Aþþan ei witeiþ þatei waldufni habaiþ sa sunus mans ana airþai
ON En suā at ēr viteþ, þat manzens son hefer makt ā iǫrþ
OE þæt gē sōþlīce witon þæt mannes sunu hæfþ anweald on eorþan
  (so) that you truly know *that man's son has power* *on earth*

Goth afletan frawaurhtins, þanuh qaþ du þamma uslíþin:
ON synder at fyrergefnar, þā sagþe hann til hins itsiūka:
OE synna tō forgyfanne, þā cwæþ hē tō þam laman,
  sins to forgive, *then said he* *to the cripple,*

Goth Urreisands nim þana ligr þeinana jah gagg in gard þeinana.
ON statt upp, tak īlegu þīna, ok gakk ī þitt hūs.
OE Ārīs and nym þīn bedd and gang on þīn hūs,
  Arise and take your bed *and go in your house,*

Goth Jah urreisands galaiþ in gard seinana.
ON Ok hann stōp upp ok fōr ī sitt hūs.
OE And hē ārās and fērde tō hys hūse.
  And he arose and *went* *to his house.*

Goth Gasaiƕandeins þan manageins ohtedun sildaleikjandans
ON En þā folkit sā undraþesk þat
OE Sōþlīce þā þā sēo mænigeo þis gesāwon, þā ondrēdon hig hym
  Truly when the multitude this saw, *then feared they (for) them(selves)*

Goth jah mikilidedun guþ.
ON ok þrīsaþe Guþ.
OE and wuldrodon God.
  and glorified God.

Identify the cognate words among the three texts. Hint: To avoid confusion, use different colored pens or pencils to underline the cognate words in each category.

Cognates shared by Gothic, ON, and OE _____

_____

_____

_____

_____

_____

_____

Cognates shared by ON and OE _____

_____

_____

_____

_____

Cognates shared by Gothic and ON _____

_____

_____

_____

_____

Cognates shared by Gothic and OE _____

_____

_____

_____

_____

_____

4.9 North Germanic and West Germanic Cognates

The Germanic languages are traditionally subdivided into three branches: East Germanic, West Germanic, and North Germanic. East Germanic is now extinct. The major West Germanic languages today are German, English, Dutch, Afrikaans, and Flemish. The major North Germanic languages are Swedish, Danish, Norwegian, and Icelandic. Sometimes the distinction between the two groups is in lexicon. For example, the normal word for "child" is *barn* in Swedish and Danish, but *kind* in Dutch and German. Often, though, the differences are only phonological. That is, words ultimately deriving from the same Germanic roots have undergone different sound changes in the two branches. In the accompanying chart, three of the languages (in addition to English) are West Germanic; (A) is one of them. The remaining three are North Germanic.

English	(A)	(B)	(C)	(D)	(E)	(F)
1. bone	been	ben	been	bein	Bein	ben
2. book	boek	bog	boek	bok	Buch	bok
3. door	deur	dør	deur	dør	Tür	dörr
4. eye	oog	øje	oog	øye	Auge	öga
5. five	vyf	fem	vijf	fem	fünf	fem
6. heart	hart	hjerte	hart	hjerte	Herz	hjärta
7. (to) help	help	hjælpe	helpen	hjelpe	helfen	hjälpa
8. moon	maan	måne	maan	måne	Mond	måne
9. house	huis	hus	huis	hus	Haus	hus
10. oak	eik	eg	eik	eik	Eiche	eik
11. over	oor	over	over	over	über	över
12. plum	pruim	blomme	pruim	plomme	Pflaume	plommon
13. (to) ride	ry	ride	rijden	ride	reiten	rida
14. (to) see	sien	se	zien	se	sehen	se
15. shoe	skoen	sko	schoen	sko	Schuh	sko
16. soul	siel	sjæl	ziel	sjel	Seele	själ
17. thin	dun	tynd	dun	tynn	dünn	tunn
18. thousand	duisend	tusind	duizend	tusen	tausend	tusen
19. wise	wys	viis	wijs	vis	weise	vis
20. word	woord	ord	woord	ord	Wort	ord

1. Which are the West Germanic languages? _____

2. Which are the North Germanic languages? _____

3. Given the information that a cognate for the English word *weapon* exists in North Germanic, what does this word begin with in North Germanic languages? _____

_____

4. Given the word *Pflaster* in language (E), what is its English cognate? _____

5. With the help of item (9), give the words for *mouse* in languages (A), (B), (C), (D), (E), and (F). (There are no irregularities.) _____

6. Of the four West Germanic languages, including English, which two seem to be most closely related to each other? _____

CHAPTER 5

OLD ENGLISH

5.1 Important Terms

1. A.D. 449
2. A.D. 878
3. A.D. 1066
4. Ælfric
5. alliteration
6. amelioration
7. Angles
8. Anglian
9. *Anglo-Saxon Chronicle*
10. back mutation
11. Benedictine Reform
12. breaking (fracture)
13. calque (loan translation)
14. case
15. compounding
16. Danelaw
17. dental preterite
18. dual pronoun
19. eth
20. Frisians
21. futhorc (runic alphabet)
22. gender
23. generalization
24. grammatical gender
25. Heptarchy
26. Insular alphabet
27. Jutes
28. Kentish
29. King Alfred
30. Mercian
31. mutated plural
32. narrowing
33. number
34. Old Norse
35. pejoration
36. preterite-present verb
37. Ruthwell Cross
38. St. Augustine
39. Saxons
40. shift in denotation
41. shift in stylistic level
42. Southern
43. strengthening
44. strong (indefinite) adjective
45. strong noun
46. strong verb
47. thorn
48. Treaty of Wedmore
49. umlaut (front mutation)
50. variation
51. Venerable Bede
52. Vikings
53. weak (definite) adjective
54. weak noun
55. weak verb
56. weakening
57. wen
58. West Saxon
59. William of Normandy
60. Wulfstan

5.2   Questions for Review and Discussion

1. What was the first Indo-European language spoken in the British Isles?
2. What was the second? Explain how it came to be used in England and when it ceased to be used.
3. Who were the Picts?
4. When did the first Germanic speakers come to England? Who were these people? Where did they come from? Where did they settle?
5. Where does the name "England" come from?
6. What was the Heptarchy? Name its members.
7. When was England Christianized? By whom?
8. Of what linguistic importance to England was Christianization?
9. Who were the Vikings? When did they first attack England?
10. What language did the Vikings speak?
11. What was the Treaty of Wedmore? What was its linguistic significance?
12. What was the Danelaw?
13. In what ways was King Alfred important to the history of English?
14. What three consonants did OE have that were not phonemic in Common Germanic?
15. What consonant *phonemes* does PDE have that were not phonemic in OE?
16. What is a long consonant?
17. What is breaking?
18. Explain why there is a difference in the vowels of OE *healdan* 'to hold' and *hylt* 'he holds'.
19. What was the first alphabet used to write Germanic languages?
20. Most surviving OE texts are written in what OE dialect?
21. What kind of affixes were most frequently used in OE inflections—infixes, prefixes, or suffixes?
22. Explain the difference between grammatical and biological gender.
23. What was the difference between OE "strong" nouns and "weak" nouns?
24. What is a mutated plural?
25. Under what grammatical circumstances were weak adjectives used? Strong adjectives?
26. Which pronouns had dual forms in OE?
27. How does the use of articles in PDE differ from that in OE?
28. What was the difference between strong verbs and weak verbs in OE?
29. How did OE preterite-present verbs differ from strong verbs? What are the PDE descendants of the OE preterite-present verbs?
30. How many inflected tenses did OE have?
31. How did OE form new adverbs?
32. In what ways did the placement of adjectival modifiers in OE differ from that in PDE?
33. Of all the possible word orders of subject (S), verb (V), and object/complement (O), what was the most commonly used order in OE for independent declarative clauses? For dependent clauses?
34. What was the major source of loanwords into OE?
35. Why were there so few loanwords from Celtic into OE?
36. List some of the processes by which speakers of OE formed new words by using the resources of their own language.
37. In semantic change in English, which is more common, generalization or narrowing? Why?

38. What are some of the types of OE texts that have survived?
39. What was the metric basis for most OE poetry?

5.3   Phonology: Pronunciation and Spelling of Consonants

Though the match between spelling and pronunciation in OE was better than that of PDE, it was by no means perfect:

1. Long consonants were spelled with double graphemes. For example, *rīnan* 'to rain' was pronounced [rīnan], and *rinnan* 'to flow' was [rin:an].
2. The graphemes ⟨p b t d k m l r w⟩ corresponded well to pronunciation; they represented [p b t d k m l r w], respectively.
3. g = [j] before or between front vowels and finally after front vowels.*
     = [ɣ] (a voiced velar fricative) between back vowels or after [l] or [r].
     = [g] elsewhere.
4. c = [č] next to a front vowel.*
     = [k] elsewhere.
5. n = [ŋ] before [k] or [g].
     = [n] elsewhere.
6. h = [h] before vowels and before [l r n w].
     = [ç] (a voiceless palatal fricative) after front vowels.
     = [x] (a voiceless velar fricative) elsewhere.
7. sc = [š].
8. cg = [ǰ].
9. f = [v] when surrounded by voiced sounds.
     = [f] elsewhere and when doubled.
10. s = [z] when surrounded by voiced sounds.
     = [s] elsewhere and when doubled.
11. ð or þ = [ð] when surrounded by voiced sounds.
     = [θ] elsewhere and when doubled.

A.   Transcribe the following words. You can transcribe the vowels as they are spelled here.

1. wita 'adviser' [wita] _____
2. limpan 'to happen' _____
3. biddend 'petitioner' _____
4. lārēow 'teacher' _____
5. ðūsend 'thousand' _____
6. kyning 'king' _____
7. heofon 'sky' _____
8. secga 'informant' _____
9. ranc 'proud' _____
10. cild 'child' _____

13. prættig 'tricky' _____
14. gesiht 'sight' _____
15. pæð 'path' _____
16. paþas 'paths' _____
17. æsc 'ash tree' _____
18. fyllan 'to fill' _____
19. fāh 'hostile' _____
20. mæsse 'mass' _____
21. brocc 'badger' _____
22. hnæpp 'bowl' _____

---

* Unless that front vowel was the result of umlaut. For simplicity's sake, no examples involving umlauted vowels are included here.

11. wrīþan 'to twist' _____   23. wlitig 'beautiful' _____
12. dimm 'dim' _____   24. boga 'bow' _____

B.   How would the following words, listed here in transcription, have been spelled in OE? (If the vowel spelling differs from the transcription, it is provided for you.)

1. [boduŋg] 'message' **boduŋg**   13. [moθ:e] 'moth' _____
2. [hæərɤ] 'temple' ___ **ea** ___   14. [mōdrije] 'maternal aunt' _____
3. [seǰan] 'to say' _____   15. [sāɤol] 'cudgel' _____
willice 4. [wil:īče] 'willingly' _____   16. [hæəvod] 'head' ___ **ea** ___
5. [jeræəvian] 'to rob' *gereaðian*   17. [θræšan] 'to crush' _____
6. [kniçt] 'boy' _____   18. [pliçt] 'danger' _____
7. [θōxt] 'thought' _____   19. [hraðe] 'quick' _____
8. [mūða] 'mouth' _____   20. [ābrazlian] 'to crash' _____
9. [pistol] 'letter' _____   21. [čēpiŋg] 'trading' _____
10. [græf] 'grave' _____   22. [spirkan] 'to sparkle' _____
11. [wašan] 'to wash' _____   23. [myǰ] 'midge' _____
12. [frēəzan] 'to freeze' ___ **ēo** ___   24. [θurx] 'through' _____

5.4   Phonology: Front Mutation

As is described on pages 72–74 of *A Biography of the English Language*, front mutation (or umlaut) occurred prior to surviving written English texts, probably in the sixth century A.D. Under front mutation, [i] or [j] in a following syllable changed the preceding vowel as follows:

[æ] > [e], for example, *sættjan > OE settan
[a] + nasal >[e]
[ā] > [ǣ]
[ǒ] > [ě]
[ŭ] > [y̆]
[e] > [i]
[ĕa] > [y̆]
[ĕo] > [y̆]

Under front mutation, only the quality of the vowel was affected, not the quantity. Long vowels remained long, and short vowels remained short.

1. For the following OE words, give the vowel *before* front mutation took place.

     a. drencan 'to drench' < *dr_____ncjan

     b. gēs 'geese' < *g_____si

     c. lǣfan 'to leave' < *l_____fjan

2. For the following OE words, give the vowel *after* front mutation had taken place.

     a. *fūsjan > f_____san 'to hasten'

     b. *fōdjan > f_____dan 'to feed'

     c. *ealdira > _____ldra 'older'

     d. *weorcjan > w_____rcan 'to work'

     c. *steliþ > st_____lþ '(he) steals'

     f. *hēahista > h_____hst 'highest'

     g. *brādjan > br_____dan 'to extend'

     h. *slægi > sl_____ge 'blow'

     i. *langiþu > l_____ngþu 'length'

     j. *morgin > m_____rgen 'in the morning'

     k. *þurstjan > þ_____rstan 'to thirst'

     l. *cēosiþ > c_____st 'she chooses'

3. Because the vowels of all words in the language, regardless of their origin, underwent front mutation under the conditions specified earlier, the presence or absence of mutation can help in dating the entrance of loanwords into English. That is, if a loanword shows mutation in its English form, it must have entered the language *before* mutation took place. If it does not show mutation, it probably was borrowed *after* front mutation had stopped operating. For the following OE words originally borrowed from Latin, indicate which ones probably entered English (or Germanic) before mutation and which ones probably entered after mutation had stopped operating.

	Latin	*Old English*	*When Was It Borrowed?*
a.	uncia	ynce 'inch'	*Before, because mutation has taken place.*
b.	radicem	rædic 'radish'	
c.	pallium	pallium 'garment'	
d.	pagella	pægel 'pail'	
e.	gloria	gloria 'doxology'	
f.	Saturni (dies)	Sætern-(dæg) 'Saturday'	
g.	pungere	pyngan 'to prick'	
h.	postis	post 'post'	
i.	pannus	pennig 'penny'	

5.5   Phonology: Vowel Correspondences Between OE and PDE

The correspondence between sound and spelling was not perfect in OE and is even worse
in PDE. Nonetheless, in many words the OE vowels have developed predictable reflexes
in PDE, and even the spelling correspondences are often regular, as the following examples
show.

OE [ǣ] ⟨æ⟩ :	PDE [i] ⟨ea⟩	OE [æ] ⟨æ⟩ :	PDE [æ] ⟨a⟩
fǣr	fear	sæp	sap
hǣð	heath	ðæc	thatch
rǣdan	to read	pæð	patch
sǣ	sea	æppel	apple

OE [ē] ⟨e⟩ :	PDE [i] ⟨ee⟩	OE [e] ⟨e⟩ :	PDE [ɛ] ⟨e⟩
hēdan	heed	spell	spell
fēfer	fever	hecg	hedge
mētan	to meet	nest	nest
cēne	keen	sellan	to sell

OE [ī] ⟨i⟩ :	PDE [ai] ⟨i - e⟩	OE [i] ⟨i⟩ :	PDE [ɪ] ⟨i⟩
līf	life	timber	timber
scrīn	shrine	fisc	fish
glīdan	to glide	hlid	lid
wīd	wide	ðing	thing

OE [ū] ⟨u⟩ :	PDE [au] ⟨ou⟩	OE [u] ⟨u⟩ :	PDE [ə] ⟨u⟩
clūd	cloud	dumb	dumb
hlūd	loud	butere	butter
mūþ	mouth	cuppe	cup
sūr	sour	hungor	hunger

OE [ā] ⟨a⟩ :	PDE [o] ⟨oa⟩	OE [ō] ⟨o⟩ :	PDE [u] ⟨oo⟩
lām	loam	mōr	moor
tāde	toad	smōþ	smooth
hār	hoar	hrōst	roost
lāþ	loath	stōl	stool

OE [ēə] ⟨eo⟩ :	PDE [i] ⟨ee⟩
bēo	bee
crēopan	to creep
wēod	weed
hlēor	leer

Examine the preceding examples and then provide the missing forms from PDE or OE in the following lists. OE long vowels have been indicated by a macron here, although they were usually not marked as long in OE texts. When writing the OE words, assume that all letters except the vowel are the same in OE as in PDE. When writing the PDE words, you will have to make minor adjustments in the spelling of some words.

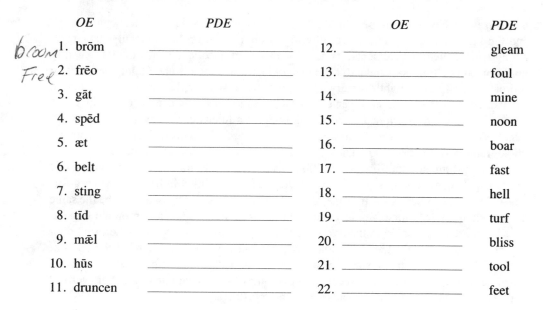

OE	PDE		OE	PDE
broom 1. brōm	_____	12.	_____	gleam
Free 2. frēo	_____	13.	_____	foul
3. gāt	_____	14.	_____	mine
4. spēd	_____	15.	_____	noon
5. æt	_____	16.	_____	boar
6. belt	_____	17.	_____	fast
7. sting	_____	18.	_____	hell
8. tīd	_____	19.	_____	turf
9. mǣl	_____	20.	_____	bliss
10. hūs	_____	21.	_____	tool
11. druncen	_____	22.	_____	feet

5.6 Graphics: *Beowulf* Manuscript

Beowulf is the best-known poem of Old English, one of the world's greatest epic poems, and the first major poem to survive in writing from any European vernacular language. Along with its fictional elements, its 3,182 lines record historical events of sixth-century northern Europe (but not England). The date of its composition is uncertain; conservative estimates put it in the eighth century. *Beowulf* survives in a single manuscript written in the late tenth or early eleventh century, which was seriously damaged by fire in 1731. However, the entire poem had been copied by Francis Junius in the seventeenth century, thus preserving many words that would otherwise have been lost. The accompanying photograph is from folio 190r, lines 2757–2782, toward the end of the poem.

Using the already transliterated portion as a guide to letter forms, transliterate the rest of the page. Illegible words from the burnt edge have been filled in for you. A word-for-word gloss appears below the transliteration. Word boundaries will not always be the same as in modern English; for example, compound nouns are not hyphenated, pronoun subjects may be written together with their verbs, prepositions may be written together with their objects, and so on. In the transliteration provided, italics indicate an expanded contraction. Though *Beowulf* is poetry, it was copied continuously, without starting a new line at every new line of verse. To help you see the alliteration that bound each line together, vertical bars have been added at line boundaries in the transliteration.

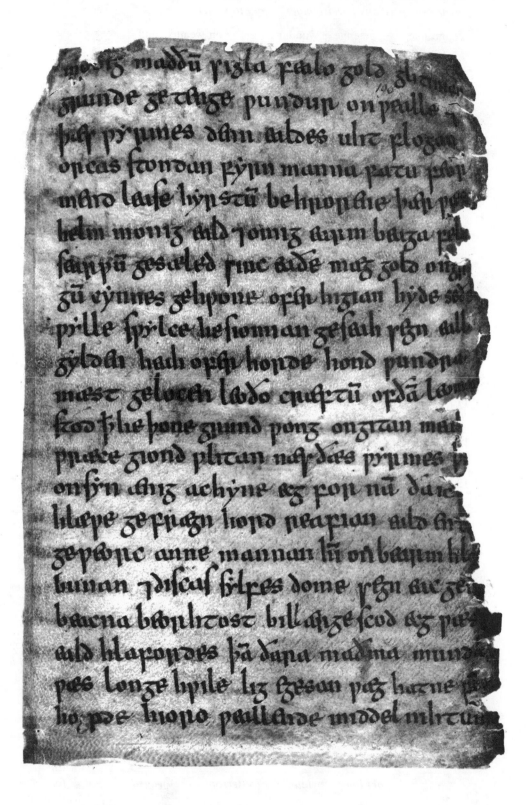

1   modig maððumsigla   fealo | gold glitinian
brave precious jewels many   gold to glitter

2   grunde   getenge | wundur   on wealle ond
(on) ground resting,   wonderful things in barrow, and

3   þæs   wyrmes denn | ealdes uht flogan
(of) the serpent's den,   (of) old dusk-flyer

4   orcas stondan | fyrn manna   fatu   feor
cups to stand,   (of) men-of-old vessels pol-

5   mend lease | hyrstum   behrorene þær wæs
isher-less   ornaments deprived of. There was

6   helm   monig | eald ond omig earmbeaga fela |
helmet many a,   old and rusty, bracelets   many

7   searwum   gesæled sinc   eaðe mæg | gold on grund
(with) skill twisted—treasure easily can,   gold in ground

8   gum cynnes gehwone | ofer higian hyde   seðe
man   any   overpower, (let) hide he who

9   _____ | _____ ____ _____ _____ _____ eall
wishes.   Likewise,   he   to lie   saw   banner   all

10   _____ | ____ ____ _____ _____ wundra
gilded,   high over   treasury, (of) hand-(crafted)   wonders

11   _____ | ____ _____ of   ðam leoman
greatest,   linked (by) hand-skills.   From   it   light

12   _____ | þæt   ____ ____ _____ _____ _____ meahte
stood   so that he   the   ground   -surface perceive   could,

13   _____ ____ ____ _____ ____ ____ _____ þær |
ornaments look   over,   Not was (of) the   serpent   there

14   ____ ____ ____ _____ _____ | ða ic on
sight any,   but him   (sword)-edge (had) destroyed.   Then I in

15   _____ _____ _____ _____ | _____ enta
barrow learned treasury   to plunder,   old   (of) giants

16   ____ _____ _____ | ____ ____ _____ hlodon
work a certain   man,   him   in   arms   to load

17   ____ ____ _____ | _____ _____ _____ eac genom
cups and dishes   (at) his own   discretion.   Standard   also (he) took

18   _____ _____ _____ _____ _____ | _____ wæs iren
(of) banners brightest.   Sword   earlier (had) injured—   edge   was iron

19   ____ _____ | _____ _____ _____ mund bora
(of) old-lord,   one who (of) the   treasures   guardian

20   _____ | _____ ____ _____ _____ | ____ for
was   (for) long   while.   Fire-terror (he) waged   hot   for

21   horde,   _____ _____ | _____ nihtum
treasury,   hostilely   welling   in middle (of) night

1. What does a line over a vowel indicate? _____

_____

2. What is the abbreviation for <u>and</u>? _____

3. The letter <u>s</u> has three distinctly different forms. What are they? _____

5.7   Graphics: The OE Runic Alphabet (Futhorc)

As your text explains, the OE runic alphabet (futhorc) was apparently used primarily for inscriptions and only rarely for longer texts. Yet, because medieval English scribes frequently inserted runes into texts written in the Latin alphabet, we know that the futhorc was familiar to the English long after it had been replaced by the Latin alphabet. One version of the futhorc is reproduced here, followed by a brief text adapted from the OE translation of Bede's story of the poet Cædmon, who was miraculously given the power to compose religious poetry in the alliterative style.

Transliterate the runic text back into the Latin alphabet. Then translate the text into modern English. Some words have been translated for you; you should be able to guess the rest of them because of their resemblance to modern English.

Rune	Equivalent	Probable Value	Rune	Equivalent	Probable Value
ᚠ	f	[f]	ᛋ	s	[s]
ᚢ	u	[u]	ᛏ	t	[t]
ᚦ	th	[θ]	ᛒ	b	[b]
ᚩ	o	[o]	ᛖ	e	[e]
ᚱ	r	[r]	ᛗ	m	[m]
ᚳ	c	[k]	ᛚ	l	[l]
ᚷ	g	[g]	ᛝ	ng	[ŋ]
ᚹ	w	[w]	ᛟ	œ	[œ]
ᚻ	h	[h]	ᛞ	d	[d]
ᚾ	n	[n]	ᚪ	a	[ɑ]
ᛁ	i	[i]	ᚫ	æ	[æ]
ᛄ	y	[j]	ᚣ	y	[y]
ᛉ	ēo	[eə]?	ᛡ	io	[io]?[iɑ]?
ᛈ	p	[p]	ᛠ	ea	[æə]
ᛣ	h	[x]			

ᛋᚢᛗ ᛗᚩᚾ ᚻᛁᚾᛖ ᚾᚪᛚᛖᛏᛏᛖ ᚩᚾᚻ ᚷᚱᛖᛏᛏᛖ ᚩᚾᚻ

sum	mon	hine			
man	him	saluted		and	

ᚻᛁᛏᛖ ᛒᛖ ᚻᛁᛋ ᚾᚪᛗᚪᚾ ᚾᛖᛗᚾᛖ: "ᚳᚪᛖᛞᛗᚩᚾ, ᛋᛁᚷ ᛖᛖ

by		name	named:	"Cædmon,	

ᚻᚢᚪᛏᚻᚹᚢᚷᚢ." ᚦᚪ ᚪᚾᛋᚹᚪᚱᛖᛞᛖ ᚻᛖ ᚩᚾᚻ ᚻᚹᚪᚦ:

something."		Then			said:

ᚾᛖ ᚻᚪᚾ ᛁᚻ ᚾᚩᚻᛏ ᛋᛁᚾᚷᚪᚾ." ᛗᛖᛏ ᚻᛖ ᚻᚹᚪᚦ:

	I	nothing		Again	

ᚾᚩᚦᚹᛖ ᚦᚢ ᛗᛖ ᛋᛁᚾᛏ ᛋᛁᚾᚷᚪᚾ." ᚦᚪ ᚻᚹᚪᚦ ᚻᛖ:

Nevertheless	thou		canst		

"ᚻᚹᚪᛏ ᛋᚻᚪᛚ ᛁᚻ ᛋᛁᚾᚷᚪᚾ?"

5.8 Morphology: Cases

In OE, the most important functions of the nominative, genitive, dative, and accusative cases were as follows:

Nominative

1. Subject   *1, 3,* _____

2. Complement after verbs like "to be"   _____

3. Direct address (vocative)   _____

Genitive

1. Possessive, including most constructions in which PDE
   would use an "of" possessive   _____

2. Expressions of measure or of larger numbers   *3,* _____

3. Direct object of some verbs, especially those expressing
   deprivation   _____

4. In certain adverbial phrases   _____

5. In special meanings after some prepositions   *5,* _____

Dative

1. Object of most prepositions   _____

2. Indirect object of verbs   _____

3. Direct object of some verbs   _____

4. With some adjectives, especially those which would
   be followed by "to" in PDE (e.g., "dear to me")   _____

5. With some possessives, especially involving parts of the body _____

6. Some time expressions (earlier instrumental case,
   and may appear with an instrumental demonstrative)   _____

Accusative

1. Direct object of verbs   _____

2. Object of prepositions expressing movement in time
   or space   *7,* _____

3. Some adverbial expressions of time or space   _____

A.   Identify the functions of the cases in the following sentences by putting the number of the sentence in the appropriate blank on the preceeding page. The cases are identified by letters following the word or phrase, which is underlined: (N) = nominative, (G) = genitive, (D) = dative, (A) = accusative. NOTE: Do not confuse the gloss with the original text. For example, the OE expression *dæges ond nihtes* might be glossed "by day and by night," but this would *not* be an example of the use of the genitive as object of a preposition in OE because the OE has no preposition. Instead, it would be an example of the use of the genitive in certain adverbial phrases.

1. Seo boc (N) com   to us binnan feowum gearum (D).
   That book   came to us within few   years.

2. He wearþ cristnum   monnum (D) swiðe hold (N).
   He was   to Christian men   very loyal.

3. Eadgar cyning (N) þone cristendom (A) gefyðrode and fela
   Edgar king   the Christendom   advanced and many

   munuclifa (G) arærde.
   monasteries   established.

4. La! leof hlaford (N), þone (A) þe þu (N) lufast ys nu   geuntrumod.
   Oh! dear lord,   the one whom you love is now become sick.

5. Ne mæg nan man (N) twam hlafordum (D) þeowian.
   Not can no man   two   lords   serve.

6. Gif mon him (D) oftihþ   ðara þenunga (G) and ðæs anwealdes (G)
   If one them takes away the attendants   and the authority

7. froxas (N) comon geond eall   Egypta (G) land (A).
   frogs   came through all (of) Egyptians' land.

8. we (N) secgað to soðan   þæt se tima (N) wæs gesælig (N) and wynsum (N)
   we   say   in truth   that that time   was happy   and joyful

   on Angelcynne (D).
   in England.

9. Windas and sæ him (D) hyrsumiaþ.
   Winds and sea him   obey.

10. Wende he (N) hine   west wiþ   Exanceastres (G).
    Turned he   himself west toward Exeter.

11. Gangaþ inn þurh   ðæt nearwe geat (A).
    Go   in through the narrow gate.

12. We cildra (N) biddaþ þe, eala lareow (N), þæt þu tæce us (D) sprecan
    We children   ask you, O teacher,   that you teach us   to speak

13. Næfde se here,   godes þonces (G), Angelcyn (A)
    Not had the army, thanks to God,   England

    ealles (G) forswiðe gebrocod.
    completely utterly crushed

14. Israhela folc (N) on hæftnede (D) Babilonisam cyninge (D) þeowde.
    (Of) Israel people in bondage   Babylonian king   served.

15. þæs halgan   Oswoldes (G) ban (N) wurdon eft   bebroht . . .
    of the holy   Oswald   bones   were   again brought

    to Myrcena (G) lande
    to Mercians'   land

16. Ond hæþne men (N) ærest ofer winter (A) sæton.
    And heathen men   first over winter   remained.

17. him (D) on bearme læg
    his   on lap   lay

18. nolde   Alexander þæs (G) getygþian.
    not wanted Alexander that   to grant.

19. Ðær wæron twa hund   and eahta and feowertig wera (G)
    There were   two hundred and eight and forty   men

20. Lætaþ us faran and offrian urum Gode (D)
    Let   us go   and sacrifice (to) our God

21. þy   ilcan geare (D) sende Ælfred cyning (N) sciphere (A) on East-Engle.
    that same year   sent Alfred king   fleet   into East Anglia.

B. Identify the case (nominative, genitive, dative, accusative) and function of the underlined words in the following phrases and sentences. If you have trouble identifying them, consult the noun, adjective, and pronoun paradigms in *A Biography of the English Language* for the endings of the cases.

1. and he wearð fornumen æfter <u>feawum dagum</u>
   and he was consumed   after few days

2. Eala, <u>oxanhyrde</u>, hwæt wyrst þu?
   O,   oxherd,   what do   you (do)?

3. God sende ða sona   <u>sumne encgel</u> him to
   God sent   then at once a certain angel him to

4. mon   towearp þone weal niþer oþ <u>þone grund</u>
   someone broke   the   wall down to the ground

5. Nis þæt   nan <u>wundor</u>
   Not is that no   wonder

6. Se   wudu is hundtwelftiges <u>mila</u> lang
   The forest is 120   miles long

7. Sum sutere   siwode <u>þæs halgan weres</u>   sceos
   A certain shoemaker sewed   the holy man's   shoes

8. ðu   ofsloge <u>him</u> fætt   cealf
   you killed   him (a) fat calf

9. Wrætlice   is þes <u>wealstan</u>
   Wondrous is this building stone

10. he <u>ðæm huse</u> genealæhte
    he the house approached

5.9   Morphology: Gender

OE had grammatical rather than biological gender. In most instances, neither the ending of the word alone nor its meaning was a reliable guide to its gender. Thus gender usually can be identified with certainty only through the form of an accompanying adjective or, especially, an accompanying demonstrative. Even with these, the gender of plural nouns may be ambiguous. By consulting paradigms of OE nouns, adjectives, and demonstratives (pages 83, 84, and 86 in *A Biography of the English Language*), identify the gender of the following nouns as masculine (M) feminine (F), or neuter (N), and state what allowed you to make the identification. If it is impossible to ascertain the gender from the form given, write (U) in the blank and state how it is ambiguous.

0. seo *byrne* 'the coat of mail'   *F – demonstrative seo is feminine*

1. þone *grund* 'the ground' _____

2. freolic *wif* 'noble woman' _____

3. on þisse *meoduhealle* 'in this mead-hall' _____

4. heoru *stow* 'pleasant place' _____

5. modiges *mannes* 'of the brave man' _____

6. þinum *broþrum* 'to your brothers' _____

7. þa *word* 'those words' _____

8. windige *weallas* 'windy walls' _____

9. æt þære *beorþege* 'at the beer-party' _____

10. þæt *anginn* 'the beginning' _____

5.10 Morphology: Noun Clauses and Inflections

A. Because so many inflectional endings in OE are identical, one cannot always identify the class and gender of a noun from its ending alone. However, a number of the endings are unique, and the class, gender, number, and case can be determined by the ending, along with the information provided by the context. For each of the following underlined nouns, give its gender, case, and number, and state whether it is an (A) *a*-stem strong noun, (B) *o*-stem strong noun, (C) *-an* weak noun, or (D) mutated-plural noun. The nominative singular form of the noun is provided in parentheses after each excerpt. If you cannot make a positive identification, explain why.

0. gesihð him   beforan . . . baþian brimfuglas,   brædan <u>feþra</u> (nom. sg. feþer)
    (he) sees him before (to) bathe   sea-birds, (to) spread wings

    feminine o-stem strong noun, accusative plural

1. And riht is   þæt ealle <u>preostas</u> . . . anræde beon   (nom. sg. <u>preost</u>)
    and proper is that all priests   persevering be

2. he geseah þa <u>hearpan</u> him nealecan (nom. sg. <u>hearpe</u>—fem.)
    he saw the   harp   him approach

3. ac hi fæstlice   wið ða <u>fynd</u> weredon   (nom. sg. <u>feond</u>—masc.)
    but they resolutely against the enemies defended

4. þa <u>flotan</u>   stodon gearowe (nom. sg. <u>flota</u>)
    the seamen stood ready

5. þeah þe <u>græf</u>   wille golde stregan   (nom. sg. <u>græf</u>)
    although (the) grave (he) may (with) gold strew

6. of þæm we begietaþ us selfum . . . fodor urum <u>horsum</u>   (nom. sg. <u>hors</u>—neut.)
    from whom we get (for) ourselves fodder (for) our horses

7. Wod under   wolcum to þæs þe he winreced,   goldsele <u>gumena</u>,
    (he) walked under clouds until he winehall,   goldhall (of) men,

    gearwost wisse   (nom. sg. <u>guma</u>—masc.)
    most readily recognized

8. he . . . his <u>leomu</u> on reste gesette ond onslepte
    he   his limbs at rest   put and fell asleep

    (nom. sg. <u>lim</u>; ignore the vowel change in the root)

_____

9. Gyf mæsseprest his agen <u>lif</u> rihtlice fadie . . .   (nom. sg. <u>lif</u>)
    If mass-priest   his own life properly arranges

_____

B.   Using the paradigms in your text and the information provided by the glosses, write
the correct form of the noun in the blank. The nominative singular form of the noun and
all other necessary information is given in the parentheses following each excerpt. (*a*-stem
and *o*-stem nouns are "strong" nouns, and *-an* nouns are "weak" nouns.)

0. he nolde fleogan fotmæl *landes*_____   (<u>land</u>: neuter <u>a</u>-stem gen. sg.)
    he wouldn't flee (a) foot's space (of) land

1. Ne acwele þu þaet _____ (<u>cild</u>: neuter <u>a</u>-stem acc.)
    Not kill   you that child

2. bæd þaet _____ gehwylc   Byrhtnoð wræce
    (he) ordered that (of the) men each Byrhtnoð avenge

    (<u>beorn</u>: masc. <u>a</u>-stem gen. pl.)

3. þonne he forð scile of _____ læded   weorðan
    when he forth must from body   brought be

    (<u>lichama</u>: masc. *-an* dat. sg.)

4. ond bi oðrum   monegum spellum þæs halgan _____
    and about other many stories   (of) the holy   writ

    (<u>gewrit</u>: neuter <u>a</u>-stem gen. sg.)

5. on þinum sæde beoð ealle _____ gebletsode (<u>þeod</u>: fem. <u>o</u>-stem nom.)
    in your offspring will be all peoples blessed

6. ðara godena wiotena ðe . . . _____ ealla be fullan geliornod hæfdon
    (of) the good wise men who books   all completely learned had

    (<u>boc</u>: fem. mutated pl.)

7. þa ceare seofdun hat ymb _____ (<u>heorte</u>: fem. *-an* acc.)
    the cares sighed hot around (my) heart

8. þæt Læden and þæt Englisc nabbað na ane wisan
    the Latin   and the English not have at all one manner

    on þære _____ fadunge (<u>spræc</u>: fem. <u>o</u>-stem gen.)
    in the language arrangement

9. Nu her þara _____ byre nathwylces . . . on flet gæð
    now here (of) killers   son some   onto floor walks

    (<u>bana</u>: masc. *-an* gen.)

5.11   Morphology: Pronouns and Demonstratives

In the following OE sentences, identify the person, gender, case, and number of the underlined personal pronouns. (First- and second-person pronouns had no gender distinction, so ignore gender for these.) For demonstrative pronouns, identify the gender, case, and number. Ignore gender in the plural for both personal and demonstrative pronouns. For interrogative pronouns, identify the case and gender. When the form is ambiguous, additional information is provided for you as necessary for a positive identification.

0.   þa geseah ic beforan unc onginnan ðeostrian ða stowe.
     Then saw I   before us   begin   to darken that place.

   ic: *1st person nom. sg.* _____   unc: _____ (dative) *1st pers. dual*

1.   Her is seo bot, hu ðu meaht þine æceras betan gif hie
     Here is the remedy, how you can your fields restore if they

     nellaþ wel weaxan.
     will not well grow.

   seo: _____   ðu: _____

   þine: _____   hie: _____

2.   cweþe ðonne nigon siþon þas word:
     say   then   nine times these words

   þas: _____

3.   ond þæs oþres þone mæstan dæl hie geridon ond him to
     and of the rest the greatest part they seized and (to) them

     gecirdon buton þæm cyninge Ælfrede.
     submitted except the king   Alfred.

   þaes: (neuter) _____   þone: _____

   hie: _____   him: _____

   þæm: (masc.) _____

4.   Her for se here to Cirenceastre of Cippanhamme. Ond þy
     Here went the army to Cirencester from Chippenham. And in that

     geare gegadrode an hloþ wicenga
     year assembled a troop (of) Vikings

   se: _____   þy: (neuter) _____

5.   Ic ahsige eow, forhwi swa geornlice leorni ge?
     I   ask you,   why   so   eagerly   study you?

   eow: (dative) _____   ge: _____

6. Hwæt sægst þu, fugelere?
   What say you, bird-hunter?

   hwæt: _____   þu: _____

7. Ic ne dear yppan þe digla ure.
   I not dare reveal (to) you secrets our.

   Ic: _____   þe: _____

   ure: _____

8. Hwa awecþ þe to uhtsancge?
   Who awakens you for matins?

   Hwa: _____   þe:_____(accusative)_____

9. ðær næs to lafe   nanðing þe   hiere wæs
   there was not remaining nothing which hers was

   hiere: _____

10. ða cristenan hine gecuron to bisceope
    the Christians him chose   as bishop

    ða: _____   hine: _____

11. Wiþ lungenadle   genim þas wyrte erifion;   gecnucude þæm
    Against lung disease take these herbs "goat's rue"; pound them

    gelice þe þu clyþan wyrce, lege to þæm sare; heo hit
    as if you poultice were making; lay on the sore; it

    gehæleþ. Nim þonne þæt wos þisse sylfan wyrte, syle
    will heal. Take then the juice (of) this same herb, give

    drincan, þu wundrast þæs mægenes þisse wyrte.
    to drink, you will marvel (at) the power (of) this herb

    þas: _____   þæm: _____
    þæm:__(neut.)_____   heo: _____
    hit: _____   þæt: _____
    þisse: _____   þæs:___(neut.)_____

12. he sende flod and besencte hie ealle
    he sent flood and drowned them all

    he: _____   hie: _____

13. on hwæs naman adræfon   eowre suna þonne?
    in whose name (do you) drive out your sons then?

    hwæs: _____   eowre: _____

5.12   Morphology: PDE Descendants of OE Pronouns

From which OE forms did the following PDE pronouns or pronominal adjectives develop?
If the PDE form does not descend from an OE form, put a dash in the blank.

Nom. *I* _____   Nom. *he* _____

Obj. *me* _____   Obj. *him* _____

Pron. Adj. *my* _____   Pron. Adj. *his* _____

Gen. *mine* _____   Gen. *his* _____

Nom. *we* _____   Nom. *she* _____

Obj. *us* _____   Obj. *her* _____

Pron. Adj. *our* _____   Pron. Adj. *her* _____

Gen. *ours* _____   Gen. *hers* _____

Nom. *you* _____   Nom. *it* _____

Obj. *you* _____   Obj. *it* _____

Pron. Adj. *your* _____   Pron. Adj. *its* _____

Gen. *yours* _____   Gen. *its* _____

Sg. *that* _____   Nom. *they* _____

Pl. *those* _____   Obj. *them* _____

Sg. *this* _____   Pron. Adj. *their* _____

Pl. *these* _____   Gen. *theirs* _____

5.13 Morphology: Strong and Weak Adjectives

Identify the underlined adjectives in the following sentences as strong (indefinite) or weak (definite), and state why each is strong or weak. Refer to page 84 of *A Biography of the English Language* as necessary.

0. þæt is æt þæm hehstan goode _Weak; preceded by demonstrative_
   that is at the highest good

1. þu woldest nu brucan ungemetlicre wrænnesse?_____
   you would now enjoy immoderate luxury?

2. heo cende   hyre frumcennedan sunu_____
   she gave birth to her first-born son

3. on midne winter_____
   in mid winter

4. þa beoð swyðe dyre mid Finnum_____
   they are very precious among the Finns

5. Eadmund se eadiga East-Engla cynincg wæs snotor_____
   Edmund the blessed of E. Angles king was wise

6. of þam diglum stowum_____
   from those secret places

5.14   Morphology: Strong Verbs

A.   OE had seven classes of strong verbs (see Figure 5.10 in *A Biography of the English Language*). There were some irregularities in all the classes, but the most typical vowels of the principal parts of each class are listed in the accompanying chart. The second- and third-person singular present indicative underwent umlaut when applicable and thus had a different vowel from the infinitive in several of the classes. Listed are the principal parts and the third-person singular present indicative for the Class 1 verb blīcan 'shine' and the infinitive and vowels for the remaining principal parts of a verb for each of the other six classes. Complete the chart by writing out the principal parts of the verbs of Classes 2 through 7. An asterisk marks verbs that had umlaut in the third-person singular present indicative. If the form is not totally predictable, it is provided for you.

	Infinitive	*3d sg. pres.*	*3d sg. pret.*	*Pret. pl.*	*Past part.*
Class 1 i a i i	blīcan 'to shine'	blīcþ '(it) shines'	blāc '(it) shone'	blicon '(they) shone'	blicen '(it has) shone'
Class 2 ēo ēa u o	drēopan 'to drip'	drȳpþ* '(it) drips'	_____ '(it) dripped'	_____ '(they) dripped'	_____ '(it has) dripped'
Class 3 i a u u	slincan 'to slink'	_____ '(it) slinks '	_____ '(it) slunk'	_____ '(they) slunk'	_____ '(it has) slunk'
Class 4 e æ ǣ o	cwelan 'to die'	_____* '(it) dies'	_____ '(it) died'	_____ '(they) died'	_____ '(it has) died'
Class 5 e æ ǣ e	swefan 'to sleep'	_____* '(it) sleeps'	_____ '(it) slept'	_____ '(they) slept'	_____ '(it has) slept'
Class 6 a ō ō a	wascan 'to wash'	_____* '(it) washes'	_____ '(it) washed'	_____ '(they) washed'	_____ '(it has) washed'
Class 7 V_1 ēo ēo V_1	feallan 'to fall'	fȳlþ* '(it) falls'	_____ '(it) fell'	_____ '(they) fell'	_____ '(it has) fallen'
V_1 ē ē V_1	blandan 'to blend'	blent* '(it) blends'	_____ '(it) blended'	_____ '(they) blended'	_____ '(it has) blended'

B.   Many of the vowels that appear in strong verbs are unique to their class. Hence, if you know the form of the verb (infinitive, third-person present, etc.), you can identify the class to which the verb belongs. Identify the class of each of the following strong verbs by placing the appropriate number in the blank to the left. (No infinitive or past participle of Class 7 verbs is included.)

0. _7_ bēonnon '(they) summoned'

1. ____ drēag '(it) endured'

2. ____ flagen '(it has) flayed'

3. ____ gælþ '(it) sings'

4. ____ gnagan 'to gnaw'

5. _4_ hæl '(it) hid'; holen '(it has) hidden'

6. ____ hēt '(it was) called'

7. ____ hrēop '(it) shouted'

8. ____ hrēowan 'to distress'

9. ____ hrinon '(they) touched'

10. ____ lēcon '(they) leapt'

11. ____ lesan 'to collect'; lesen '(it has) collected'

12. ____ nuton '(they) used'; noten '(it has) used'

13. ____ slōgon '(they) slew'

14. ____ sniden '(it has) cut'

15. ____ spunnen '(it has) spun'

16. ____ stīgþ '(it) ascends'

17. ____ swīcan 'to fight'

18. ____ swincan 'to labor'

19. ____ wæg '(it) carried'; wegen '(it has) carried'

20. ____ wann '(it) struggled'

21. ____ wōd '(it) waded'

22. ____ wrāþ '(it) writhed'

23. ____ þweran 'to stir'; þworen '(it has) stirred'

C.   The OE seven classes of strong verbs have not survived intact in PDE because of sound changes, the tendency of strong verbs to become weak, and analogical changes. In addition, PDE has only three principal parts (infinitive, past tense, and past participle), having lost the distinction between singular and plural in the past tense. Nevertheless, a few strong verbs still reflect their earlier class membership. For each of the PDE descendants of OE strong verbs, list at least one other verb with the same vowel alteration in the principal parts.

OE Class 1: PDE ride, rode, ridden [ai o ɪ] _drive_

OE Class 3: PDE bind, bound, bound [ai au au]_____

   PDE drink, drank, drunk [ɪ æ ə]_____

OE Class 4: PDE bear, bore, borne [ɛ ɔ ɔ]_____

OE Class 5: PDE speak, spoke, spoken [i o o] _____

OE Class 6: PDE shake, shook, shaken [e u e] _____

OE Class 7: PDE blow, blew, blown [o u o] _____

5.15 Morphology: Derivative Prefixes

As in PDE, suffixes in OE tended to change the part-of-speech category while prefixes tended to change the meaning of the base word in some way. Examine the glosses of the following nonprefixed and prefixed pairs, and determine the probable meaning of the prefix.

0. *for-*
   bærnan 'burn'   forbærnan 'burn up'
   hogian 'think about'   forhogian 'despise'
   hætan 'heat'   forhætan 'overheat'
   sendan 'send'   forsendan 'banish'
   giefan 'give'   forgiefan 'give, forgive'

   Meaning of prefix _"very much"; intensifier_

1. *ymb(e)-*
   sittan 'sit'   ymbsittan 'besiege'
   hycgan 'think'   ymbhycgan 'consider'
   hweorfan 'move, turn'   ymbhweorfan 'revolve'
   sniþan 'cut'   ymbsniþan 'circumcise'
   faran 'go'   ymbfaran 'surround'

   Meaning of prefix _____

2. *el-*
   land 'land, country'   elland 'foreign country'
   reord 'speech'   elreord 'barbarous'
   þeod 'people'   elþeod 'strange people'
   (ge)hygd 'mind, thought'   elhygd 'distraction'

   Meaning of prefix _____

3. *wan-*
   hal 'healthy'   wanhal 'sick'
   hygdig 'thoughtful'   wanhygdig 'careless'
   sped 'prosperity'   wansped 'poverty'
   fot 'foot'   wanfota 'pelican'
   fah 'dyed, shining'   wanfah 'dark-hued'

   Meaning of prefix _____

4. *to-*
   weorpan 'throw'   toweorpan 'destroy'
   licgan 'lie'   tolicgan 'separate'
   lucan 'close, lock'   tolucan 'wrench apart'
   fleotan 'swim, sail'   tofleotan 'carry off by flood'
   hælan 'heal'   tohælan 'weaken'

   Meaning of prefix _____

5. *to-*
   cuman 'come, go'   tocuman 'arrive'
   don 'do, put'   todon 'apply'
   geteon 'pull'   togeteon 'attract, draw'
   smeagan 'think, reflect'   tosmeagan 'inquire into'

   Meaning of prefix _____

6. *sam-*   grene 'green'   samgrene 'immature'
             hal 'healthy'   samhal 'weakly'
             wis 'wise'   samwis 'stupid'
             (ge)boren 'born'   samboren 'premature'
             bærned 'burnt'   sambærned 'half-burnt'

Meaning of prefix _____

5.16   Morphology: Derivative Suffixes

The following are examples of several common OE derivative suffixes. By examining the patterns of the first two items in each group, you can supply the missing items. Note that umlaut (mutation) is involved in some of the sets.

I. Nouns from Adjectives, Verbs, and Other Nouns

Suffix	Adjective		Noun	
-nes	æðel 'noble'		æðelnes 'nobility'	
	swet 'sweet'		swetnes 'sweetness'	
	_____	'holy'	halignes 'holiness'	
	mildheort 'merciful'		_____ _____	
	_____	'bright'	beorhtnes _____	
-þu	hean 'lowly'		hynþnu 'humiliation'	
	fah 'hostile'		fæhþu 'hostility'	
	heah _____		hyhþu 'height'	
	_____	'long'	lengþu _____	
	earm 'wretched'		_____	'misery'

Suffix	Verb		Noun	
-ung	bletsian 'to bless'		bletsung 'blessing'	
	earnian 'to earn'		earnung 'merit'	
	heofian _____		heofung 'lamentation'	
	_____	'to lie'	leasung 'falsehood'	
	weorðian _____		_____	'honor'

Suffix	Noun		Noun	
- had	preost 'priest'		preosthad 'priesthood'	
	geoguþ 'youth'		geoguþhad 'time of youth'	
	woruld _____		_____	'secular life'
	_____	'child'	cildhad _____	
	mægþ 'maiden'		_____	'virginity'

II. Adjectives from Nouns or Adjectives

Suffix	Noun or Adjective		Adjective	
-sum	wynn 'pleasant'		wynsum 'pleasant'	
	lang 'long'		langsum 'enduring'	
	fryþ _____		_____	'peaceful'
	_____	'abundance'	genyhtsum _____	

	Noun	*Adjective*
-lic	woruld 'world'	woruldlic 'worldly'
	torht 'brightness'	torhtlic 'bright'
	deofol 'devil'	_____ 'diabolical'
	_____ 'joy'	hyhtlic 'joyful'
	_____ 'power'	þryþlic 'strong'
-ig	blod 'blood'	blodig 'bloody'
	mod 'courage'	modig 'bold'
	dust _____	_____ 'dusty'
	_____ 'skill'	cræftig _____
	wlite 'beauty'	wlitig _____
- en	ator 'poison'	ætren 'poisonous'
	seolfor 'silver'	sylfren 'made of silver'
	Crist _____	cristen 'Christian'
	wulf 'wolf'	wylfen _____
	stan _____	_____ 'made of stone'

III. Verbs from Adjectives or Nouns

Suffix	*Adjective or Noun*	*Verb*
-sian	yrre 'angry'	yrsian 'to be angry'
	mære 'famous'	mærsian 'to become famous'
	clæne 'clean'	_____ 'to cleanse'
	ege 'fear'	_____ 'to frighten'
	_____ 'powerful'	ricsian _____

	Adjective	*Verb*
-an	wod 'mad'	wedan 'to be mad'
	cuþ 'known, familiar'	cyþan 'to make known'
	brad _____	brædan 'to extend'
	eald 'old'	_____ 'to delay'
	_____ 'full'	fyllan _____

5.17 Syntax

Among the differences between OE syntax and that of PDE are that, in OE,

A. titles used with proper names often followed the name.
B. if a noun had two modifiers, one often preceded and the other followed the noun.
C. prepositions sometimes followed their objects.
D. impersonal verbs (with no expressed nominative subject) were common.
E. in clauses or sentences preceded by an adverbial, the verb frequently preceded the subject.
F. pronoun objects often preceded the verb, especially in subordinate clauses.
G. in subordinate clauses, the finite verb was often at the end.

For the following excerpts, decide which of the above rules applies and enter the appropriate letter(s) in the blank to the left. (In several instances, more than one rule applies.) Then rewrite the excerpt in acceptable PDE.

B, E 0. þa comon on sumne sæl ungesælige þeofas eahta on anre
then came at certain time unfortunate thieves eight on one

nihte to þam arwurþan halgan . . .
night to   the venerable   saint

Then, at a certain time, eight unfortunate thieves came to the venerable saint on one night.

_____ 1. se wæs Ælfredes cyninges godsunu . . .
he was Alfred's   king('s) godson

_____ 2. Nis eac nan wundor, þeah us mislimpe, forðam we witan
Not is also no wonder,   if   us goes wrong because we know

ful georne þæt . . .
very well that

_____ 3. Ond þa salde se here him foregislas ond micle aþas . . .
And then gave the army him hostages and great oaths

_____ 4. Mid þy þe se cyngc þæt geseah, he bewænde hine . . .
When the king that   saw,   he turned himself

———— 5. Se cyng . . . aræde hi up and hire to cwæð: "Leofe dohtor . . ."
The king lifted her up   and her to said: "Beloved daughter"

———— 6. **And sona þeræfter com Tostig eorl** . . . mid swa miclum liðe,
And at once thereafter came Tostig earl with as big fleet

swa he begitan mihte.
as he get could

———— 7. Gif man **gewundud sy,** genim wegbrædan sæd, gnid to
*If someone **wounded is** take waybread seed, grind to*

duste & scead on **þa wunde** . . .
powder & sprinkle on the wound

———— 8. **þa gefengon hie þara þreora scipa tu æt ðæm muðan**
Then seized they (of) the 3 ships 2 at the mouth

uteweardum . . .
outside

———— 9. And **utan** . . . sume **getrywða** habban us betweonan butan
And let us some fidelity keep us between without

uncræftan
deceit

———— 10. ond hu him ða **speow ægðer** ge mid wige ge mid
*and how them then **succeeded** both with battle and with*

wisdome . . .
wisdom

———— 11. **þa gemette hie Æþelwulf aldorman** on Engla-felda, ond him
Then met they Athelwulf alderman at Englefield, and him

þær wiþ gefeaht . . .
there against fought

5.18   Lexicon: Fossilized Survivals

Although much of the OE vocabulary has been lost, a number of items survive as parts of compounds. For each of the following words, use a dictionary to identify the OE etymon and meaning of the italicized portion.

0.   ear*wig* *OE wicga "insect"*　　6.   god*send* _____

1.   a*jar* _____　　7.   *hench*man _____

2.   black*mail* _____　　8.   mid*riff* _____

3.   cow*slip* _____　　9.   *mid*wife _____

4.   after*math* _____　　10.   *war*lock _____

5.   *gar*lic _____　　11.   *stir*rup _____

5.19   Lexicon: Acquisition of New Words

The chief means of acquiring new lexical items in OE were compounding and affixing, with loanwords being a minor source of new vocabulary. For each of the following items that have survived from OE into PDE, indicate whether OE acquired the word by compounding (C), affixing (A), or borrowing (B). Use a dictionary to find the etymologies.

0. pope _Latin papas -- B_
0. learner _OE leorn + ere -- A_
0. waterway _OE wæter + weg -- C_
1. bastard _____
2. bequeath _____
3. bloodless _____
4. cheekbone _____
5. childish _____
6. daytime _____
7. fatherland _____
8. homestead _____
9. husband _____

10. landlord _____
11. martyr _____
12. mighty _____
13. misread _____
14. outlaw _____
15. oversee _____
16. quicksilver _____
17. radish _____
18. table _____
19. unfriendly _____
20. woodcock _____

5.20   Lexicon: Continuity of English Basic Vocabulary

Although many OE words have been lost from the language, and although many thousands of new words have entered English since OE times, a large proportion of the most common words of OE have survived and remain among the most frequently used words of PDE. Listed are fifty of these words in their OE spelling. You should be able to guess the modern form of most of these words, some of which are even spelled the same today. Write the contemporary spelling of each in the blank to the right. Hint: Most OE infinitives ended in -an.

0.   æfter _after_____

1.   and _____

2.   blōd _____

3.   dōn _____

4.   eald _____

5.   eall _____

6.   ende _____

7.   eorþe _____

8.   fæder _____

9.   folc _____

10. for _____

11. forþ _____

12. full _____

13. gōd _____

14. gold _____

15. grund _____

16. hām _____

17. hand _____

18. heofon _____

19. heorte _____

20. hūs _____

21. hwǣr _____

22. land _____

23. lang _____

24. līf _____

25. lȳtel _____

26. manig _____

27. mann _____

28. nama _____

29. niht _____

30. of _____

31. ofer _____

32. on _____

33. oðer _____

34. sendan _____

35. sittan _____

36. standan _____

37. strang _____

38. strēam _____

39. þær _____

40. under _____

41. wæter _____

42. wel _____

43. weorc _____

44. weorold _____

45. wīd _____

46. wīf _____

47. willan _____

46. word _____

49. yfel _____

5.21 Semantics: Semantic Change

Listed below are a number of English words that have undergone semantic change over the centuries. For each word, state whether the change has been (a) generalization, (b) narrowing, (c) amelioration, (d) pejoration, (e) strengthening, (f) weakening, (g) shift in stylistic level, or (h) shift in denotation. For some items, you may feel that more than one of these types of changes has occurred. If so, indicate this.

0. OE lāst 'track, sole of foot, footprint' (PDE last [noun])   *b*
    Hie ðæs laðan last sceawedon 'They inspected the track of the foe'

1. OE nēah 'near(ly)' (PDE nigh)   _____
    feor oððe neah 'far or near'

2. OE bana 'killer, murderer' (PDE bane)   _____
    Hie næfre his banan folgian noldan 'they would never follow his murderer'

3. OE sellan 'give, supply' (PDE sell)   _____
    Hie him sealdon attor drincan 'They gave him poison to drink'

4. OE fēond 'enemy, devil, the Devil, fiend' (PDE fiend)   _____
    Eowre fynd feallaþ beforan eow 'Your enemies fall before you'

5. OE mōdig 'bold, brave, proud' (PDE moody)   _____
    Ðæt wæs modig secg 'That was (a) brave man'

6. OE drēorig 'bloody, gory, grievous, sorrowing' (PDE dreary)   _____
    Wæter stod dreorig and gedrefed 'Water stood gory and roiled up'

7. OE botm 'ground, physically lowest part' (PDE bottom)   _____
    Heo to ðæs fennes botme com 'She came to the bottom of the fen'

8. OE godsibb 'godparent or godchild' (PDE gossip)   _____
    Nan man on his godsibbe ne wifige 'No man should marry his godchild'

9. OE cwellan 'kill, murder' (PDE quell)   _____
    Ða cwelleras ne woldan hine cwellan 'The executioners did not want to kill him.'

10. OE ādela 'filth, urine, dirt' (PDE addled)   _____
    Ðæt her yfle adelan stinceþ 'That here it stinks of filth'

11. OE smeortan 'to smart' (PDE smart [verb and adjective])   _____
    Ðenne wile his heorte aken and smerten 'Then his heart will ache and smart'

12. OE mægden 'maiden, virgin, girl' (PDE maiden)   _____
    He nam ðæs mædenes modor 'He took the girl's mother'

13. OE morðor 'violent deed, crime, homicide, punishment, manslaughter' _____
    (PDE murder)
    Seo sawl sceal mid deoflum drohtnoþ habban in morþre and on mane 'The soul shall have company with devils in great sin and in crime'

5.22   Semantics: Kinship Terms

Listed below are some of the kinship terms in OE.

brōðor 'brother'   mōdorcynn 'maternal descent'
dohtor 'daughter'   mōdrige 'maternal aunt'
ēam 'maternal uncle'   suhterga 'brother's son; uncle's son'
fæder 'father'   sunu 'son'
fædera 'paternal uncle'   sweostor 'sister'
fæderencnōsl 'father's kin'   geswigra 'sister's son'
faðe 'paternal aunt'   wæpnedhand 'male line'
mōdor 'mother'   wīfhand 'female line'

1. What cultural similarities and differences between the Anglo-Saxon kinship system and that of contemporary American culture does this list suggest? _____

_____

_____

_____

2. Where did English get the terms *uncle, aunt, niece,* and *cousin?*_____

_____ Why might English have borrowed all these terms, yet none of the terms for members of the nuclear family?_____

_____

_____

5.23 OE Illustrative Texts

I. The OE Heptateuch

The OE Heptateuch (first seven books of the Old Testament) is a collection of Biblical translations by the Old English scholar, cleric, and writer Ælfric. The translations are in lucid prose that still manages to follow the Latin original fairly closely. The selection here is from Joshua 6:1–4, 12–19, 21–25, 27.

¹Hiericho seo burh wæs mid weallum ymbtrymed & fæste belocen
Jericho   the city was with walls surrounded and firmly locked

for ðes folces tocyme, & hi ne dorston ut faran ne in faran
against the people's arrival, & they not dared out go nor in go

for him.   ²Drihten cwæð ða to Iosue: Ic do ðas buruh
because of them. The Lord said then to Joshua: I put this city

Hiericho on ðinum gewealde & ðone cyning samod & ða strengstan
Jericho into your power   & the king together & the strongest

weras ðe wuniað on hyre. ³Farað nu six dagas symble ymb ða
men who dwell in   it. Go now six days continually around the

burh, ælce dæg æne & ealle suwigende; ⁴& seofon sacerdas blawan
city,   each day once & all keeping silent; & seven priests   blow

mid byman eow ætforan. ¹²Iosue ða swa dyde, & sacerdas bæron
with trumpets before you. Joshua then thus did, & priests bore

ðæt Godes scrin ymbe ða burh, ælce dæge æne. ¹³& oðre seofon
the God's ark around the city, each day once.   & another seven

blewon mid sylfrenum byman. ¹⁴& hi ealle to fyrdwicon ferdon
blew with silver trumpets.   & they all to (the) camp went

æfter ðam. ¹⁵On ðam seofoðan dæge hi ferdon seofon siðon ymb
after them.   On the seventh day   they went seven times around

ða burh. ¹⁶& on ðam seofoðan ymbfærelde, ða ða sacerdas blewon,
the city. & on the seventh circuit,   when the priests blew,

& ðæt folc eall hrymde, swa swa Iosue him rædde, ða burston
& the people all cried out, as   Joshua them advised, then burst

ða weallas, ðe ða burh behæfdon, endemes to grunde, & hi
the walls, which the city surrounded, completely to ground, & they

ða in eodon, ælc man swa he stod on ðam ymbgange. ¹⁷Iosue
then in went, each man as he stood at the circumference. Joshua

ða clypode, & cwæð to ðam folce: Sy ðeos burh amansumod & eall
then spoke, & said to the people: Let this city be cursed   & all

ðæt bið on hyre, buton Raab ana libbe & ða ðe lociað to hyre,
that are in it, except Rahab alone live & those who belong to her,

for ðan ðe heo urum ærendracum arfæstnysse cydde. ¹⁸& ge
because she (to) our messengers mercy showed.   & you

nan ðingc ne hreppon on reafe ne on feo,   ðæt ge ne beon scyldige
nothing not touch   as plunder nor as property, lest you be guilty

sceamlicre forgægednysse,   && Israhela fyrdwic for synne beo gedrefed.
of disgraceful transgression, & Israelite camp for sin be afflicted.

[19]Swa hwæt swa her goldes byð, ðæt beo Gode gehalgod, & on
Whatever here (of) gold is,   that be to God consecrated, & in

seolfre oððe on are, eall in to his hordum. [21]Hi ofslogon ða sona
silver or in brass, all into his treasuries.   They slew then at once

mid swurdes ecge weras & wifmen & ða wepende cild, hryðera &
with sword's edge men & women & the weeping children, oxen &

scep, assan & ealle ðingc. [22]Iosue cwæð ða syððan to ðam foresædum
sheep, asses & all things.   Joshua said then later to the foresaid

ærendracum: Gað nu to ðam huse, ðær ge behydde wæron, &
messengers: Go now to the house where you hidden were, &

lædað ut ðæt wif, ðe eowrum life geheolp, & ða ðe
lead out the woman who your life supported, & that which

hyre to lociað, lædað of ðisre byrig. [23]Hy dydon ða swa swa him
belongs to her, take from this town. They did then as them

gedihte Iosue, & læddon hi of ðære byrig mid eallum hyre magum,
ordered Joshua, & led her from the town with all her kinsmen,

& hi syððan leofodon mid sibbe betwux him. [24]Hi forbærndon ða
& they afterward lived with peace among them. They burned then

ða burh & ðæt ðe binnan hyre wæs. [25]& Iosue bæd ðus: Beo
the city and what within it was.   & Joshua ordered thus: Be

se awyrged, ðe æfre eft geedstaðelie ðas buruh Hiericho. [27]God wæs
he cursed, who ever again reestablishes this city Jericho. God was

ða mid Iosue on eallum his weorcum, & his nama wearð
then with Joshua in all his works,   & his name became

gewidmærsod wide geond ðæt land.
celebrated widely throughout the land.

II. The OE Herbarium

Several medical texts in OE have survived, among them an *herbarium*, or a collection of descriptions of plants useful for medical purposes. This selection, a description of the medicinal uses of rue, is from MS. V. London, British Library, Cotton Vitellius CIII.

Ðeos wyrt þe man rutam montanam & oþrum naman þam gelice
This herb which one Ruta montana *& another name to it similar*

rudan nemneþ byþ cenned on dunum & on unbeganum stowum.
rude *calls   is produced on hills   & in uncultivated places.*

    1. Wið eagena dymnysse & wið yfele dolh   genim þysse wyrte
        Against eyes' dimness & against bad wound take this herb

leaf þe we rutam montanam nendun on ealdum wine gesodene, do
leaf that we Ruta montana *named in old   wine boiled, put (it)*

þonne on an glæsen fæt, smyre syþþan þærmid.
then in a glass vessel,   rub   then   with (it).

     2.   Wiþ ðæra breosta   sare genim þas ylcan wyrte rutam
       Against of the breasts pain take this same herb Ruta

siluaticam, cnuca on trywenan fæte, nim þonne swa micel swa ðu
silvatica,   pound in wooden vessel,   take then as   much as you

mid ðrim fingron gegripan mæge, do on an fæt & þærto anne scenc
with three fingers grasp   can,   put in a vessel and to it a cup

wines & twegen wæteres, syle drincan, gereste hyne þonne sume
of wine & two of water, give to drink, let him rest then for a

hwile, sona he byð hal.
while, at once he will be healthy.

     3.   Wið lifersare   genim þysse ylcan wyrte anne gripan & oþerne
       Against liver-pain take (of) this same herb   a handful & another

healfne sester wæteres & ealswa mycel huniges, wyll tosomne,
half measure of water & also a lot of honey,   boil together,

syle drincan þry dagas, ma gyf him þearf sy, þu hine miht
give to drink   3 days, more give him if need be, you him can

gehælan.
cure.

III. Riddles Nos. 24 and 47

The Exeter Book, a manuscript preserving numerous OE poems, contains ninety-five metrical riddles varying greatly in length, subject matter, elegance, and decency. Some of them are based on Latin riddles; others are apparently original compositions. The answers to the two reproduced here, Nos. 24 and 47, are "magpie" and "bookworm," respectively. Riddle No. 24 contains six runic characters, which, rearranged, spell out *higoræ*, the OE word for jay or magpie.

Riddle No. 24

    Ic eom wunderlicu wiht,   wræsne mine stefne,
    I am wonderful creature,   modulate my voice,

hwilum beorce swa hund,   hwilum blæte swa gat,
sometimes bark like dog,   sometimes bleat like goat,

hwilum græde swa gos,   hwilum gielle swa hafoc,
sometimes cry out like goose, sometimes shriek like hawk,

hwilum ic onhyrge   þone haswan   earn,
sometimes I imitate   the gray   eagle,

guðfugles hleoþor, hwilum   glidan   reorde
bird of war's song, sometimes (like) vulture speak

muþe gemæne,   hwilum mæwes song,
(with) mouth universal, sometimes sea-gull's song,

þær ic glado sitte. ᛝ mec nemnað,
where I joyful sit. G   me names,

swylce ᚠ ond ᚱ ᚾ fullesteð,
also   Æ   and R   O   supports,

·ℕ· ond ·/· Nu ic haten eom
H   and I   Now I called am

swa þa siex stafas   sweotule becnaþ.
as the six characters   clearly signify.

Riddle No. 47

Moððe word fræt.   Me þæt þuhte
(A) moth words ate. (To) me it seemed

wrætlicu wyrd, þa ic þæt wundor gefrægn,
curious event,   when I the marvel heard of,

þæt se wyrm forswealg wera gied sumes,
that the worm devoured the song of certain men

þeof in þystro, þrymfæstne cwide
thief in dark,   illustrious utterance

ond þæs strangan staþol.   Stælgiest   ne wæs
and of the strong position. Thievish stranger not was

wihte þy gleawra, þe he þam wordum swealg.
a bit the wiser,   though he the words swallowed.

IV. The Peterborough Chronicle

One of the most interesting surviving prose works of OE is the *Anglo-Saxon Chronicle,* the umbrella title given to several different but related chronicles. King Alfred probably initiated the writing of the Chronicle toward the end of the ninth century, and some of the regional chronicles were kept up to date until well after the Norman Conquest. The following passage is the entry for 1085 in the Peterborough Chronicle, telling about the instituting of the Domesday Book. Note the indignation of the scribe at this point—the people suspected the king was up to no good with his census; they rightly feared new taxes.

On þisum geare menn cwydodon & to soðan sædan þet Cnut
In this   year men   declared & in truth   said that Canute

cyng of Denmearcan, Swægnes sune cynges, fundade hiderward
king of Denmark,   King Swegn's son,   set out toward this place

& wolde gewinnan þis land mid Rodbeardes eorles fultume of
& wanted to conquer this land with Earl Rotbert's help of

Flandran, forðan þe Cnut heafde Rodbeardes dohter. Ða Willelm
Flanders, because Canute had Rotbert's daughter. When William

Englalandes cyng, þe þa wæs sittende on Normandige forðig he
England's king,   who   was dwelling in Normandy because he

ahte ægðer ge Englaland ge Normandige, þis geaxode, he ferde into
held both   England and Normandy, this learned, he went into

Englalande mid swa mycclan here ridendra manna & gangendra
England with so great (an) army (of) horsemen & foot soldiers

of Francrice and of Brytlande swa næfre ær þis land ne gesohte,
from France and from Wales as never before this land approached,

swa þet menn wundredon he þis land mihte eall þone here afedan;
so that men marveled how this land could all the army support;

ac se cyng let toscyfton   þone here geond eall þis land to
but the king ordered to distribute the army through all this land to

his mannon, & hi fæddon þone here, ælc be his
his men,   and they fed the army, each according to his

landefne.   & Men heafdon mycel geswinc þæs geares. & Se
proportion of land. & men had great hardship this year.   And the

cyng lett   awestan þet land abutan þa sæ, þet gif his
king ordered to lay waste the land around the sea, so that if his

feond comen upp þet hi næfdon   na on hwam   hi
enemies came up that they would have nothing on which they

fengon swa rædlice.   Ac þa se cyng geaxode to soðan þet his
could seize so quickly. But when the king learned in truth that his

feond gelætte wæron & ne mihten na   geforðian heora fare,
enemies departed were & not could at all carry out their attack,

þa lett he sum þone here faren to heora agene lande, & sum he
then had he part of the army go to their own land, & part he

heold on þisum lande ofer winter. Ða to þam Midewintre wæs
held in this land over winter.   Then at Midwinter was

se cyng on Gleaweceastre mid his witan & heold þær his hired
the king at Gloucester with his councillors & kept there his retinue

v dagas. & Syððan þe arcebiscop & gehadode men hæfden sinoð
5 days.   & afterward the archbishop & ordained men had (a) synod

þreo dagas. Ðær wæs Mauricius gecoren to biscope on Lundene &
three days. There was Mauricius chosen as bishop of London and

Willelm to Norðfolce, & Rodbeard to Ceasterscire: hi wæron ealle
William of Norfolk, and Rotbert of Cheshire: they were all

þæs cynges clerecas. Æfter þisum hæfde se cyng mycel geþeaht
the king's clerks.   After this had the king great counsel

& swiðe deope spæce wið his witan   ymbe þis land, hu hit
& very serious speech with his councillors about this land, how it

wære gesett oððe mid hwylcon mannon. Sende þa ofer eall
was settled or   by which people.   (He) sent then over all

Englaland into ælcere scire his men & lett agan ut hu fela
England into   each shire his men & had find out how many

hundred hyda wæron innon þære scire, oððe hwet se cyng himsylf
hundred hides were within the shire, or what the king himself

hæfde landes & orfes innan þam lande, oððe hwilce gerihtæ he
had of land and livestock in the land, or which privileges he

ahte to habbanne to xii monþum of ðære scire. Eac he lett
ought to have for   12 months from the shire. Also he ordered to

gewritan hu mycel landes his arcebiscopas hæfdon & his
write   how much land his archbishops   had and his

leodbiscopas & his abbodas & his eorlas, &, þeah ic hit lengre telle,
provincials   & his abbots   & his earls, &, though I it longer tell,

hwæt oððe hu mycel ælc mann hæfde þe landsittende wæs innan
what or how much each man had who occupying land was inside

Englalande, on lande oððe on orfe,   & hu mycel feos hit wære
England,   in land or in livestock,   and how much money it was

wurð. Swa swyðe nearwelice he hit lett ut aspyrian þet næs
worth. So very strictly he it ordered to investigate that not was

an ælpig hide ne an gyrde landes,   ne furðon—hit is sceame
one single hide nor one quarter hide of land, nor even—it is shame

to tellanne, ac hit ne þuhte him nan sceame to donne— an oxe ne
to tell,   but it not seemed to him no shame to do—one ox nor

an cu   ne an swin   næs belyfon þet næs gesæt on
one cow nor one swine not was spared that was not set down in

his gewrite. & Ealle þa gewrita wæron gebroht to him syððan.
his document. & all the documents were brought to him afterwards.

V. *Alexander's Letter to Aristotle*
The *Beowulf* manuscript (MS. Cotton Vitellius A XV) also contains the prose *Alexander's Letter to Aristotle*, a fictional work ultimately based on an early Greek original. It is particularly interesting because it reveals a knowledge of and taste for Eastern romances in Anglo-Saxon England.

Swelce eac laforas þær cwoman unmætlicre micelnisse & monig
Moreover leopards there came (of) enormous size   & many

oþer wildeor   & eac tigris us on þære nihte þær abisgodon.
other wild animals & also tigers us in the night there kept busy.

Swelce þær eac cwoman hreaþemys. þa wæron in culefrena gelic-
Further there also came bats   which were in pigeons' like-

nesse swa micle. & þa on ure ondwlitan sperdon & us pulledon.
ness so big,   & they in our faces   struck & us pecked.

hæfdon hie eac þa   hreaþemys teð in monna gelicnisse.   & hie
Had   they also the bats'   teeth in men's shape.   And they

mid þæm þa men wundodon & tæron. Eac ðæm oþrum bisgum
with them then men wounded & tore. Also (to) the other afflictions

& geswencnissum þe us on becwom.   þa cwom semninga swiðe micel
& troubles   that (to) us happened, then came suddenly very big

deor sum mare þonne þara oðra ænig hæfde þæt deor þrie hornas
animal greater than (of) the others any. Had that animal 3 horns

on foran heafde & mid þæm hornas wæs egeslice gewæpnod. þæt
on front (of) head & with the horns was dreadfully armed. That

deor indeos hatað dentes tyrannum. hæfde þæt deor horse heafod.
animal Indians call "tyrant teeth." Had that animal horse head,

& wæs blæces heowes. Ðis deor mid þy ðe hit þæs wætres ondronc
& was dark in color. This animal, while it (of) the water drank,

þa beheold hit þa ure wicstowe. & þa semninga on us & on ure
then saw it there our camp, & then suddenly on us & on our

wicstowe ræsde. Ne hit for þæm bryne wandode þæs hatan leges
camp rushed. Not it because of the fire flinched of the hot flame

& fyres þe him wæs ongean ac hit ofer eall wod & eode. Mid þy
& fire which it was facing, but it over all walked & went. Thereupon

ic þa getrymede þæt mægen greca heriges, & we us wið him
I then exhorted the troop (of) Greek army & we us against it

scyldan woldon þa hit ofsloh   sona   minra þegna
to defend wanted, then it struck down at once (of) my warriors

•xxvi• ane ræse   & •lii• hit oftræd. & hie to loman gerenode.
26 (in) one attack & 52 it trampled & them to earth drove down,

þæt hie mec   nænigre note nytte beon meahton. & we hit þa
so that they to me not any use beneficial be could.   & we it then

unsofte   mid strælum & eac mid longsceaftum sperum of
with difficulty with arrows & also with long-shafted spears from

scotadon & hit ofslogon & acwealdon. þa hit wæs foran to uhtes.
shot   and it slew and destroyed.   Then it was early toward dawn.

þa æteowde þær wolberende lyft hwites hiowes. & eac missenlices
Then appeared there pestilential air (of) white color, & also diversely

wæs heo on hringwisan fag. & monige men for heora þæm
was it in rings variegated.   & many men because of the

wolberendan stence swulton mid þære wolberendan lyfte   þe
pestilential stench perished with the pernicious atmosphere which

þær swelc æteowde þa   ðær cwoman eac indisce mys in þa
there such appeared then; there came also Indian mice into the

fyrd in foxa gelicnisse . . .
camp in foxes' likeness . . .

VI. *Deor*

This 42-line poem is typically OE in its somewhat gloomy emphasis on misfortune and depression, but unusual in its stanzaic form with a refrain. Deor was a *scop*, or poet, who formerly had served his lord for many years, but then was supplanted by another *scop*, Heorrenda. The six examples of misfortunes that were overcome or outlived refer to various stories from Germanic history and legend.

Welund him be wurman   wræces cunnade,
Weland from the Vermars exile experienced,

anhydig eorl   earfoþa dreag,
resolute warrior torments suffered,

hæfde him to gesiþþe   sorge ond longaþ
had as his companions sorrow and longing,

wintercealde wræce;   wean oft onfond,
wintry cold exile;   misery (he) often suffered,

siþþan hine Niðhad on   nede legde,
after Niðhad on him   fetters laid,

swoncre seonobende   on syllan monn.
supple sinew-bonds   on (a) better man.

    þæs ofereode,   þisses swa mæg!
    That passed away, so may this!

Beadohilde ne wæs   hyre broþra deaþ
(To) Beadohild not was her brothers' death

on sefan swa sar   swa hyre sylfre þing,
in heart so painful as her own state,

þæt heo gearolice   ongieten hæfde
when she clearly   perceived had

þæt heo eacen wæs;   æfre ne meahte
that she pregnant was; (she) never could

þriste geþencan,   hu ymb þæt sceolde.
without shame think; (of) how it must (end).

    þæs ofereode,   þisses swa mæg!
    That passed away, so may this!

We þæt Mæðhilde   monge gefrugnon
We for Mæðhild   many (of us have) heard

wurdon grundlease   Geates frige,
(that was) bottomless Geat's love,

þæt hi seo sorglufu   slæp ealle binom.
That him the sad love sleep all deprived.

    þæs ofereode,   þisses swa mæg!
    That passed away, so may this!

Ðeodric ahte þritig wintra
Ðeodric ruled thirty years

Mæringa burg;   þæt wæs monegum cuþ.
Merovingians' stronghold; that was to many known.

    þæs ofereode,   þisses swa mæg!
    That passed away, so may this!

We geascodan   Eormanrices
We have heard of Eormanric's

wylfenne geþoht;   ahte wide folc
wolf-like mind;   (he) ruled widely (the) people

Gotena rices.   þæt wæs grim cyning.
Goths' kingdom. He was (a) savage king.

Sæt secg monig   sorgum gebunden,
Sat many a man   (by) sorrows bound,

wean on wenan,   wyscte geheahhe
despair in mind,   (he) wished often

þæt þæs cynerices   ofercumen wære.
that this kingdom   overthrown would be.

þæs overeode, þisses swa mæg!
That passed away, so may this!

Siteð sorgcearig, sælum bidæled,
Sits sad-faced (one) of joys deprived,

on sefan sweorceð, sylfum þinceð
in heart grieves, (to) him (it) seems

þæt sy endeleas earfoða dæl.
that is endless of sufferings (his) share.

Mæg þonne geþencan, þæt geond þas woruld
(He) can then think, that throughout this world

witig dryhten wendeþ geneahhe,
wise Lord changes often

eorle monegum are gesceawað,
(to) many a man favor shows,

wislicne blæd, sumum weana dæl.
wise spirit, (to) some (a) portion of woes.

þæt ic me sylfum secgan wille,
This I about myself want to say,

þæt ic hwile wæs Heodeninga scop,
that I once was (of) Heodenings (the) bard,

dryhtne dyre. Me wæs Deor noma.
(to a) lord dear. My name was Deor ['wild animal'].

Ahte ic fela wintra folgað tilne,
Had I many years employment good,

holdne hlaford, oþþæt Heorrenda nu,
gracious lord, until Heorrenda now,

leoðcræftig monn londryht geþah,
skilled-in-song man land-rights took,

þæt me eorla hleo ær gesealde.
that (to) me warriors' protector earlier had given.

þæt ofereode, þisses swa mæg!
That passed away, so may this!

VIII. A Ninth-Century Charter

A number of legal documents in OE have survived, among them a Kentish charter that specifies one Abba's division of his inheritance. An abridged version of this charter is reproduced here.

ic abba geroefa cyðe & writan hate hu min will is
I Abba officer make known & order to write how my will is

þæt mon ymb min ærfe gedoe æfter minum dæge.
that people about my property should do after my day.

ærest ymb min lond þe ic hæbbe, & me god lah, & ic
First about my land that I have, & (to) me God granted, & I

æt minum hlafordum begæt, is min willa, gif me god bearnes unnan
from my lords obtained, is my will, if (to) me God child grant

wille, ðæt hit foe to londe æfter me & his bruce mid minum
will, that it take to (the) land after me & it use with my

gemeccan, & sioððan swæ forð min cynn ða hwile þe god wille
wife, & afterward thus forth my family as long as God may will

ðæt ðeara ænig sie þe londes weorðe sie & land gehaldan cunne.
that (of) them any be who (of) land worthy be & land hold can.

gif me ðonne gifeðe sie ðæt ic bearn begeotan ne mege, þonne is min
If (to) me then granted be that I child beget not can, then is my

willa þæt hit hæbbe min wiif ða hwile ðe hia hit mid clennisse
will that it have my wife as long as she it with chastity

gehaldan wile, & min broðar alchher hire fultume & ðæt lond hire
wants to keep, & my brother Alchhere her help & the land (to) her

nytt gedoe. & him man selle an half swulung
use put. & (to) him people should give a half sulung [land mea-

ciollan dene to habbanne & to brucanne, wið ðan ðe he ðy
sure] in Cioll valley to have & to use, provided that he the

geornliocar hire ðearfa bega & bewiotige. & mon selle
more willingly her needs attend to & care for. & people should give

him to ðem lond IIII oxan, & II cy, & L scepa, & ænne horn. gif min
him for the land 4 oxen, & 2 cows, & 50 sheep, & one horn. If my

wiif ðonne hia nylle mid clennisse swæ gehaldan, & hire liofre
wife then she not wants chastity thus to keep, & her more agreeable

sie oðer hemed to niomanne, ðonne foen mine megas to ðem londe,
be another marriage to take, then let take my kinsmen the land,

& hire agefen hire agen. gif hire ðonne liofre sie
& (to) her return her own. If (to) her then more agreeable be to a

. . . nster to ganganne oðða suð to faranne, ðonne agefen hie twægen
nunnery to go or south to go, then yield (to) her two

mine megas, alchher & æðel. . . . hire twa ðusenda & fon him to
my kinsmen, Alchhere & Æðel . . . her two thousand & take them

ðem londe. & agefe mon to liminge L cawa & V cy fore hie,
the land. & people should deliver to Liming 50 ewes & 5 cows for it,

& mon selle to folcanstane in mid minum lice X oxan, & X cy, &
& one should give to Folkstone with my body 10 oxen, & 10 cows, &

C eawa, & C swina, & higum an sundran D pend' wið ðan
100 ewes, & 100 swine, & to monks separately 500 pennies provided

ðe min wiif þær benuge innganges swæ mid minum lice swæ
that my wife there have entry whether with my body or

sioððan yferran dogre, swæ hwæder swæ hire liofre sie.
after at a later date, whichever (to) her preferable may be.

gif higan ðonne oððe hlaford þæt nylle hire mynsterlifes
If monks then or lord that not want (to) her monastic life

geunnan, oðða hia siolf nylle,   & hire oðer ðing
to allow, or she herself not wants, & (to) her another thing

liofre sie,   þonne agefe mon   ten hund pend' inn
preferable be, then one should bestow 10 hundred pennies inside

mid minum lice me wið   legerstowe & higum an sundran
with my body in return for burial place & to monks separately

fif hund pend' fore mine sawle.
five hundred pennies for my soul.

   & ic bidde & bebeode swælc monn se ðæt min lond hebbe
   & I ask & command such man as   my land may have

ðæt he ælce gere agefe ðem higum æt folcanstane L ambra maltes,
that he each year give the monks at Folkstone 50 pails of malt,

of VI ambra gruta, & III wega   spices & ceses, & CCCC hlafa, &
& 6 pails of groats, & 3 measures of bacon & cheese, & 400 loaves, &

an hriðr, & VI scep. & swælc monn se ðe to minum ærfe foe,
one cow, & 6 sheep. & such man   as to my property takes,

ðonne gedele   he ælcum messepreoste binnan cent mancus
then should distribute he to each mass-priest inside 100 mancus

goldes, & ælcum   godes ðiowe   pend', & to sancte petre min
of gold, & (to) each of God's servants (a) penny, & to St. Peter my

wærgeld twa ðusenda. . . . & gif þæt gesele þæt min cynn to ðan
wergeld (of) two thousand. . . . & if it happens that my family after-

   clane   gewite ðæt   ðer ðeara nan ne sie ðe
ward completely depart so that there (of) them none be who (of)

londes weorðe sie, þonne foe se hlaford to & ða higan æt kristes
land worthy be, then take (it) the lord & monks at Christ's

cirican, & hit minum gaste nytt gedoen. . . .
church, & it (to) my soul's use put. . . .

   ic ciolnoð mid godes gefe ærcebiscop ðis write & ðeafie, &
   I Ciolnoð by God's grace archbishop this write & approve, &

mid cristes redetacne hit festniæ. ic beagmund pr' ðis ðeafie
with Christ's sign of cross it confirm. I Beagmund priest this confirm

& write. ic wærhard pr' ðis ðeafie & write.   ic abba geroefa ðis
& write. I Wærhard priest this approve & write. I Abba officer this

write & festnie mid Kristes rodetacne.   ic æðelhun pr' ðis
write & confirm with Christ's sign of cross. I Æðelhun priest this

ðeafie & write. ic abba pr' ðis þeafie & write. . . .
confirm & write. I Abba priest this confirm & write. . . .

   heregyð hafað ðas wisan binemned ofer hire deg & ofer abban.
   Heregyð has this director named over her day & over Abba's.

ðæm higum et cristes cirican of londe et cealflocan: ðæt is ðonne
(To) the monks at Christ's church from land at Cealfloc: *it is then*

ðritig ombra alað, ðreo hund   hlafa, ðeara bið   fiftig
thirty pails of ale, & three hundred loaves, of which will be fifty

hwitehlafa, an weg   spices & ceses, an ald hrið, feower
white loaves, 1 measure (of) bacon & cheese, one old ox, four

weðras, an suin oððe weðras,   sex gosfuglas, ten hennfuglas,
wethers, one swine or six wethers, six geese,   ten hens,

ðritig teapera, gif hit wintres deg sie, sester fulne huniges,
thirty tapers, if it winter's day be, measure full (of) honey,

sester fulne butran,   sester fulne saltes.   & heregyð bibeadeð
measure full (of) butter, measure full (of) salt. & Heregyð instructs

ðem mannum ðe efter hire to londe foen on godes noman ðæt hie
the people who after her to land take in God's name that they

fulgere witen   ðæt hie ðiss gelesten   ðe on ðissem gewrite
very well take care that they this carry out which in this document

binemned is ðem higum to cristes cirican . . .
named is (to) the monks at Christ's church . . .

VIII. Ælfric's Lives of the Saints: St. Cecilia

The prolific Ælfric was also the author of thirty-seven homilies detailing the suffering, martyrdom, and miracles of saints. These saints' lives are written in an alliterative prose that so resembles alliterative verse that early editors often printed them as verse. The selection here is the closing lines of his life of St. Cecilia.

Almachius hire andwyrde, "Awurp þine dyrstignysse and geoffra
Almachius her answered: "Cast aside your insolence and offer

þam godum arwurðlice onsægednysse." Cecilia him cwæð to, "Cunna
to the gods honorable sacrifice."   Cecilia to him said,   "Test

mid grapunge hwæðer hi stanas synd and stænene anlicnysse, þa
by touching whether they stones are and stone idols,   those

þe þu godas gecigst, begotene mid leade, and þu miht swa witan
which you gods call, covered with lead, and you can thus find out

gewislice mid grapunge gif ðu geseon ne miht þæt hi synd stanas.
for sure by touching   if you see not can that they are stones.

Hi mihton wel   to lime gif man hi lede on ad. Nu
They would completely (turn) to lime if one them put in fire. Now

hi ne fremiað him sylfum, ne, soðlice, mannum, and hi mihton
they not help themselves, nor, truly, men, and they would

     to lime gif hi man lede on fyr."
(turn) to lime if them one put in fire.

     þa   wearð se arleasa dema deoflice   gram and het
Then became the wicked judge diabolically angry and ordered

hi lædan sona and seoðan on wætere on hire agenum huse for þæs
her led at once and boiled in water in her own house for the

hælendes naman. þa dydon þa hæþenan swa swa hi het
Savior's name. Then did the heathens just as them ordered

almachius; and heo læg on þam bæðe bufan byrnendum fyre
Almachius; and she lay in that bath over (a) burning fire

ofer dæg and niht   ungederodum lichaman, swa swa on cealdum
throughout day & night (with) uninjured body, as if   in cold

wætere, þæt heo ne swætte furðon. Hi cyddon þa almachie hu
water, so that she not sweat even. They told then Almachius how

þæt mæden þurh-wunode on þam hatum baðe mid halum
the maiden persevered   in the hot bath   with healthy

lichaman, and furþon butan swate. þa sende he ænne cwellere
body,   and even without sweat. Then sent he an executioner

to   and het hi beheafdian on þam hatan wætere. Se cwellere
to (her) & ordered to behead her in the hot water. The executioner

hi sloh þa mid his swurde, æne eft, and þryddan siðe, ac hire swura
her struck with his sword, once again, & third time, but her neck

næs forod.   and he forlet hi sona   swa samcuce
not was cut through. And he left her immediately as half-alive

licgan forþam-þe witan cwædon þæt nan cwellere ne sceolde feower
to lie because counselors said that no executioner not should four

siðan slean to þonne man sloge scyldigne. Heo leofode þa þry dagas,
times strike   when one struck (a) criminal. She lived then 3 days,

and þa geleaffullan tihte and hire mædena betæhte   þam maran
and the faithful (she) taught & her maids entrusted (to) the splendid

papan and hire hus wearð gehalgod to haligre cyrcan. þær wurdon
pope and her house was sanctified as holy church. There were,

þurh god wundra gelome   and urbanus se papa bebyrigde hi
through God, miracles often (done), and Urban the pope buried her

arwurðlice to wuldre   þam ælmihtigan þe on ecnysse rixað.
honorably to (the) glory (of) the Almighty who in eternity reigns.

CHAPTER 6

MIDDLE ENGLISH

6.1 Important Terms

1. analytic language
2. Anglo-French
3. back-formation
4. Black Death
5. blend (portmanteau)
6. Carolingian minuscule
7. clipping
8. closed syllable
9. compounding
10. cumulative sentence
11. Danelaw
12. digraph
13. double possessive
14. East Midland dialect
15. folk etymology
16. group possessive
17. Hundred Years' War
18. impersonal verb
19. Insular hand
20. London dialect
21. Middle English dialects
22. Norman Conquest
23. noun adjunct
24. open syllable
25. perfect infinitive
26. periodic sentence
27. periphrastic construction
28. progressive tense
29. quasi-modal
30. Scandinavian loans
31. synthetic language
32. voiced fricative
33. William the Conqueror

6.2   Questions for Review and Discussion

1. Summarize the effects of the Norman Conquest on the English language.
2. What happened to the use of French in England over the course of the ME period?
3. Norman French, and later Anglo-French, differed from Central (Parisian) French. What were the implications of this fact for the English language?
4. What influence did the Hundred Years' War have on the history of English?
5. How did the Black Death affect the English language?
6. What were the effects of the Danelaw settlement on the English language?
7. When and where did a "standard" English begin to arise?
8. On what dialect was the rising new standard based?
9. We have few texts that show a linguistic continuity between OE and ME. Explain.
10. How did the consonant phonemes of English change during the ME period?
11. What happened to the OE diphthongs during ME?
12. Explain the influence of open and closed syllables on ME vowels.
13. How was English word stress influenced by the thousands of French loanwords introduced during ME?
14. Summarize the changes in the English alphabet during ME.
15. What influence did the French have on English spelling?
16. What change in handwriting styles took place during ME?
17. What are some of the probable reasons for the nearly total loss of English inflections during ME?
18. What happened to OE strong and weak adjectives in ME?
19. Where did the PDE forms of the third-person plural pronouns come from?
20. Where did the PDE form *she* come from?
21. What happened to the OE demonstrative adjectives/pronouns during ME?
22. Describe the development of OE strong verbs during ME.
23. Did the number of English prepositions increase or decrease during ME?
24. Where did the indefinite article *a/an* come from?
25. List a few PDE syntactic features that originated during ME.
26. How did the use of the negative in ME differ from its use in PDE?
27. What are the probable origins of the PDE progressive tense?
28. What happened to impersonal verbs during ME?
29. How did the word order of sentences with pronoun objects in ME differ from that of PDE?
30. What were the major sources of loanwords during ME?
31. How did Scandinavian loanwords differ from French loans?
32. Which foreign influence provided new place-name elements in ME?
33. What were some of the minor ways of forming new words during ME?
34. Was the majority of the OE vocabulary retained in ME?
35. Suggest reasons why narrowing was the commonest type of semantic change from OE to ME.
36. What are the traditional five major dialectal areas of ME? Why is this division unsatisfactory?
37. What major change in English poetics occurred during ME?

6.3   Phonology: Voiced Fricatives Become Phonemic

As is explained in the text, there was no *phonemic* distinction in OE between voiced and voiceless fricatives. Fricatives were voiced when surrounded by voiced sounds and were voiceless otherwise. During ME, phonemicization took place as voiced fricatives appeared in previously voiceless environments for various reasons:

A.   French loanwords that had voiced fricatives in initial or final position in a word, for example, *villain*.

B.   Dialect mixture. Southern dialects were voicing initial fricatives as early as OE, for example, ME Southern *zinne* 'sin' versus E. Midlands *sinne*.

C.   Voicing of fricatives in lightly stressed common words, for example, *is*.

D.   Loss of final vowels that left voiced fricatives in a previously voiceless position, for example, OE *risan* [rīzan] 'to rise' versus ME *rise* [rīz].

Identify the reason (A–D) for the voiced fricative in ME in each of the following words. The words are given in their PDE forms. You will need to consult a dictionary to determine the origin of some of the words.

_____ 1. weave

_____ 2. slave

_____ 3. vixen

_____ 4. was

_____ 5. of

_____ 6. freeze

_____ 7. pave

_____ 8. this

_____ 9. verse

_____ 10. seethe

_____ 11. valley

_____ 12. there

_____ 13. lose

_____ 14. carve

_____ 15. seize

_____ 16. clothe

_____ 17. has

_____ 18. vat

_____ 19. ease

_____ 20. cave

6.4 Phonology: Lengthening and Shortening of Vowels in Stressed Syllables

I.   In ME, the quantity of the stressed vowels in many words was different from what it had been in OE. The following developments were responsible for these changes in length.

  A. In late OE, short vowels lengthened before certain consonant clusters. The resulting long vowels remained in ME in the following combinations:
   1. *i, o + mb;* for example, OE *climban*, ME *clīmbe(n)*
   2. *i, u + nd;* for example, OE *grindan*, ME *grīnde(n)*
   3. any vowel + *ld;* for example, OE *milde*, ME *mīlde*
  B. In the thirteenth century, *a, e,* and *o* lengthened in open syllables, that is, syllables ending in a vowel. If a single consonant comes between two vowels, the consonant goes with the second vowel and the first syllable is open, as in OE *stelan* 'to steal', ME *stē-le(n)*.
  C. In late OE and in ME, long vowels (with the exception of those included under [A] above) shortened in closed syllables, that is, syllables ending in one or more consonants. If two consonants come between vowels, the first consonant goes with the first syllable, making it a closed syllable. The second consonant goes with the second syllable, as in OE *sōfte* 'soft', ME *sof-te*.
  D. In ME, if two or more unstressed syllables followed the stressed syllable, the vowel of the stressed syllable always shortened, regardless of whether it was open or closed and regardless of the following consonants, as in ME *brēke(n)* 'to break' versus *brekefast* 'breakfast'.

The stressed vowel (the first vowel) in each of the following ME words differs in quantity from its earlier form in OE. Indicate which of the developments listed above (A–D) caused the change in the length of the vowel.

___ bīnde(n) 'to bind'	___ hāre 'hare'	___ rīnde 'rind'
___ blast	___ holiday	___ rust
___ blīnd	___ hōse 'hose'	___ smōke
___ bōde(n) 'to bode'	___ hūnd 'hound'	___ stepchild
___ ēven	___ lefte 'left'	___ wākien 'to wake'
___ fedde 'fed'	___ mēle 'meal'	___ wīlde 'wild'
___ fōunden 'found'	___ mēte 'meat'	___ wōmbe 'womb'
___ frend 'friend'	___ rāke 'rake'	___ yīelde(n) 'to yield'
___ gōld	___ redeles 'riddle'	

II.   Each of the following PDE words has a vowel different from that of another, related PDE word. The difference in the vowels ultimately goes back to one of the changes described above, even though PDE no longer distinguishes vowels on the basis of quantity. For each of the following words, give a related PDE word with a different vowel. In some cases, you may need to refer to a dictionary to determine the origin of the word.

gossamer _____   sheriff _____

holiday _____   southern _____

kindred _____   stealth _____

Lammas _____   throttle _____

lit _____   utter (extreme) _____

nostril _____   width _____

6.5   Phonology: Sporadic Sound Changes

In addition to systematic changes in consonants and vowels, ME experienced numerous sporadic sound changes that involved only a limited number of words. Among the types of sporadic sound changes were the following:

A. Addition of unetymological consonants, as when PDE *drowned* is pronounced [drɑʊndɪd]

B. Loss of consonants, as when PDE *husband* is pronounced [həzbən]

C. Dissimilation, when one of two similar or identical sounds in a word is changed, as when Latin *turtur* became English *turtle*

D. False division, when the boundary between two words that frequently appear together is shifted, as when PDE *ice cream* is pronounced as if it were *I scream*

E. Metathesis, or the inversion of the order of two sounds in a word, as when PDE *nuclear* is pronounced [nukələr]

Each of the following words underwent one of the listed changes (A–E) during ME. Use a college dictionary to determine the earlier form of the word and put it in the blank to the right. Identify the type of change in the blank to the left. Some words may show more than one type of change.

0. *E*   dirt   *ME drit < ON drit*

1. _____ pomander _____

2. _____ sister _____

3. _____ spindle _____

4. _____ fresh _____

5. _____ slumber _____

6. _____ custard _____

7. _____ launder _____

8. _____ hasp _____

9. _____ messenger _____

10. _____ marble _____

11. _____ passenger _____

12. _____ adder (snake) _____

13. _____ curl _____

14. _____ scrimmage _____

15. _____ harbinger _____

16. _____ newt _____

17. _____ mulberry _____

18. _____ tine _____

19. _____ eyas _____

20. _____ thrill _____

6.6   Graphics: Changes in the Spelling of Consonants

A.   Listed below are a number of OE words with digraphs (two letters representing a single sound, as in PDE ⟨ch⟩ = [č]), along with typical spellings of these same words in ME. By examining the list, decide how the OE digraphs were changed in ME. Note that some of them were spelled in more than one way in ME.

  OE ecg 'edge'; ME egge, edge
  OE fisc 'fish'; ME fishsh, fischche, etc.
  OE hricg 'ridge'; ME rigge, ridge
  OE hwæl 'whale'; ME whale
  OE hwæte 'wheat'; ME whete
  OE hweol 'wheel'; ME wheele
  OE hwit 'white'; ME white
  OE mycg 'midge'; ME migge, mydge
  OE nahwær 'nowhere'; ME nowher
  OE scal 'shall'; ME schal, ssel, shal, xal, etc.
  OE scearp 'sharp'; ME scharp, sharp, ssarp, etc.
  OE scield 'shield'; ME shild, schilde, etc.
  OE scort 'short'; ME short, schort, etc.
  OE wecg 'wedge'; ME wegge
  OE wyscan 'wish'; ME wisshen, wisse, whysshe, etc.

OE *cg* ➔ ME _____

OE *sc* ➔ ME _____

OE *hw* ➔ ME _____

B.   Listed below are a number of words in their OE and ME spellings. By examining the list, you should be able to describe the graphic (spelling) environments that determined the change in spelling of OE *c* during ME.

  OE candel 'candle'; ME candel
  OE castel 'castle'; ME castel
  OE cese 'cheese'; ME chese
  OE cest 'chest'; ME chest
  OE ciele 'chill'; ME chile
  OE cild 'child'; ME child
  OE clæg 'clay'; ME clay
  OE cleofan 'cleave'; ME cleven
  OE cnif 'knife'; ME knif
  OE cniht 'knight'; ME kniht
  OE corn 'corn'; ME corn
  OE crypel 'cripple'; ME crepel
  OE cuppe 'cup'; ME cuppe
  OE cwacung 'quaking'; ME quakinge
  OE cwealm 'qualm'; ME qualm
  OE cwellan 'quell'; ME quell
  OE (a)cwencan 'quench'; ME quenchen
  OE cweorn 'quern'; ME quern
  OE cycene 'kitchen'; ME kichene

OE kynd 'kind'; ME kind
OE cyrnel 'kernel'; ME kernell

OE *c* → ME *c* _before ⟨a⟩,_ _____
OE *c* → ME *ch* _____
OE *c* → ME *k* _____
OE *c* → ME *q* _____

C. The graphemes *g* and *h* each represented more than one sound in OE, though the distinction was not made in writing. In ME, these sounds came to be spelled differently, although not necessarily consistently. Examine the following lists and determine the written environments under which the ME spellings of OE *g* and *h* appeared.

OE behindan 'behind'; ME behinde(n)
OE beorht 'bright'; ME brycht, briʒt, brigth, etc.
OE feohtan 'to fight'; ME fiʒten, fyghte, fecht, fyþt, etc.
OE frogge 'frog'; ME frog(e), frogge, etc.
OE gærs 'grass'; ME grasse, grase, etc.
OE gamen 'game'; ME game(n)
OE gearn 'yarn'; ME ʒern, yarn, etc.
OE geolu 'yellow'; ME ʒelwa, ʒealwe, yelow, etc.
OE gielpan 'yelp'; ME yelpe, ʒelpen, etc.
OE giet 'yet'; ME ʒit, ʒet, yet, etc.
OE gif 'if'; ME ʒif, yef, etc.
OE glæs 'glass'; ME gles, glas(e), etc.
OE gnæt 'gnat'; ME gnatte, gnet, etc.
OE gold 'gold'; ME gold(e)
OE grædig 'greedy'; ME gredie, gredy, gredi, etc.
OE gylt 'guilt'; ME gult(e), gelte, guilt(e), etc.
OE heah 'high'; ME hegh, heeʒ, hye, heich, heigh, etc.
OE hefig 'heavy'; ME heui, heuy, hevye, etc.
OE hlid 'lid'; ME lede, lid(e)
OE hliehhan 'laugh'; ME leuhwen, lahʒhhen, lauch, lawhe, etc.
OE hnecca 'neck'; ME nekke, necke
OE hogg 'hog'; ME hogge, hog
OE hring 'ring'; ME ring(e), reynge, ryng, etc.
OE hulu 'hull'; ME hul, hull
OE mæg 'may'; ME mai, may
OE oferherian 'overhear'; ME ouerhere(n)
OE pægel 'pail'; ME payle, paille, payelle, etc.
OE ruh 'rough'; ME rowgh, roch, rowhe, rough, etc.
OE sarig 'sorry'; ME sary, sori, etc.
OE segl 'sail'; ME sail(le)
OE sihþ 'sight'; ME sihthe, syhte, sycht, siʒhte, siʒt, etc.
OE singan 'to sing'; ME singe(n)
OE unhalig 'unholy'; ME unholi, vnholy, vnhooli, etc.

OE *g* → ME *g* _____
OE *g* → ME *ʒ, i, y* _____
OE *h* → ME *h* _____
OE *h* → ME *ch, gt, ʒh, ʒ, wh,* etc. _____
OE *h* → ME ∅ _when OE ⟨h⟩ preceded ⟨r, n, l⟩ at beginning of syllable_

6.7   Graphics: ME Handwriting

The text reproduced here is the top part of a page from the Bodley Rawlinson D.99 manuscript of *Mandeville's Travels,* a popular medieval narrative (see p. 188, *A Biography of the English Language*). The manuscript was written in the first half of the fifteenth century. The handwriting is exceptionally clear and legible for this late date.

   The first five lines of the passage have been transliterated for you, and a word-for-word gloss of the entire text is provided. Complete the transliteration of the passage.

Courtesy Bodleian Library, Oxford, U.K. Copyright.

ƷE shal vnderstonde þat this Babylonye þat I speke of where þe
Ye shall understand that this Babylon that I speak of where the

Sawdoun dwelleþ is a gret Cite and fair enhabited. but it is noƷt
Sultan dwells is a great city and fair inhabited but it is not

the Babilonye where the confusiouñ and dyuersite of tungis was made
the Babylon where the confusion and diversity of tongues was made

whanne the Tour of Babilonye was in makinge the wiche is in deserte
when the Tower of Babylon was in making the which is in desert

of Arabie. ffor it is long tyme sithenes þat any man durst þider goen
of Arabia. For it is long time since that any man dared there go

_____
to visit that same wretched place For it is full of vermin and dragons

_____
and adders and many other venom(ous) beasts for the vengeance that God

_____
took at the beginning of that tower (so) that no man dares come there. ¶and

_____
the circle of that tower with the compass of the city of Babylon that there

_____
was once contains 25 miles around. But nevertheless if it be

_____
called a tower, yet there was once in that circle many fair edifi-

_____
ces that now is destroyed and become all wilderness and that same tower

                                                      Nembrok
of Babylon founded the king that (is) called Nimrod that was king of that

_____
land and thereof he was the first king that ever was on earth. ¶And that

                                                      Ryuere
same Babylon was once set on a fair plain field upon the River

1. What major differences in graphics do you find here from the OE facsimile in the preceding chapter?

_____

_____

_____

2. Are any OE letters missing? _____

If so, what has replaced them? _____

Are there any new letters? _____

3. Do *y* and *i* have different sound values? _____

How do you know? _____

_____

4. What evidence for a lack of fixed spelling do you find? _____

_____

5. The letter *s* has three different physical forms in this passage. What are they? _____

Is their distribution arbitrary? Explain. _____

_____

6. The letter *z* appears only once. To what other letter is it very similar? _____

7. What is unusual about the formation of the sequences *da, de,* and *do*? _____

_____

8. What does a wavy line over a vowel mean? _____

_____

9. What is the abbreviation for *er* (lines 3, 6, 9, 10, 14)? _____

_____

6.8   Morphology: Adjective Inflections

During ME, all the OE adjectival inflections were lost except for a trace of the earlier strong versus weak declensions. Even here, the distinction was retained only for monosyllabic adjectives ending in a consonant. For these, a strong singular adjective had no ending; strong plural adjectives and both singular and plural weak adjectives ended in -e:

	Strong	Weak
Sg.	*blind*	*blinde*
Pl.	*blinde*	*blinde*

Adjectives were weak if they appeared

    a.   after a definite article, a demonstrative adjective, a possessive pronoun, or a possessive noun

    b.   in direct address

Adjectives were strong if they appeared

    a.   without a preceding definite article, demonstrative, or possessive

    b.   in predicate adjective position

This remaining inflectional distinction was breaking down during ME, and texts frequently show incorrect forms (although sometimes a seemingly incorrect form can also be interpreted as a remnant of an OE dative).

For the following sentences or phrases, state whether the italicized adjective is *strong* or *weak,* and identify the reason as (a) or (b) as outlined above. If the distinction does not apply because the adjective is polysyllabic or ends in a vowel, write *not applicable* in the blank. Finally, note whether the usage is correct or incorrect according to the rules described above. The base form of the adjective is provided for you.

0. Alss *wise* men haue writen the wordes before. (Base form: *wis*)
    As

Strong, (a), correct plural

1. Bothe failet hym the fode and the *fyne* clothes (Base: *fyn*)
    he lacked   *food*

2. Ethiope is departed in two *princypall parties (Base: princypall)*
          divided   *parts*

3. God . . . chargiþ not siche song, but . . . *goode* werkis (Base: *good*)
        orders   *such singing*   *works*

4. Goth henne swiþe, *fule* þeues! (Base: *ful*)
    Go away quickly, foul thieves

5. Of *green* jaspe and *rede* corale (Bases: *gren, red*)
    green jasper   *red coral*

Both are Strong-(a)-Incorrect, but could be remnants of a dative ending

6. Rideʒ þurʒ þe *roʒe* bonk ryʒt to þe dele (Base: *roʒ*)
   Rides through rough slope   valley

---

7. þai counted no course of the *cold* stormys (Base: *cold*)
   took no account

---

8. þat him   was so *hard* grace yʒarked (Base: *hard*)
   to him   (a) fate ordained

---

9. þat welle ys . . . noʒt *deop* bote to þe kneo (Base: *deop*)
   not deep just   knee

---

10. þat with   the Grekys was *gret,* and of Grice comyn (Base: *gret*)
    that (one)   great   from Greece come

---

11. þe Franche men er *fers*   and *fell* (Bases: *fers, fell*)
    fierce   cruel

---

12. þe *swifte* barge was Duk Henri (Base: *swyft*)
    Duke Henry's

---

13. þes foolis schullen lerne what is *actif* lif and *contemplatif*
    (Bases: *actif, contemplatif*)

---

14. þis *goode* schip I may remene (Base: *good*)
    interpret

---

15. This Yris, fro   the *hihe* stage (Base: *hih*)
    Iris, from   high

---

16. Vnder a *fair* ympe-tre (Base: *fair*)
    sapling

---

17. when þe weder was *clere* and *briʒt* (Bases: *clere, briʒt*)
    weather

6.9 Morphology: Personal Pronouns

For each of the underlined pronouns, identify the person (first, second, or third), case (nominative, objective, or genitive), and number (singular or plural). For third-person pronouns, identify the gender (masculine, feminine, neuter). Give the PDE equivalent of each pronoun.

1. "Hule, þu axest me," ho seide, "ȝif Ich kon eni oþer dede . . ."
   "Owl,   ask   said, "if   know any other thing

   þu _2d pers. sg. nom., thou_   me _____

   ho _____   Ich _____

2. Whan hi beþ fur fram þe abbei, Hi makiþ ham nakid forto plei.
   When   are far from the abbey,   make   naked to play.

   hi _____   Hi _____

   ham _____

3. We redith i þo holi godespelle of tedei ase ure Louerd God
   *   read in the holy gospel for today how   Lord God*

   Almichti ibore was of ure Lauedi Seinte Marie.
   Almighty born was of   Lady Saint Mary.

   We _____   ure _____

   ure _____

4. Mend   ȝow sone of ȝowre misdede: ȝowre _____
   Reform at once of   wrong-doing:

   care es comen,   will ȝe it ken.
   misery has come, will   know.

   ȝow _____   ȝowre _____

   ȝowre _____   ȝe _____

   it _____

5. His light is on vs laide, / He comes oure cares to kele.
   *   light is on   put   comes   cares to assuage.*

   His _____   vs _____

   He _____   oure _____

6. þe maidens durst   hir nouȝt awake, Bote lete hir ligge and rest take.
   The maidens dared   not awake,   but let   lie and rest take

   So sche slepe til afternone.
   So   slept till afternoon.

   hir _____   hir _____

   sche _____

7. But þei wolen not ȝeue here almes to prestis and children.
   But   want not give   alms to priests and children.

   þei _____   here _____

8. For I am wel awroke now of wastoures, þorw þi myȝte. Ac I
   For am well avenged now on rogues, through   power. But

   preye þe, ar þow passe . . .
   pray before   go away . . .

   I _____   þi _____

   I _____   þe _____

   þow _____

9. Natheles it befalleth often tyme þat the gode dyamond leseth his
   Nonetheless, happens oftentimes that the good diamond loses

   vertue.
   quality.

   it _____   his _____

10. þat was myn owne syster Aue, þat y wende y myȝt a saue.
    That was   own sister Ave, that   thought   could have saved.

    myn _____   y _____

    y _____

11. The thyrde es þat scho kepes clene and bryghte hire wyngeȝ.
    The third is that   keeps clean and bright   wings.

    scho _____   hire _____

12. And he let sende for the man, and axede him hou that it was.
    And   caused to send for the man, And asked   how that was.

    he _____   him _____

    it _____

6.10   Morphology: Strong and Weak Verbs

A.   During ME, many verbs that had been strong in OE became weak, though the period still had many more strong verbs than does PDE. In a very few instances, previously weak verbs became strong. The following sentences are from ME texts from the thirteenth through the fifteenth centuries. An (S) after the underlined verb means that it was strong in OE; a (W) means that it was weak. (OF) means that it was a French loan into ME, and (ON) means that it was a Norse loan. Indicate by an (S) or a (W) whether the verb is strong or weak in the ME excerpt, and then indicate whether it is strong or weak in PDE.

1.   And feendes . . . stode (S) _S, S_ on iche halfe on hym and shewed (W) ____
     And fiends   stood   on each side of him and showed

     vnto hym all is liff . . . and weyden (S) ____ þem in a balaunce.
     to him all his life   and weighed   them in a balance.

2.   Suilk als þei brued (S) ____ now ha þai dronken (S) ____.
     Such as they brewed   now have they drunk.

3.   Gnattes gretely me greuede (OF) ____ and gnewen (S) ____ myn eghne.
     Gnats greatly me grieved   and gnawed   my eyes.

4.   þo wex (S) ____ her hertes niþful and bold, /
     Then waxed   their hearts envious and bold

     Quanne he hem adde is dremes told (W) ____ .
     when he them had his dreams told.

5.   Scho wippe (S) ____ and hir hondis wronge (S) ____ .
     She wept   and her hands wrung.

6.   He had lepte (S) ____ in to the ryver and drowned (ON) ____
     He had leapt   into the river and drowned

     hym-self . . . Thei did his comaundement and lepe
     himself . . . They did his commandment and leapt

     (S) ____ to horse.
     to horse.

7.   And whan þis creatur was þus gracyowsly comen (S) ____
     And when this creature was thus graciously come

     ageyn to hir mende, sche thowt (W) ____ she was bowndyn
     again to her mind,   she thought   she was bound

     (S) ____ to god.
     to God.

8.   hir yonge sone Iulo, / And eke Ascanius also, / Fledden (S) ____ .
     her young son Iulus, And also Ascanius also,   Fled.

9.   Lewed men leued (W) ____ hym wel and lyked (W) ____
     Laymen believed   him well and liked

     his wordes, Comen (S) ____ vp knelyng to kissen his bulles.
     his words, came   up kneeling to kiss his documents.

10.   The ladye <u>lough</u> (S) _____ a loud laughter, / As shee <u>sate</u> (S) _____ by the king.
     The lady laughed   a loud laughter   As she sat   by the king.

11.   I have <u>yelded</u> (S) _____ you agen that ye <u>lended</u> (W) _____ me right now.
     I have yielded (repaid) you back what you lent   me right now.

12.   þey <u>founde</u> (S) _____ a mannis hede in þat place while þey digged (OF) _____ .
     They found   a man's head in that place while they dug.

13.   Y <u>dwelled</u> (W) _____ yn þe pryorye fyftene ȝere yn cumpanye.
     I dwelt   in the priory fifteen years in company.

14.   He seynge the citee, <u>wepte</u> (S) _____ on it.
     He seeing the city,   wept   about it.

15.   and so long he <u>knawed</u> (S) _____ it that the lace <u>brake</u> (S) _____ .
     and so long he gnawed   it that the lace broke.

16.   He set ane sege thar-to stoutly, / And <u>lay</u> (S) _____
     He set a siege thereto stoutly,   And lay

     thair quhill it <u>ȝolden</u> (S) _____ was.
     there until it yielded   was.

17.   þenne þe burde byhynde þe dor for busmar <u>laȝed</u> (S) _____ .
     Then the girl behind   the door for scorn laughed.

18.   þi best cote . . . Hath many moles and spottes; it most be <u>ywasshe</u> (S) _____ .
     Your best coat has many stains and spots;   it must be washed.

B.   A number of verbs in PDE are strong when intransitive (e.g., *shine/shone/shone*) but weak when transitive *(shine/shined/shined)*. Other verbs have variant strong forms (e.g., *it shrank* or *it shrunk*) or variant weak forms (e.g., *I dreamt* or *I dreamed*). A few verbs have, in at least one of their principal parts, alternative strong and weak forms. One example is *show*, with variant past participles *showed* and *shown*. List a few more PDE verbs of this last type. _____

_____

6.11   Syntax

Reproduced here are two English translations of the gospel of St. John, 3:1–17, the first from OE and the second from ME. The OE text is from the Anglo-Saxon Gospels, c. 1000, and the ME text is from the Wycliffite version, 1389. Punctuation is modern. A complete gloss of the OE text is provided, along with a partial gloss of the ME text.

John 3:1–17, Old English

[1]Soþlice sum Phariseisc man wæs, genemned Nichodemus, se wæs
Truly a certain Pharisee man was, named   Nicodemus, who was

Iudea ealdor.   [2]Ðes   com to him on niht, and cwæþ to him,
(of) Jews leader. This (one) came to him at night, and said to him,

Rabbi, ðæt is lareow, we witon, ðæt ðu come fram Gode; ne mæg
Rabbi, that is teacher, we know that you come from God; not can

nan man ðas tacn wyrcan ðe ðu wyrcest, buton God beo mid him.
no man these tokens work that you work unless God be with him.

[3]Se Hælend him andswarode, and cwæþ, Soþ, ic ðe secge, buton
The Savior him answered   and said,   True, I (to) you say, unless

hwa beo edniwan gecenned, ne mæg he geseon Godes rice. [4]Ða
someone be anew born,   not can he see God's kingdom. Then

cwæþ Nichodemus to him, Hu mæg man beon eft acenned, ðonne he biþ
said Nicodemus to him,   How can one be again born,   when he is

eald? Cwyst ðu mæg he eft cuman on his moder innoþ, and beon
old? Say you can he again come   in his mother's womb, and be

eft acenned? [5]Se Hælend him andswarode and cwæþ, Soþ, ic ðe
again born?   The Savior him answered and said,   True, I (to) you

secge, buton hwa beo ge-edcenned of wætere, and of Haligum Gaste,
say, unless one be re-created   by water, and by Holy Ghost,

ne mæg he in-faran on Godes rice.   [6]Ðæt ðe acenned is of flæsce,
not can he go in into God's kingdom. That which born is of flesh,

ðæt ys flæsc; and ðæt ðe of gaste   is acenned, ðæt is gast. [7]Ne
that is flesh; and that which of spirit is born, that is spirit. Not

wundra ðu, forðam ðe ic sæde ðe,   Eow gebyraþ ðæt ge beon
marvel you, because I said (to) you, (To) you befits that you be

acennede edniwan. [8]Gast oreðaþ ðar he wile, and ðu gehyrst his
born   again.   Spirit breathes where it wishes, & you hear its

stefne, and ðu nast,   hwanon   he cymþ, ne hwyder he gæþ;
voice, and you do not know, from where it comes, nor where it goes;

swa is ælc ðe acenned is of gaste. [9]Ða andswarode Nichodemus, and
thus is each who born is of spirit. Then answered Nicodemus and

cwæþ, Hu magon ðas þing ðus geweorðan? ¹⁰Se Hælend andswarode,
said, How can these things thus happen?   The Savior answered

and cwæþ to him, Ðu eart lareow Israhela folce,   and ðu
and said to him, You are teacher (of) Israel people, and you

nast ðas þing?   ¹¹Soþ, ic ðe secge, ðæt we sprecaþ, ðæt
not know these things? True, I (to) you say, what we speak, that

we witon, and we cyðaþ, ðæt we gesawon, and ge ne underfoþ ure
we know, and we proclaim what we saw,   and you not receive our

cyðnesse. ¹²Gif ic eow eorþlice þing sæde, and ge ne gelyfaþ,
testimony. If I (to) you earthly things said, and you not believe,

humeta gelyfe ge, gif ic eow heofenlice þing secge? ¹³And nan man
how believe you, if I (to) you heavenly things say? And no man

ne astihþ to heofenum, buton se ðe   nyðer com of heofenum,
not ascends to heaven, except he who down came from heaven,

mannes sunu se ðe com of heofenum. ¹⁴And swa swa Moyses ða
man's son   who came from heaven. And just as Moses the

næddran up-ahof on ðam westene, swa gebyraþ ðæt mannes sunu
serpent up-raised in the desert,   so befits that man's son

beo up-ahofen, ¹⁵Ðæt nan ðara ne forweorðe, ðe on hyne belyfþ,
be up-raised,   That none of those not perish, who on him believe,

ac hæbbe ðæt ece lif.   ¹⁶God lufode middan-eard swa, ðæt he sealde
but have the eternal life. God loved world   so, that he gave

his an-cennedan sunu,   ðæt nan ne forweorðe ðe on hine belyfþ, ac
his only-born son,   that none not perish   who in him believes, but

hæbbe ðæt ece lif. ¹⁷Ne sende God his sunu on middan-eard, ðæt
have the eternal life. Not sent God his son into   world that

he demde middan-earde, ac ðæt middan-eard sy gehæled þurh hine.
he judge world,   but that world   be saved through him.

John 3:1 17, Middle English

¹Forsothe ther was a man of Pharisees, Nicodeme bi name, a prince
Truly   by

of Jewis. ²He cam to Jhesu in the nyʒte, and seide to him, Raby,
                          Jesus   night   Rabbi

we witen, for of God thou hast come a maister; sothli no man may
    know because from   teacher; truly   can

do thes signes that thou dost, no but God were with him. ³Jhesu
                              unless

answeride, and seyde to him, Treuli, treuli, I seye to thee, no but
                          Truly, truly,   unless

a man schal be born aʒen, he may not se the kyngdom of God.
        again,   can   see

⁴Nycodeme seide to him, How may a man be born, whanne he is
                              can   *when*

olde? wher he may entre aȝen in to his modris wombe, and be
       whether can   again   mother's

born aȝein? ⁵Jhesus answeride, Treuli, treuli, I seie to thee, no but
     again?   say   unless

a man schal be born aȝen of watir, and of the Hooly Gost, he may
                    again by   by   can

not entre in to the kyngdom of God. ⁶That that is born of fleisch, is
                                          which

fleisch; and that that is born of spirit, is spirit. ⁷Wondre thou not,
                                                     Do not marvel,

for I seye to thee, It behoueth ȝou for to be born aȝein. ⁸The spirit
                               behooves   again.

brethith wher it wole, and thou heerist his vois, but thou wost not,
breathes   wishes,   hear its voice   know

fro whennis he cometh, or whidir he goth; so is ech man that is
    where it   where it goes   is (for) each

borun of the spirit. ⁹Nycodeme answeride, and seide to him, Hou
born

mown thes thingis be don? ¹⁰Jhesu answeride, and seyde to him,
can these

Art thou a maister in Israel, and knowist not thes thingis? ¹⁴Treuli,
          teacher

treuli, I seye to thee, for that that we witen, we speken, and that
                                       know   speak

that we han seyn, we witnessen, and ȝe taken not our witnessing.
    have seen   testify   you accept

¹²If I haue seid to ȝou ertheli thingis, and ȝe bileuen not, how if I
        said you   believe

schal seie to ȝou heuenli thingis, schulen ȝe bileue? ¹³And no man
                 heavenly   shall you believe?

styeth to heuene, no but he that cam doun fro heauene, mannis sone
ascends   except   from   man's son

that is in heuene. ¹⁴And as Moyses reride vp a serpent in desert, so
                         just as   raised up

it bihoueth mannus sone for to be areysid vp, ¹⁵That ech man that
  behooves man's son   raised   each

bileueth in to him, perische not, but haue euerelastinge lyf.
believes in

¹⁶Forsothe God so louede the world, that he ȝaf his oon bigetun
  Truly   loved   gave   one begotten

sone that ech man that bileueth in to him perische not, but haue
son so that

euere lasting lyf. [17]Sothli God sente not his sone in to the world,
Truly

that he iuge the world, but that the world be sauyd by hym.
judge   *saved*

 For each of the categories listed below, note what changes in English syntax have occurred between the OE and the ME translations. (See *A Biography of the English Language*, pp. 156–65, for general remarks about ME syntax.) Be sure to base your answers on the syntax of the original text, not on that of the gloss.

A.   The Syntax of Phrases

1. Position of noun modifiers _____

_____

2. Use of definite and indefinite articles _____

_____

3. Position of adverbial modifiers _____

_____

4. Negation of verbs _____

_____

5. Prepositional phrases (frequency; number of different prepositions used) _____

_____

6. Verb phrases

 a. Use of perfect tense (*have* + past participle) _____

_____

 b. Formation and use of passive _____

_____

 c. Formation and use of future _____

_____

 d. Use of modal auxiliaries _____

_____

 e. Expression of passive infinitive _____

_____

B.   The Syntax of Clauses

1. Word order in independent clauses _____

_____

2. Word order in subordinate clauses _____

_____

3. Word order of questions _____

_____

4. Word order of imperatives _____

_____

5. Impersonal verbs and "dummy" subjects (*there; it*) _____

_____

_____

    Reproduced here is the text of the same passage from the Revised Standard Version of the Bible of 1952.

    [1]Now there was a man of the Pharisees, named Nicodemus, a ruler of the Jews. [2]This man came to Jesus by night and said to him, "Rabbi, we know that you are a teacher come from God; for no one can do these signs that you do, unless God is with him." [3]Jesus answered him, "Truly, truly, I say to you, unless one is born anew, he cannot see the kingdom of God." [4]Nicodemus said to him, "How can a man be born when he is old? Can he enter a second time into his mother's womb and be born?" [5]Jesus answered, "Truly, truly, I say to you, unless one is born of water and the Spirit, he cannot enter the kingdom of God. [6]That which is born of the flesh is flesh, and that which is born of the Spirit is spirit. [7]Do not marvel that I said to you, 'You must be born anew.' [8]The wind blows where it wills, and you hear the sound of it, but you do not know whence it comes or whither it goes; so it is with every one who is born of the Spirit." [9]Nicodemus said to him, "How can this be?" [10] Jesus answered him, "Are you a teacher of Israel, and yet you do not understand this? [11]Truly, truly, I say to you, we speak of what we know, and bear witness to what we have seen; but you do not receive our testimony. [12]If I have told you earthly things and you do not believe, how can you believe if I tell you heavenly things? [13]No one has ascended into heaven but he who descended from heaven, the Son of man. [14]And as Moses lifted up the serpent in the wilderness, so must the Son of man be lifted up, [15]that whoever believes in him may have eternal life." [16]For God so loved the world that he gave his only Son, that whoever believes in him should not perish but have eternal life. [17]For God sent the Son into the world, not to condemn the world, but that the world might be saved through him.

C.   Compare the syntax of the ME text with that of the PDE text. Is the syntax of the ME text more similar to that of the OE or to that of the PDE text? Give specific examples.

_____

_____

_____

_____

_____

_____

6.12 Lexicon: Loanwords and Native Words

The Norman Conquest changed the entire fabric of the English vocabulary, partly through the thousands of French loanwords that resulted directly from the Conquest and partly because English thereafter became permanently receptive to loanwords from virtually any source. Today it is difficult to write even a paragraph without using at least a few loanwords. Still, it can be done.

On a separate piece of paper, rewrite the following paragraph using only native English words. In your dictionary, these will have *O.E.* or *A-S* (and perhaps also *Germanic*) listed as their ultimate source. To save time in looking up etymologies, treat all personal pronouns; the conjunctions *and, but,* and *or;* all parts of the verbs *to be* and *to have;* and all prepositions of four or fewer letters as native words (even this is not quite accurate because *they, them, and their* are from Old Norse). If a word is affixed, look up the base; for example, for the word *unsuccessfully,* look up *success.* Leave all proper nouns as they are in the passage. Whenever your dictionary lists the direct source of one of the words in the passage as a language other than English, look the word up in the *OED,* note the date of its first recorded appearance in English, and enter the word and the date on the appropriate line.

By the eleventh century, the English and the Norse had achieved an uneasy peace, and the Norse settlers were becoming assimilated into English society. But in 1066, another invasion occurred that was to have a great effect on the history of English. Taking advantage of a somewhat dubious claim to the throne of England, William of Normandy (William the Conqueror) successfully invaded and then took over England. William and most of his followers were racially Germanic, but their ancestors had abandoned their original language for French when they settled in Normandy during the ninth and tenth centuries A.D. Hence the language brought to England by William was French. French became the official language of the court, of law, and of administration for the next 300 to 350 years. However, there were many more English people than French people in England, and the conquered English continued to speak their native language. Many natives surely learned to speak French, but the French also had to learn at least some English in order to be able to speak to their English servants. The English spoken and written from about 1100 (that is, shortly after the Conquest) until about 1500 is called Middle English.

French Loanwords

_____   _____   _____
_____   _____   _____
_____   _____   _____
_____   _____   _____
_____   _____   _____
_____   _____   _____

_____ _____ _____

_____ _____ _____

_____ _____ _____

Latin Loanwords

_____ _____ _____

_____ _____ _____

_____ _____ _____

Old Norse Loanwords

_____ _____ _____

_____ _____ _____

1. Which words did you find it most difficult to replace with native equivalents? _____

_____

2. How does your "translation" differ from the original passage? _____

_____

_____

3. Comment on the date of entry into English of the words from French, Latin, and Old
Norse. _____

_____

_____

4. How do the Norse loans differ from the French and Latin loans? Suggest reasons for
this difference. _____

_____

_____

6.13   Lexicon: Minor Processes of Word Formation

I. Among the minor processes of word formation in ME were

A. **Clipping,** in which the latter part of a word (as in PDE *recap* from *recapitulation*) or the first part (as in PDE *mum* from *chrysanthemum*) is dropped, creating a new, shorter word.

B. **Back-formation,** in which a new word is formed by mistakenly interpreting an existing word as having been derived from it, as in PDE *peeve* from *peevish*.

C. New words from **proper nouns,** as in PDE *limerick* from Limerick, Ireland, or *farad* from (Michael) Faraday.

D. **Folk etymology,** in which an unfamiliar word is altered to make it seem more familiar or to fit English patterns more closely, as in PDE *alewife* (fish) from earlier *allowes*.

Using a college dictionary, check the etymologies of the following words that first appeared in ME. (In some instances, the process took place prior to the word's being borrowed into English.) Write the original form in the space to the right. Indicate which process is involved by writing the appropriate letter (A–D) in the space to the left.

a. ____ pamphlet _____   k. ____ gentry _____

b. ____ mace (spice) _____   l. ____ gun _____

c. ____ slant _____   m. ____ fiddle (violin) _____

d. ____ satin _____   n. ____ peal (ring) _____

e. ____ nuthatch _____   o. ____ gad (run about) _____

f. ____ lapwing _____   p. ____ polecat _____

g. ____ pheasant _____   q. ____ sample _____

h. ____ noisome _____   r. ____ magnet _____

i. ____ die (cube) _____   s. ____ patter _____

j. ____ chat _____   t. ____ wall-eyed _____

II. The following new words in ME, some native and some borrowed, are all derived from either phrases or other parts of speech. Find the origin of each in a dictionary and write it in the space to the right.

a. placebo _____

b. bastard _____

c. constable _____

d. debonair _____

e. memento _____

f. ado _____

III. All of the following words borrowed during ME ultimately derive from animal names. Identify the animals.

a.   arctic _____

b.   cockney _____

c.   pedigree _____

d.   musket _____

e.   spermaceti _____

f.   chameleon _____

6.14   Lexicon: Lost Vocabulary

Biblical translations tend to be highly conservative in their language, partly because of the religious nature of the texts and partly because of translators' awareness of previous translations. For example, the language of the King James Bible was old-fashioned by the time it first appeared in 1611; the same is true of much of the language of the Revised Standard Version of 1952. Consequently, when we find lexical replacements from one translation to a later one, we can at least suspect that the words used in the earlier translation were no longer suitable (though, of course, words are also sometimes replaced because of the stylistic preferences of the translators). The following excerpts are from a late OE and a ME translation of Matthew 13:44–46.

Anglo-Saxon Gospels, c. 1000

[44]Heofona rice is gelic   gehyddum gold-horde on ðam æcere,
Heaven's kingdom is like hidden treasure   in the field,

ðone behyt se man   ðe hine fint; and for his blysse gæþ, and
which hides the man who it finds; and because of his joy goes, and

sylþ eall ðæt he ah,   and gebigþ ðone æcer. [45]Eft is heofena
sells all that he owns, and buys that field.   Again is heaven's

rice gelic ðam mangere,   ðe sohte ðæt gode meregrot; [46]Ða he
kingdom like the monger, who sought the good pearl;   When he

funde ðæt an deorwyrðe   meregrot, ða eode he, and sealde eall ðæt
found the one precious   pearl,   then went he, and sold all that

he ahte,   and bohte ðæt meregrot.
he owned, and bought that pearl.

Wycliffite Gospels, 1389

[44]The kyngdame of heuenes is lijk to tresour   hid in a feeld,
The kingdom of heaven   is like to treasure hidden in a field,

the whiche a man that fyndith, hidith; and for ioye of it he goth,
the which a man   that finds, hides;   and for joy of it he goes,

and sellith alle thingis that hath,   and bieth the ilk feeld. [45] Eftsones
and sells   all things that (he) has, and buys the same field. Again

the kyngdam of heuenes is lic to a man marchaunt,   seekyng good
the kingdom of heaven   is like to a man merchant,   seeking good

margarytis; [46]Sothely oo preciouse margarite founden, he wente,
pearls;   Truly one precious   pearl found,   he went,

and solde alle thingis that he hadde, and bouȝte it.
and sold all   things that he had,   and bought it.

1. The following words from the Anglo-Saxon version have been replaced in the Wycliffite version. Look each of them up in the *OED* and note the *latest* citation given there for each in the meaning intended in the OE text.

rice _____

gold-horde (gold-hoard) _____

æcere (acre) _____

blysse (bliss) _____

ah (owe) _____

mangere (monger) _____

deorwyrðe (dearworth) _____

eode (look under *go*) _____

2. The following words from the Wycliffite version replace the words listed in item 1. Check the origin and first citation in English of each in the *OED*. If the word was used in its meaning here in OE, simply write OE.

kyngdame _____

tresour _____

feeld _____

ioye _____

hath _____

marchaunt _____

preciouse _____

wente _____

3. What is the first citation in the *OED* for *acre* in the meaning of a definite measure of land? _____ How might this have affected the decision of the translators of the Wycliffite version to use the word *field* instead? _____

_____

4. Which of the replaced words from the Anglo-Saxon passage are totally lost (in all meanings) today? _____

_____

5. What are the sources of the newly appearing words in the Wycliffite passage? _____

_____

6 What type of semantic shift in the meaning of *mangere* (monger) was already taking place by the time of the Wycliffite text? _____

_____

7. Both the King James Bible (1611) and the Revised Standard Version (1952) use the word *joy* in Matthew 13:44. What type of semantic shift has *bliss* undergone that makes it unsuitable in this context today? _____

_____

6.15 Semantic Change

Many of the words borrowed during the ME period had already undergone significant semantic change from their etymons in Latin or Greek. Using a good dictionary, find the *ultimate* root of the following loanwords in ME.

1. comet _____

2. coward _____

3. faucet _____

4. noise _____

5. pupil (of the eye) _____

6. story (floor) _____

7. tercel _____

6.16   ME Dialects

As your text explains, the dialectal picture during the ME period was very complex. After the Norman Conquest, dialectal differences proliferated, partly because, with French as the official language, English was written down less frequently than before, and there was no standard for English to serve as a brake on linguistic change. The different regions of England developed their own scribal habits and traditions to some extent, but how closely these reflected differences in speech is uncertain.

Despite all the complexities, one can usually, with a little experience, identify the general area in which a text was written, although more specific location of texts requires specialized knowledge and practice beyond the scope of the novice.

Reproduced here are four texts, all written within approximately a 25-year period and all reasonably pure representatives of their regions of origin, which we can call North, South, East Midlands, and West Midlands. Following the texts is a chart outlining some of the typical characteristics of each region. You will not find all of the features in any one text and you will encounter anomalies. Nonetheless, you should be able to identify the general geographical area in which each of the four texts originated.

Text No. 1 (c. 1365)

Hunger in haste þo hent Wastour bi þe mawe,
            then seized   stomach

And wronge hym so bi þe wombe þat bothe his eyen wattered;
                        belly   eyes

He buffeted þe Britoner aboute þe chekes,

þat he loked like a lanterne al his lyf after.
so that

He bette hem so bothe he barste nere here guttes;   *5*
    beat them   nearly their

Ne hadde Pieres with a pese-lof preyed Hunger to cesse,
If Piers had not   loaf of peas-bread

They hadde ben doluen bothe, ne deme þow non other
        would have been buried   think you (= no 2 ways about it)

'Suffre hem lyue,' he seyde, 'and lete hem ete with hogges,
Let them

Or elles benes and bren ybaken togideres,
        beans   bran

Or elles melke and mene ale': þus preyed Pieres for hem . . .   *10*
        milk   inferior

        þanne hadde Peres pite and preyed Hunger to wende
                                go

Home into his owne erde and holden hym þere—
                land   keep himself

'For I am wel awroke now of wastoures, þorw þi myȝte.
     avenged   *through power*

Ac I preye þe, ar   þow passe,' quod Pieres to Hunger,
     before   *go*

'Of beggeres and of bidderes, what best be to done?   15
      beggars   *is*   *do*

For I wote wel, be þow went, þei wil worche ful ille:
      if thou goest   *work very badly*

For myschief it maketh þei beth so meke nouthe,
   trouble   *they are*   *now*

And for defaute of her fode þis folke is at my wille.
     lack   *their*

þei are my blody brethren,' quod Pieres, 'for God bouȝte vs alle;
     blood

Treuthe tauȝte me ones to louye hem vchone,   20
       once   *love them each one*

And to helpen hem of alle þinge ay   as hem nedeth.
              always   *is necessary for them*

And now wolde I witen of þe what were þe best,
      want I to know from you what would be

And how I myȝte amaistrien hem and make hem to worche.'
      govern

Text No. 2 (c. 1375)

Ant heere þe freris wiþ þer fautours seyne þat it is heresye to
      friars   *supporters say*

write þus goddis lawe in english, & make it knowun to lewid men.
   thus God's   *lay*

& fourty signes þat þey bringen for to shewe an heretik ben not
                 in order to show

worþy to reherse, for nouȝt groundiþ hem but nygromansye.
    repeat   *nothing supports them*   *conjuring*

It semyþ first þat þe wit of goddis lawe shulde be tauȝt   5
      meaning

in þat tunge þat is more knowun, for þis wit is goddis word.
               meaning

whanne crist seiþ in þe gospel þat boþe heuene & erþe shulen passe
    says

but his wordis shulen not passe, he vndirstondith bi his woordis his
                     means

wit. . . . Sum men seyn þat freris trauelen & þer fautours in þis
meaning   *say*   *work*   *supporters*

cause for þre chesouns, þat y wole not aferne, but god woot   *10*
       three reasons   *affirm*   *God knows*

wher þey ben soþe. First þey wolden be seun so nedeful to þe
whether are true   *seen*

engliȝschmen of oure reume þat singulerly in her wit layȝ
           kingdom   *their knowledge lies*

þe wit of goddis lawe, to telle þe puple goddis lawe on what maner
meaning   *people*

euere þey wolden. & þe secound cause herof is seyd to stonde in þis

sentense: freris wolden lede þe puple in techinge hem goddis   15

lawe, & þus þei wolden teche sum, & sum hide, & docke sum. For
                                         curtail

þanne defautis in þer lif shulden be lesse knowun to þe puple, &
      faults

goddis lawe shulde be vntreweliere knowun boþe bi clerkis & bi
              less truly

comyns.   þe þridde cause þat men aspien stondiþ in þis, as þey
common men   *see*

seyn: alle þes newe ordris dreden hem þat þer synne shulde   *20*
            orders of friars fear

be knowun, & hou þei ben not groundid in god to come into þe

chirche; & þus þey wolden not for drede þat goddis lawe were

knowun in engliȝsch, but þey myȝten putte heresye on men ȝif
                                            in

engliȝsch toolde not what þey seyden.

Text No. 3 (c. 1340)

    The bee has thre kyndis. Ane es þat scho es neuer ydill, and
             qualities.   *she*   *idle*

scho es noghte with thaym þat will noghte wyrke, bot castys thaym
    (= has nothing to do with)

owte and puttes thaym awaye. Anothire es þat when scho flyes

scho takes erthe in hyr fette, þat scho be noghte lyghtly
               feet   *easily*

ouerheghede in the ayere of wynde. The thyrde es þat scho   5
raised too high   *air by*

kepes clene and bryghte hire wyngeȝ. Thus ryghtwyse men þat
                               righteous

lufes God are neuer in ydyllnes; for owthyre þay ere in trauayle,
love   *either*   *are*   *toil*

prayand, or thynkande, or redande, or othere gude doande, or
praying   *reading*   *doing*

withtakand ydill mene and schewand thaym worthy to be put fra
scolding   *men*   *showing*   *from*

þe ryste of heuene, for þay will noghte trauayle here.   *10*
    rest   *heaven*   *work*

    þay take erthe, þat es, þay halde þamselfe vile and erthely,
                   themselves

that thay be noghte blawene with þe wynde of vanyte and of
          blown by

pryde. Thay kepe thaire wynges clene, that es, þe twa commande-

mentes of charyte þay fulfill in gud concyens, and thay hafe othyre

vertus, vnblendyde with þe fylthe of syne and vnclene luste.   *15*
    unmingled

    Arestotill sais þat þe bees are feghtande agaynes hym þat will
      says   *fighting against*

drawe þaire hony fra thaym. Swa sulde we do agaynes deuells þat
                Thus should

afforces thame to reue fra us þe hony of poure lyfe and of grace.
endeavor   *rob*   *poor*

For many are þat neuer kane halde þe ordyre of lufe ynence þaire
                   love toward

frendys, sybbe or fremmede; bot outhire þay lufe þaym ouer   *20*
    related   *unrelated*   *either*

mekill, settand thaire thoghte vnryghtwysely on thaym, or þay luf
much

thayme ouer lyttill, yf þay doo noghte all as þey wolde till þame.
                   toward

Swylke kane noghte fyghte for thaire hony, forthy þe deuelle turnes
Such   *because*

it to wormode, and makes þeire saules oftesythes full bitter in
    wormwood   *often*   *very*

angwys and tene and besynes of vayne thoghtes and oþer   *25*
anguish   *pain*   *busy-ness*

wrechidnes. For thay are so heuy in erthely frenchype þat þay
                friendship

may noghte flee intill þe lufe of Iesu Criste, in þe wylke þay moghte
       into   *which*   *might*

wele forgaa þe lufe of all creaturs lyfande in erthe.
    forgo   *living on*

Text No. 4 (c. 1340)

Sleȝþe zayþ, "Hyt lykeþ þet   þou zayst. Ac uor of echen of þe holy
Prudence says It is pleasing what   say   But because each

ordres wondres þou hest yzed, we byddeþ þet þou zigge ous huet is
              hast said   say (to) us what

hare dede ine mennesse and huet is þe conversacion of uelaȝrede;
their deed in common   (holy) life   fellowship

zay ous!" þe Wylyngge of þe Lyue wyþoute end zayþ, "Vor zoþe ich
    Desire   Life   says   Forsooth I

wylle zygge. þe dede of alle ine mennesse ys zeueuald: hy   5
   say   sevenfold they

lybbeþ, hy smackeþ, he louyeþ, hy byeþ glede, he heryþ, he byeþ
live   experience they love   are glad   praise   are

zuyfte, hy byeþ zikere." Sleȝþe zayþ, "þaȝ ich somdel þis onder-
swift   secure Prudence   though I somewhat

stonde, uor ham þet lhesteþ of echen zay."
    for them   listen about each tell

    Wylnynge of þe lyue wyþoute ende zayþ, "zuo by hyt. Hy
    Desire   life   so be it.   They

lybbeþ be lyue wyþoute ende, wyþoute enye tyene, wyþoute   10
live according to life   pain

enye lessinge, wyþoute enye wyþstondynge. Hyre lyf is þe zȝyþe
  decrease   adversity   Their   sight

and þe knaulechynge of þe holy trinyte, ase zayþ oure lhord iesus.
    knowledge   as says   lord

þis is þet lyf wyþoute ende, þet hy knawe þe zoþe god and huam þe
                                   true   him that

zentest, iesu crist. And þeruore ylyche hy byeþ, uor hy yzyeþ ase
sent   alike they are   see (Him)

he is. Hy smackeþ þe redes and þe domes of god. Hy   15
    they know   counsels   judgments

smackeþ be kendes and the causes and þe begynnynges of alle
      by natures

þynges. Hy louyeþ god wyþoute enye comparisoun, uor þet hy
                   beyond   because they

wyteþ huerto god his heþ ybroȝt uorþ. Hy louyeþ ech oþren ase
know wherefore   has brought forth

ham zelue. Hy byeþ glede of god   onzyginde; hy byeþ glede of zuo
themselves   are glad because of God unstintingly   so

moche of hare oȝene holynesse; and uor þet ech loueþ oþren   20
    their own   because

ase him zelue, ase moche blisse heþ ech of oþres guode ase of his
as   has each because of other's good

oȝene. . . . Yef þanne on onneaþe nymþe al his blisse, hou   ssel he
If then one scarcely (can) receive   shall

nyme zuo uele and zuo manye blyssen? And þeruore hit is yzed,
receive numerous   said

'guo into þe blysse of þyne lhorde' . . .
                                thy

FEATURES OF ME DIALECTS

	North	South	East Midlands	West Midlands
a. 3d sg. pres. ind.	-(e)s[1]	-(e)þ[2]	-(e)þ[2]	-(e)þ[2]
b. 3d. pl. pres. ind.	-(e)s, -e	-(e)þ	-(e)n	-(e)þ,-n,-e
c. Pres. part.[3]	-and(e)	-ind(e), later -ing(e)	-end(e), later -ing(e)	-end(e), later -ing(e)
d. 3d pl. pronouns[4]	they, them, their	hi, hem, hire	they, hem, hire	they, hem, hire
e. she[5]	scho, sco	heo, he	sche	scho,he,ho,ha
f. Pres. pl. 'to be'	er, are, es	be(n)	be(n), are(n)	be(n), beþ
g. Past pl. 'to be'	ware	weren	weren	weren
h. Noun pls.	-(e)s(s)	-(e)n, -(e)s	-(e)n, -(e)s	-(e)n, -(e)s
i. Prep. with infin.	at, to, ø	to, ø	to, ø	to, ø
j. Infin. ending	ø	ø	-(e)n	-(e)n
k. Strong past part.	-(e)n	ø	-(e)n, ø	-(e)n, ø
l. Weak past part.	-it, -d	-(e)d	-(e)d	-(e)t, -(e)d
m. Past part. prefix	ø	i-, y-	i-, y-, ø	y-, i-, ø
n. OE [ā]	ā[6]	ō	ō	ō
o. OE [k]	[k] ⟨c,k⟩	[č] ⟨ch⟩	[č] ⟨ch⟩	[č] ⟨ch⟩
p. OE [ă] + [m,n][7]	a	a	a	o
q. OE [ў][8]	⟨i,y⟩ [ɪ,i]	⟨u⟩ [y] ⟨e⟩ [e] (Kent)	⟨i,y⟩ [ɪ,i]	⟨u⟩ [y]
r. OE initial ⟨f,s⟩	⟨f,s⟩	⟨v,z⟩	⟨f,s⟩	⟨f,s⟩
s. OE ⟨hw⟩	⟨qu,quh⟩	⟨hu⟩, later ⟨w⟩	⟨w,wh⟩	⟨hw⟩, later ⟨wh⟩
t. OE [š] in 'shall, should'	⟨s⟩	⟨ss⟩	⟨s,sh,sch⟩	⟨sh⟩

[1] Parentheses mean the sound or letter may or may not appear. Note that square brackets indicate sound values and angled brackets indicate spelling values.

[2] ⟨t⟩ or ⟨th⟩ may appear instead of ⟨þ⟩.

[3] By later ME, all dialects had -ing.

[4] The spelling of everything after the initial consonant may vary.

[5] Only a few of the many different forms in each dialect area are listed here.

[6] If the word has an ⟨a⟩ where PDE has ⟨o⟩, it is probably an example of this.

[7] If the word has ⟨om⟩ or ⟨on⟩ where PDE has ⟨am⟩ or ⟨an⟩, it is probably an example of this.

[8] The PDE words would normally be pronounced with [ɪ] or [i]. A ⟨u⟩ spelling indicates that the vowel is still rounded in these dialects.

WORKSHEET FOR ME DIALECTS

	No. 1	No. 2	No. 3	No. 4
a. 3d sg. pres. ind.				
b. 3d pl. pres. ind.				
c. Pres. part.				
d. 3d pl. pronouns				
e. she				
f. Pres. pl. 'to be'				
g. Past pl. 'to be'				
h. Noun pls.				
i. Prep. with infin.				
j. Infin. ending				
k. Strong past part.				
l. Weak past part.				
m. Past part. prefix				
n. OE [ā]				
o. OE [k]				
p. OE [ă] + [m,n]				
q. OE [y̆]				
r. OE initial ⟨f,s⟩				
s. OE ⟨hw⟩				
t. OE [š] in 'shall, should'				

1. Fill in the blank chart with examples of the specific features from each text. (You will not find examples of every feature in every text.)

2. Identify the probable dialect area from which each text comes by writing "North," "South," "East Midlands," or "West Midlands" at the top of the appropriate column.

3. Did you find any anomalies or evidence of dialect mixture? _____

_____

_____

4. Which passage(s) do you find it easiest to read in the original? _____

_____

The hardest? _____

Can you offer any explanations for your answers here? _____

_____

5. One of these texts is a translation from French; the other three are original English compositions. Which one do you think is the translation and why? _____

_____

6. Which text seems to have the highest proportion of loanwords from French? _____ The lowest proportion? _____ Since all of the texts were written at roughly the same time, what might account for the difference in the proportions?

_____

_____

6.17   ME Illustrative Texts

I.   The Peterborough Chronicle

The Peterborough Chronicle was continued for almost a century after the Norman Conquest, well into the ME period. The following is the final entry, that for the year 1154. Though at first glance the text may look like OE, many changes in the language have taken place since even the entry for 1085. Note in particular the undeclined definite article and such French loanwords as *court* and *procession*.

On þis gær wærd þe king Stephne ded & bebyried þer his
In this year was the king Stephen   dead & buried where his

wif & his sune wæron bebyried æt Fauresfeld; þaet ministre hi
wife & his son were buried at Faversham;   that minster they

makeden. þa þe king was ded,   þa was þe eorl beionde sæ;
founded. When the king was dead, then was the earl overseas;

& ne durste nan man don oþer bute god for þe micel eie of him.
& not dared no man do other but good for the great fear of him.

þa he to Engleland com,   þa was he underfangen mid micel
When he to England came, then was he received with great

wurtscipe, & to king   bletcæd in Lundene on þe Sunnendæi beforen
honor,   & as king   ordained in London on the Sunday before

Midwintre Dæi, & held þære micel curt.   þat ilce dæi þat
Midwinter Day,   & held there great court. That same day that

Martin abbot of Burch   sculde þider faren, þa sæclede he,
Martin abbot of Peterborough was to go there,   then took sick he,

& ward ded iiii Nonarum Ianuarii. & Te munekes innen dæis cusen
& was dead 4 the nones January. & the monks within a day chose

oþer of heomsælf,   Willelm de Walteruile is gehaten,
another from themselves, William of Walterville is called,

god clerc & god man   & wæl luued of þe king & of alle gode men;
good cleric & good man & well loved by the king & by all good men;

& on morgen byrieden þabbot hehlice. & Sone þe cosan abbot
& in morning buried   the abbot nobly. & at once the elected abbot

ferde, & te muneces mid him, to Oxenforde to þe king; & he iaf
went, & the monks   with him, to Oxford   to the king; & he gave

him þat abbotrice. & He ferde him   sone to Lincol, & wæs
him the abbacy.   & he took himself at once to Lincoln, & was

þær bletcæd to abbot   ær he ham come;   & sithen was
there ordained as abbot before he home came; & afterward was

underfangen mid micel wurtscipe at Burch   mid micel
received   with great honor at Peterborough with great

processiun; & sau   he was alsua at Ramsæie,   & at Torneie, & at
procession; & thus he was also at Ramsey,   & at Thorney, & at

Cruland & Spallding,   & at S. Albanes & F. . . . & Nu is abbot &
Crowland & Spalding,   & at St. Albans & F. . . . & now is abbot &

fair haued begunnon: Xrist him unne þus enden!
fair had begun: Christ him grant thus (to) end!

II. *Hali Meidenhad*

Hali Meidenhad, or "Holy Virginity," is a prose homily in praise of virginity. It is one member of a five-text group (the others are *Seinte Marharete, Seinte Iuliene, Seinte Katerine*, and *Sawles Warde*) collectively termed The Katherine Group. All date from the late twelfth or early thirteenth century and are written in a West Midlands dialect.

Ga we nu forthre   ant loki we hwuch   wunne ariseth threfter
Go we now further and look what sort of delight arises thereafter

i burtherne of bearne   hwen thet streon   in the awakeneth ant
in pregnancy of (a) child when that offspring in you quickens and

waxeth ant hu monie earmthen anan awakeneth therwith, the
grows and how many miseries immediately spring up with it, that

wurcheth the wa inoh,   fehteth o thi seolve flesch ant weorrith with
occupy you woe enough, fight in your own flesh   and struggle with

feole weanan o thin ahne cunde. Thi rudie neb schal leanin   ant
many woes in your own flesh.   Your rosy face will grow lean and

ase gres grenin,   thine ehnen schule doskin ant underneothe
as grass turn green, your eyes will become dim and underneath

wonnin,   ant of thi breines turnunge thin heaved aken sare;
become dark, and of your brain's activity your head ache sorely;

inwith i thi wombe   swelle thi butte   the bereth the forth
inside in your womb swells your belly, which sticks out in front of

as a weater-bulge;   thine thearmes thralunge, ant stiches i
you like a water-barrel; of your guts pain,   and stitches in

thi lonke, ant i thi lendene sar eche rive,   hevinesse in
your side, and in your loins painful ache prevalent, heaviness in

euch lim; thine breostes burtherne o thine two pappes ant te milc-
every limb; your breasts' weight   in your two nipples and the milk-

strunden the the of striketh.   Al is with a weolewunge thi wlite
streams which you from flow. All is with a nausea   your face

overwarpen. Thi muth is bitter   ant walh al thet tu cheowest,
downcast.   Your mouth is bitter and insipid all that you chew,

ant hwetse thi mahe   hokerliche underveth, thet is with
and whatever your stomach nauseatedly receives, it is with

unlust, warpeth hit eft ut.   Inwith   al thi weole ant ti
distaste, throws it back out. In the midst of all your joy and your

weres wunne forwurthest.   A wrecche! The cares
husband's pleasure, [you are] perishing. Ah, wretch! The anxieties

ayein thi pinunge thrahen bineometh the nahtes slepes. Hwen hit
about your pain spasms deprive   you of night's sleep. When it

thenne therto kimeth,   thet sore sorhfule angoise,   thet stronge ant
then thereto comes,   that painful sorrowful agony, that strong and

stikinde stiche, thet unroles uvel,   thet pine   over pine,
piercing spasm, that restless misery, that torment after torment,

thet wondrinde yeomerunge, hwil thu swenchest terwith i thine
that amazing lamentation,   while you labor therewith in your

deathes dute scheome teke   thet sar with the alde wifes
death's fear shame (in addition to) that pain with the old women's

scheome creft, the cunnen of   thet wa-sith, hwas help the
shame skill, who are familiar with that woe-time, whose help to you

bihoveth ne beo hit neaver se uncumelich; ant nede most hit tholien
is necessary not be it never so unseemly;   and needs must it endure

thet te   therin itimeth.   Ne thunche the nan uvel of, for we ne
what to you therein happens. Not seem to you no evil of, for we not

edwiteth nawt wifes hare   weanen thet ure alre modres drehden
reproach not women their woes which all our mothers suffered

on us seolven,   ah we schawith ham forth forte warni meidnes
through ourselves, but we reveal them forth to   warn maidens

thet ha beon the leasse efterwart swuch thing ant witen herthurh
that they be the less afterward such things   and know thereby

the betere hwet ham beo to donne.
the better what to them is to do.

    Efter al this kimeth of thet bearn   ibore thus wanunge ant
    After all this comes from that child born thus lamentation and

wepunge, the schal abute midniht   makie the to wakien other theo
weeping, that will around midnight make you to wake or those

the hire stude halt the thu most forcarien.   Ant hwet
who her place holds that you must worry about. And what about

the cader-fulthen ant bearmes: unbestunde to feskin ant to
the baby-filth and (your) breasts: at times to swaddle and to

fostrin hit se moni earmhwile?   Ant his waxunge se let ant
nurse it so many wretched times? And its growth so late and

se slaw his thriftre, ant eaver habbe   sar care ant lokin efter
so slow its growth, and always having vexing care and looking after

al this hwenne hit forwurthe ant bringe on his moder sorhe. Thah
all this when it dies   and brings on its mother grief. Though

thu riche beo ant nurrice habbe, thu most as moder carien for al
you rich be and (a) nurse have, you must as mother care for all

thet hire limpeth to donne. Theose ant othre earmthen the of
that she ought to do.   These and other miseries which from

wedlac awakenith Seinte Pawel biluketh in ane lut wordes,
wedlock arise   St. Paul   expresses in a few words,

Tribulaciones carnis, et cetera. Thet is on Englisch 'Theo thet
Tribulation in the flesh, etc.   That is in English, 'Those that

thulliche beoth schulen derf drehen.' Hwase thencheth on al this
such be must cruel suffer.'   Whoever thinks about all this

ant o mare thet ter is ant nule   withbuhe thet thing thet
and of more that there is and not wants to avoid that thing that

hit al of awakeneth, ha is heardre iheortet then adamantines stan
it all springs from,   she is harder hearted than adamantine stone

ant mare amead, yef ha mai,   than is meadschipe seolf, hire ahne
and more mad, if she can (be), than is insanity itself, her own

fa ant hire feont,   heateth hire seolfen.
foe and her enemy, hates herself.

III. Lyrics

The lyric as we know it today makes its first appearance in English during the ME period. The subject matter may be religious or secular; of the four reproduced here, only the second is secular in theme. Their dates range from the twelfth to the fifteenth century. Note that all of these lyrics use end rhyme to tie the lines together instead of the OE alliteration.

St. Mary Virgin

Sainte Marye Virgine,
St.   Mary   Virgin

Moder Jesu Christes Nazarene,
Mother of Jesus Christ the Nazarene

Onfo, schild, help thin Godric,
Receive, defend, help your Godric,

Onfang, bring heyilich with thee in Godes Riche.
Take, bring on high   with you into God's kingdom.

Sainte Marye, Christes bur,
St. Mary, Christ's chamber,

Maidenes clenhad, moderes flur,
Virgins' purity, motherhood's flower,

Dilie min sinne, rix in min mod,
Wipe out my sin, rule in my heart,

Bring me to winne with the self God.
Bring me to joy with that same God.

Merry it is

Mirie it is, while sumer ilast,
Merry it is, while summer lasts,

With fugheles song.
With birds' song.

Oc nu necheth windes blast,
But now approaches wind's blast,

And weder strong.
And weather strong.

Ey! ey! what this night is long!
Alas! Alas! how long this night is!

And ich, with well michel wrong,
And I, because of very great wrong,

Soregh and murne and fast.
Sorrow and mourn and fast.

When I see on the rood

Whanne ic se on Rode
When I see on (the) cross

Jesu, my lemman,
Jesus, my lover,

And besiden him stonden
And beside him stand

Marye and Johan,
Mary and John,

And his rig iswongen,
And his back scourged,

And his side istungen,
And his side pierced,

For the luve of man;
For the love of man;

Well ou ic to wepen,
Well ought I to weep,

And sinnes for to leten,
And sins to abandon,

Yif ic of luve can,
If I of love know,

Yif ic of luve can,
If I of love know,

Yif ic of luve can.
If I of love know.

Adam lay bound

Adam lay ibounden,
Adam lay bound,

Bounden in a bond:
Bound in a bond:

Foure thousand winter
Four thousand years

Thought he not too long.
Thought he not too long.

And all was for an apple,
And all was because of an apple,

An apple that he tok,
An apple that he took,

As clerkes finden
As clerics find

Wreten in here book.
Written in their book.

Ne hadde the apple take ben,
(If) not had the apple taken been,

The apple taken ben,
The apple taken been,

Ne hadde never our Lady
(Then) not had never our Lady

A ben Hevene Quen.
Have been heaven's queen.

Blissed be the time
Blessed be the time

That apple take was!
That apple taken was!

Therfore we moun singen,
Therefore we may sing,

'Deo gracias!'
'Thanks be to God!'

IV. Proclamation of Henry III
Though the official language of England was French after the Conquest, English continued
to be the language of the great majority of the people. In recognition of this fact, some
official documents were written in both French and English, as was the case of this 1258
proclamation of King Henry III.

Henri, þurȝ godes fultume king on Engleneloande, lhoauerd on
Henry, through God's help, king in England,   lord in

Yrloande, duk on Normandie, on Aquitaine, and eorl on Aniow send
Ireland, duke in Normandy, in Aquitaine,   and earl in Anjou, sends

igretinge to alle hise holde, ilærde and ileawede, on Huntendoneschire.
greeting to all his faithful, clerical and lay,   in Huntingtonshire.

þæt witen ȝe wel alle, þæt we willen and vnnen þæt þæt vre
That know you well all, that we wish and grant that, that our

rædesmen alle, oþer þe moare dæl of heom, þæt beoþ ichosen þur3
counselors all, or the greater part of them,   that are chosen by

us and þur3 þæt loandes folk on vre kuneriche, habbeþ idon and
us and by the land's people in our   kingdom, have done and

schullen don in þe worþnesse of gode and on vre treowþe for þe
shall do in the   honor of God and in our faith   for the

freme of þe loande, þur3 þe besi3te of þan to-foren inseide redesmen,
profit of the land,   through the provision of the aforesaid counselors,

beo stedefæst and ilestinde in alle þinge a buten ænde.
be steadfast and stable   in all things always without end.

And we hoaten alle vre treowe   in þe treowþe þæt heo vs
And we command all our faithful in the fidelity that they us

o3en, þæt heo stedefæstliche healden and swerian to healden and
owe, that they steadfastly   hold   and swear   to hold and

to werien þo isetnesses þæt beon imakede and beon to makien þur3
to defend those statutes that are made   and are to (be) made by

þan to-foren iseide rædesmen, oþer þur3 þe moare dæl of heom,
the aforesaid   counselors, or by   the greater part of them,

alswo alse hit is biforen iseid; and þæt æhc oþer helpe þæt
also as it is before said; and that each (the) other help that

for to done bi þan ilche oþe a3enes alle men ri3t for to done and to
to do by the same oath toward all men right   to do and to

foangen; and noan ne nime of loande ne of e3te,   wherþur3
take;   and none not take from land nor from property,   by which

þis besi3te mu3e beon ilet   oþer iwersed on onie wise.
this provision can be hindered or damaged in any way.

And 3if oni   oþer onie cumen her on3enes, we willen and
And if any one or ones come here against,   we want and

hoaten þæt   alle vre treowe heom healden deadliche ifoan.
command that all our faithful them consider deadly foes.

And for þæt we willen, þæt þis beo stedefæst and lestinde, we
And because we want that this be steadfast and lasting,   we

senden 3ew þis writ open, iseined wiþ ure seel, to halden a-manges 3ew ine hord.
send   you this writ open, marked with our seal, to keep amongst   you in treasury.

Witnesse vs seluen æt Lundene þane e3tetenþe day on the
Witness ourselves at London   the eighteenth day in the

monþe of Octobre, in þe two and fowerti3þe 3eare of vre cruninge.
month of October, in the two and fortieth   year of our crowning.

And þis wes idon ætforan vre isworene redesmen: Boneface,
And this was done before our sworn counselors: Boniface,

archebischop on Kanterburi; Walter of Cantelow, bischop on
archbishop in Canterbury;   Walter of Cantelow, bishop in

Wirechestre; Simon of Muntfort, eorl on Leirchestre; Richard of
Worcester;   Simon of Montfort, earl in Leicester;   Richard of

Clare, eorl on Glowchestre and on Hurtforde; Roger Bigod, eorl on
Clare, earl in Gloucester and in Hertford;   Roger Bigod, earl in

Northfolke and marescal on Engleneloande; . . .
Norfolk   and Marshal in England; . . .

And al on þo ilche worden is   isend in-to æurihce oþre schire
And all in those same words is (to be)   sent into every other shire

ouer al þære kuneriche on Engleneloande, and ek in-tel Irelonde.
over all the kingdom   of England   and also into Ireland.

V. *Sir Orfeo*

During the ME period, romances, adventure tales usually in verse, became popular in England. Many of them were translations of French originals. A subdivision of the romance was the Breton lai, usually a short romance emphasizing love and the supernatural. *Sir Orfeo,* one of the most charming of the English Breton lais, retells the classical story of Orpheus and Eurydice—and gives it a happy ending. The manuscript from which this excerpt was taken was written about 1335.

Orfeo was a king,
Orpheus was a king,

In Inglond an heiʒe lording,
In England a high lord,

A stalworþ man and hardi bo,
A valiant man and hardy both,

Large and curteys he was also.
Generous and well-bred he was also.

His fader was comen of King Pluto,
His father was descended from King Pluto,

And his moder of King Juno,
And his mother from King Juno,

þat sum time were as godes yhold,
That once were as gods considered,

For auentours þat þai ded and told.
For feats that they did and told.

Orpheo most of ony þing
Orpheus most of any thing

Louede þe gle of harpyng;
Loved the minstrelsy of harping;

Syker was euery gode harpoure
Certain was every good harpist

Of hym to haue moche honoure.
From him to have much honor.

Hymself loued for to harpe,
(He) himself loved to (play the) harp,

And layde þeron his wittes scharpe.
And applied to it his wits sharp.

He lernyd so,   þer noþing was
He learned so (well), there nothing was

A better harper in no plas;
A better harpist in no place;

In þe world was neuer man born
In the world was never man born

þat ones Orpheo sat byforn,
That once Orpheus sat in front of,

And he myȝt of his harpyng here,
If he could of his harping hear,

He schulde þinke þat he were
He would think that he was

In one of þe ioys of Paradys,
In one of the joys of Paradise,

Suche ioy and melody in his harpyng is.
Such joy and melody in his harping is.

þis king soiournd in Traciens,
This king lived in Thrace,

þat was a cité of noble defense;
That was a city of good fortification;

For Winchester was cleped þo
For Winchester was called then

Traciens wiþouten no.
Thrace undoubtedly.

þe king hadde a quen of priis,
The king had a queen of excellence

þat was ycleped Dame Herodis,
That was called Dame Eurydice,

þe fairest leuedi, for þe nones,
The fairest lady, to be sure,

þat miȝt gon on bodi and bones,
That could walk in body and bones,

Ful of loue and of godenisse;
Full of love and of goodness;

Ac no man may telle hir fairnise.
But no man can describe her beauty.

Bifel   so in þe comessing of May,
(It) happened so in the beginning of May,

When miri and hot is þe day,
When merry and hot is the day,

And oway beþ winter-schours,
And away are winter showers,

And eueri feld is ful of flours,
And every field is full of flowers,

And blosme breme on eueri bouȝ
And blossom glorious on every bough

Oueral wexeþ miri anouȝ,
Everywhere grows merry enough

þis ich quen, Dame Heurodis,
This same queen, Dame Eurydice,

Tok to maidens of priis,
Took two maidens of worth,

And went in an vndrentide
And went in a morning

To play bi an orchard side,
To play by an orchard side,

To se þe floures sprede and spring,
To see the flowers spread and spring,

And to here þe foules sing.
And to hear the birds sing.

þai sett   hem   doun al þre
They set themselves down all three

Vnder a fair ympe-tre,
Under a lovely sapling,

And wel sone þis fair quene
And very soon this fair queen

Fel on slepe opon þe grene.
Fell asleep upon the green.

þe maidens durst hir nouȝt awake,
The maidens dared her not awake,

Bot lete hir ligge and rest take.
But let her lie   and rest take.

So sche slepe til afternone,
So she slept till afternoon,

þat vndertide was al ydone.
That morning was all done.

Ac as sone as sche gan awake,
But as soon as she did awake,

Sche crid and loþli bere gan make,
She cried and horrible outcry did make,

Sche froted hir honden and hir fet,
She rubbed her hands and her feet,

And crached hir visage, it bled wete;
And scratched her face, it bled wet;

Hir riche robe hye al torett,
Her rich robe noble all tore to pieces,

And was reueysed out of hir witt.
And was driven out of her wits.

þe tvo maidens hir biside
The two maidens her beside

No durst wiþ hir no leng abide,
Not dared with her no longer stay,

Bot ourn to þe palays ful riȝt,
But ran to the palace immediately,

And told boþe squier and kniȝt
And told both squire and knight

þat her quen awede wold,
That their queen go mad would,

And bad hem go and hir athold.
And bade them go and her restrain.

Kniȝtes vrn, and leuedis also,
Knights ran, and ladies also,

Damisels sexti and mo,
Damsels sixty and more,

In þe orchard to þe quen hye come,
In the orchard to the queen they came,

And her vp in her armes nome,
And her up in their arms took,

And brouȝt hir to bed atte last,
And brought her to bed at last,

And held hir þere fine fast;
And held her there very fast;

Ac euer sche held in o cri,
But always she kept up the same cry,

And wold vp and owy.
And wanted up and away.

VI. Barbour's *Bruce*
John Barbour, a Scottish cleric, was the author of *The Bruce*, a long, quasi-historical verse chronicle of the deeds of Robert Bruce, king of Scotland. It was written in the Northern dialect in 1376. The following passage from the early part of the poem tells of the famous battle of Bannockburn.

And fra schir amer with the king
And after Sir Aymer with the king

Wes fled,   wes nane that durst abyde,
Had fled, (there) was none that dared stay,

Bot fled, scalit on ilka syde.
But fled, dispersed on every side.

And thair fais thame presit fast,
And their foes them pressed diligently,

Thai war, to say   suth, all agast,
They were, to tell (the) truth, all terrified,

And fled swa richt effrayitly
And fled in such a frightened way

That of thame a full gret party
That of them a very great party

Fled to the wattir of forth; and thar
Fled to the water of Forth; and there

The mast part of thame drownit [war].
The most part of them drowned were.

And bannokburn, betuix the braiß,
And Bannockburn, between the banks,

Of horß and men so chargit waß,
Of horses and men so loaded was,

That apon drownit horß and men
That upon drowned horses and men

Men mycht paß dry atour it then.
Men could pass dry across it then.

[And] laddis, swanys, and rangall,
And lads, peasants, and camp-followers,

Quhen thai saw vencust the battall,
When they saw vanquished the battalion,

Ran emang thame and swa can sla
Ran among them and so did slay

Thai folk, that no defens mycht ma,
Those people, who no defense could make,

That it war pite for to se.
That it was pity to see.

I herd neuir quhar, in na cuntre,
I heard never where, in no country,

Folk at swa   gret myschef war stad;
People in such great misfortune were beset;

On a syde thai thair fais had,
On one side they their foes had,

That slew thame doune vithout mercy,
That slew them   down without mercy,

And thai had on the tothir party
And they had on the other side

Bannokburne, that sa cummyrsum was
Bannockburn, that so hard to cross was

Of slyk, and depnes for till pas,
With slime, and depth to pass,

That thair mycht nane atour it ryde.
That they could none across it ride.

Thame worthit,   magre thairis,   abyde;
It behooved them, despite themselves, (to) remain;

Swa that sum slayne, sum drownit war;
So that some slain, some drowned were;

Micht nane eschap that euir com thar.
None could escape that ever came there.

The quhethir mony gat avay,
Nevertheless, many got away,

[That ellis-whar fled], as I herd say.
That elsewhere fled,   as I heard say.

The kyng, with thame he with him had,
The king, with them he with him had,

In a rout till the castell raid,
In a band to the castle rode,

And wald haue beyn tharin, for thai
And wanted to have been therein, for they

Wist nocht quhat gat to get avay.
Knew not what way to get away.

VII. Chaucer's "Second Nun's Tale"
Chaucer's "Second Nun's Tale," a version of the legend of St. Cecilia, was probably written in the 1370s. Reproduced here are the closing lines. You might compare this version with the OE one by Ælfric, written roughly four centuries earlier.

"Do wey thy booldnesse," seyde Almachius tho,
"Leave off your boldness," said Almachius then,

"And sacrifice to oure goddes er thou go.
And sacrifice to our gods before you go.

I recche nat what wrong that thou me profre,
I care not what wrong that you (to) me present,

For I kan suffre it as a philosophre,
For I can suffer it as a philosopher,

"But thilke wronges may I nat endure
"But those wrongs can I not endure

That thou spekest of oure goddes heere," quod he.
That you speak of our gods here,"   said he.

Cecile answerde,   "O nyce creature!
Cecilia answered, "O foolish creature!

Thou seydest no word syn thou spak to me
You said no word since you spoke to me

That I ne knew therwith thy nycetee;
That I knew not thereby your foolishness;

And that thou were, in every maner wise,
And that you were, in every way,

A lewed officer and a veyn justise.
An ignorant officer and an ineffectual justice.

"Ther lakketh no thyng to thyne outter eyen
"There lacks nothing in your outer eyes

That thou n'art blynd, for thyng that we seen alle
That you aren't blind, with regard to things that we all see

That it is stoon—that men may wel espyen—
That it is stone—that men can easily spot—

That ilke stoon a god thow wolt it calle.
That same stone a god you will it call.

I rede thee, lat thyn hand upon it falle
I advise you, let your hand upon it fall

And taste it wel and stoon thou shalt it fynde,
And feel it well and stone you shall it find,

Syn that thou seest nat with thyne eyen blynde.
Since that you see not with your eyes blind.

"It is a shame that the peple shal
"It is a shame that the people must

So scorne thee and laughe at thy folye,
So scorn you and laugh at your folly,

For communly men woot it wel overal
For commonly men know it well overall

That myghty God is in his hevenes hye.
That mighty God is in his heavens high.

And thise ymages, wel thou mayst espye
And these images, easily you can spot

To thee ne to hemself ne mowen noght profite,
To you nor to themselves not can nothing profit,

For in effect they been nat worth a myte."
For in effect they are not worth a mite."

Thise wordes and swiche othere seyde she,
These words and such others said she,

And he weex wrooth and bad men sholde hir lede
And he grew angry and ordered men should her lead

Hom til hir hous, and "In hire house," quod he,
Home to her house, and "In her house," said he,

"Brenne hire right in a bath of flambes rede."
"Burn her completely in a bath of flames red."

And as he bad, right so was doon in dede;
And as he ordered, just so was done in deed;

For in a bath they gonne hire faste shetten,
For in a bath they did her firmly shut,

And nyght and day greet fyr they under betten.
And night and day great fire they under fed.

The longe nyght and eek a day also
The long night and moreover a day also

For al the fyr and eek the bathes heete
For all the fire and also the bath's heat

She sat al coold and feelede no wo;
She sat all cold and felt no woe;

It made hire nat a drope for to sweete.
It made her not a drop to sweat.

But in that bath hir lyf she moste lete,
But in that bath her life she had to leave,

For he Almachius, with ful wikke entente,
For he Almachius, with very wicked intent,

To sleen hire in the bath his sonde sente.
To slay her in the bath his messenger sent.

Thre strokes in the nekke he smoot hire tho,
Three strokes in the neck he struck her then,

The tormentour, but for no maner chaunce
The tormenter, but for no manner of chance

He myghte noght smyte al hir nekke atwo.
He could not strike all her neck in two.

And for ther was that tyme an ordinaunce
And because there was that time an ordinance

That no man sholde doon man swich penaunce
That no man should do anyone such punishment

The ferthe strook to smyten, softe or soore,
The fourth stroke to smite, soft or hard,

This tormentour ne dorste do namoore,
This tormenter not dared do no more,

But half deed, with hir nekke ycorven there,
But half dead, with her neck carved there,

He lefte hir lye, and on his wey he went.
He left her lie, and on his way he went.

The Cristen folk which that aboute hire were
The Christian people that around her were

With sheetes han the blood ful faire yhent.
With sheets have the blood very well caught.

Thre dayes lyved she in this torment,
Three days lived she in this torment,

And nevere cessed hem the feith to teche
And never ceased them the faith to teach

That she hadde fostred. Hem she gan to preche,
That she had fostered. Them she began to preach,

And hem she yaf hir moebles and hir thyng,
And them she gave her furniture and her things,

And to the Pope Urban bitook hem tho,
And to Pope Urban entrusted them then,

And seyde, "I axed this at Hevene Kyng,
And said, "I asked this from Heaven's King,

To han respit thre dayes and namo,
To have respite three days and no more,

To recomende to yow er that I go
To recommend to you before I go

Thise soules, lo, and that I myghte do werche
These souls, lo, and that I could have made

Heere of myn hous perpetuelly a cherche."
Here of my house perpetually a church."

Seint Urban with his deknes prively
St. Urban with his deacons secretly

The body fette and buryed it by nyghte
The body fetched and buried it by night

Among his othere seintes honestly.
Among his other saints honorably.

Hir hous the chirche of Seinte Cecilie highte.
Her house the church of St. Cecilia called.

Seint Urban halwed it as he wel myghte,
St. Urban consecrated it as he well could,

In which into this day in noble wyse
In which up to this day in noble fashion

Men doon to Crist and to his seinte servyse.
Men do to Christ and to his saint service.

VIII. Caxton's Introduction to Chaucer's *Canterbury Tales*
England's first printer, William Caxton, printed about a hundred works, some of which
he himself had translated from French into English. Among the books he published was
Chaucer's *Canterbury Tales* (1484). Reproduced here is the first part of the introduction
he wrote to his edition of the *Canterbury Tales*.

Grete thankes, laude, and honour ought to be gyuen vnto the
Great thanks, praise, and honor ought to be given to the

clerkes, poetes, and historiographs, that haue wreton many noble
clerks, poets, and historians   that have written many noble

bokes of wysedom of the lyues, passions, and myracles of holy
books of wisdom of the lives,   passions, and miracles of holy

sayntes, of hystoryes, of noble and famous actes and faittes, and of
saints, of histories,   of noble and famous acts and deeds, and of

the cronycles sith the begynnyng of the creacion of the world vnto
the chronicles since the beginning of the creation of the world up to

thys present tyme, by whyche we ben dayly enformed and have
this present time, by which   we are daily informed and have

knowleche of many thynges, of whom we shold not haue knowen,
knowledge of many things,   of which we should not have known,

yf they had not left to vs theyr monumentis wreton. Emong whom
if they had not left to us their documents   written. Among whom

and inespecial to-fore alle other we ought to gyue a synguler laude
and in particular before all others we ought to give a special praise

vnto that noble and grete philosopher Gefferey Chaucer, the whiche
to that noble and great philosopher   Geoffrey Chaucer, who,

for his ornate wrytyng in our tongue may wel haue the name of a
for his ornate writing in our tongue can well have the name of a

laureate poete.
laureate poet.

    For to-fore that he by hys labour enbelysshyd, ornated, and
    For, before   he by his labor embellished, decorated, and

made faire our Englisshe,   in thys royame was had rude speche and
made beautiful our English, in this realm was had rude speech and

incongrue, as yet it appiereth by olde bookes, whyche at thys day
incongruous, as yet it appears in old books,   which in this day

ought not to haue place ne be compared emong ne to hys
ought not to have place nor be compared among nor to his

beauteuous volumes and aournate writynges, of whom he made
beautiful volumes and ornate writings, of which he made

many bokes and treatyces of many a noble historye as wel in metre
many books and treatises of many a noble history in meter as well

as in ryme and prose, and them so craftyly made, that he
as in rhyme and prose, and them so skillfully made, that he

comprehended hys maters in short, quyck, and hye sentences,
comprised his matters in short, vivid, and lofty sentences,

eschewyng prolyxyte, castyng away the chaf of superfluyte, and
eschewing prolixity, casting away the chaff of superfluity, and

shewyng the pyked grayn of sentence, vtteryd by crafty and sugred
showing the refined grain of judgment, uttered by skillful and sweet

eloquence, of whom emonge all other of hys bokes I purpose
eloquence, of which among all other of his books I intend

temprynte by the grace of god the book of the Tales of
to print by the grace of God the books of the Tales of

Cauntyrburye, in whiche I fynde many a noble hystorye of euery
Canterbury, in which I find many a noble story of every

astate and degre.   Fyrst rehercyng the condicions and tharraye of
estate and degree. First describing the conditions and the order of

eche of them as properly as possyble is to be sayd, and after
each of them as properly as possible is to be said, and afterward

theyr tales whyche ben of noblesse, wysedom, gentylesse, myrthe,
their tales, which are of nobility, wisdom, gentility, mirth,

and also of veray holynesse and vertue, wherin he fynysshyth thys
and also of true holiness and virtue, with which he finishes this

sayd booke; whyche book I haue dylygently ouersen and duly
said book;   which book I have diligently looked over and fitly

examyned, to thende that it be made accordyng vnto his owen
examined, to the end that it be made according   to his own

makyng.
making.

For I fynde many of the sayd bookes, whyche wryters haue
For I find many of the said books, which writers have

abrydgyd it and many thynges left out; and in somme place haue
abridged it and many things left out; and in some places have

sette certayn versys, that he neuer made ne sette in hys booke. Of
put certain verses that he never made nor put in his book. Of

whyche bookes so incorrecte was one brought to me ·vj· yere
which books so incorrect was one brought to me six years

passyd, whyche I supposed had ben veray true and correcte. And
past, which I assumed had been completely true & correct. And

accordyng to the same I dyde do enprynte a certayn nombre of
accordingly   I had a certain number of them printed,

of them, whyche anon were sold to many and dyuerse gentyl-men,
which at once were sold to many and diverse gentlemen,

of whome one gentylman cam to me, and said, that this book was
of whom one gentleman came to me and said that this book did

not accordyng in many places vnto the book that Gefferey Chaucer
not accord in many places to the book that Geoffrey Chaucer

had made. To whom I answerd, that I had made it accordyng to
had made. To whom I answered that I had made it according to

my copye, and by me was nothyng added ne mynusshyd.
my copy, and by me was nothing added nor removed.

CHAPTER 7

EARLY MODERN ENGLISH

7.1 Important Terms

1. Joseph Aickin
2. assibilation
3. Nathaniel Bailey
4. Thomas Blount
5. John Bullokar
6. William Caxton
7. Chancery scribes
8. Chaucerisms
9. Sir John Cheke
10. Henry Cockeram
11. Elisha Coles
12. diacritic
13. double negative
14. doublet
15. Sir Thomas Eliot
16. enclitic
17. Alexander Gil
18. gloss
19. glossary
20. Great Vowel Shift
21. John Hart
22. inkhorn terms
23. Samuel Johnson
24. King James Bible
25. Robert Lowth
26. Richard Mulcaster
27. oversea language
28. Edward Philipps
29. Joseph Priestley
30. proclitic
31. reduplication
32. spelling pronunciation
33. two-part verb
34. universal grammar
35. John Wallis
36. Noah Webster
37. Jeremiah Wharton
38. zero derivation

7.2 Questions for Review and Discussion

1. What were some of the effects of the introduction of printing on the English language?
2. How did the EMnE translations from classical languages affect English?
3. Upon what aspect of English has the King James Bible had the most influence?
4. Explain how the enclosures affected the English language.
5. How did the Industrial Revolution have an effect on English vocabulary?
6. What was the most important scholarly language in England at the beginning of the EMnE period? At the end?
7. Summarize the EMnE dispute over vocabulary.
8. What effect did the EMnE spelling reformers have on the subsequent history of English?
9. Why had there been no English-to-English dictionaries prior to the EMnE period?
10. What is the difference between a gloss and a translation?
11. Who were the most important dictionary makers of EMnE?
12. Why did the English never establish an English Academy?
13. Why did the early grammarians consider existing English grammar to be very corrupt?
14. What language was the most important "model" for English grammars during EMnE?
15. Compare and contrast the attitudes toward English grammar of (a) Robert Lowth, (b) Joseph Priestley, and (c) Noah Webster.
16. What changes in the English consonant phonemes took place during EMnE?
17. Give some examples of assibilation.
18. Give some examples of spelling pronunciation.
19. Summarize the operation of the Great Vowel Shift (GVS), including date, details, and order in which the changes took place.
20. Explain apparent exceptions to the GVS such as *threat* [θrɛt] rather than predicted [θrit] or *blood* [bləd] rather than predicted [blud].
21. How has the use of proclitic and enclitic contracted forms changed between EMnE and PDE?
22. By what time were PDE punctuation patterns established?
23. How did possessive constructions in EMnE differ from those in PDE?
24. What changes in the use of relative pronouns occurred between ME and EMnE?
25. How did the formation of the perfect tense in EMnE differ from that in PDE?
26. Compare the nature of the Latin loanwords into English in EMnE with that of French loanwords into English in ME.

7.3   Phonology: Minor Consonant Changes

Numerous minor changes in consonants occurred during EMnE, some of them permanent, some of them to be reversed later in the standard language, some of them to remain in some dialects but not in others. Among these are:

1. Assibilation, whereby poststress /sj/, /zj/, /tj/, and /dj/ became /š/, /ž/, /č/, and /ǰ/, respectively. For example, earlier /fɔrtjən/ 'fortune' became /fɔrčən/.
2. Loss of preconsonantal /r/ (especially after back vowels) and of final unstressed /r/. For example, earlier /rɛkərdz/ 'records' became /rɛkədz/. Also, development of nonetymological intrusive /r/, as in /marθər/ 'Martha'.
3. Loss of /t/ and /d/ in consonant clusters and finally after other consonants. For example, earlier /nɛkst/ 'next' became /nɛks/.
4. Loss of /l/ after a low vowel and before a labial or velar consonant. For example, /tɔlk/ 'talk' became /tɔk/.
5. Loss of [ç] and [x] as allophones of /h/ after a vowel. For example, [brɪçt] 'bright' became [braɪt].
6. Continued loss of the phonemic distinction between /hw/ and /w/. For example, earlier /hwɪč/ 'which' became /wɪč/.

Because the standard spelling had become fixed at the beginning of the EMnE period, it is difficult to see these changes in the writings of educated people. However, the misspellings of the semiliterate can be very revealing. That is, if such people frequently write *lan* for *land*, we can be reasonably certain that they did not pronounce a final /d/ in this word. Reverse spellings are also instructive. For example, if writers spell *gallons* as *gallonds*, we can assume they knew that many words ending in /n/ in speech have an additional consonant in spelling; in the case of *gallonds*, they just guessed wrong.

All of the following items are taken from texts by semiliterate EMnE writers. Identify by number which of the minor consonantal changes described above is illustrated by the misspelling.

a. _5_ drigh (dry)

b. ___ suffishent (sufficient)

c. ___ grinstone (grindstone)

d. ___ whome (home)

e. ___ matte (matter)

f. ___ memorander (memoranda)

g. ___ haf (half)

h. ___ wite (white)

i. ___ behing (behind)

j. ___ menchened (mentioned)

k. ___ sighned (signed)

l. ___ Leonad (Leonard)

m. ___ Norwack (Norwalk)

n. ___ eastwart (eastward)

o. ___ wilst (whilst)

p. ___ tweney (twenty)

q. ___ nit (night)

r. ___ trashewer (treasurer)

s. ___ whithin (within)

t. ___ andvell (anvil)

u. ___ Indjans (Indians)

v. ___ imbercillity (imbecility)

w. ___ prudencshall (prudential)

x. ___ assistand (assistant)

7.4 Phonology: The Great Vowel Shift

Beginning in late ME and continuing throughout the EMnE period, all of the long vowels (from whatever source) of ME underwent a qualitative shift, that is, a shift in their point of articulation. Ignoring a few irregularities in the development of the mid vowels, the changes were as follows:

ME PDE   *as in*

ī → ai   ME [tīd]   → PDE [taid] 'tide'
ē → i   ME [dēp]   → PDE [dip] 'deep'
ɛ̄ → i   ME [hɛ̄tə]   → PDE [hit] 'heat'
ā → e   ME [tālə]   → PDE [tel] 'tale'
ū → au   ME [dūn]   → PDE [daun] 'down'
ō → u   ME [fōl]   → PDE [ful] 'fool'
ɔ̄ → o   ME [smɔ̄kə] → PDE [smok] 'smoke'

A. Give the standard spelling of the PDE reflexes of the following ME words written in phonetic transcription. There are no irregularities.

ME	PDE	ME	PDE	ME	PDE
0. [stɔ̄n]	*stone*	8. [klɛ̄n]	_____	16. [grēt]	_____
1. [jɛ̄ld]	_____	9. [θrē]	_____	17. [stōl]	_____
2. [brōd]	_____	10. [tōθ]	_____	18. [komplɛ̄t]	_____
3. [bīt]	_____	11. [rākə]	_____	19. [fūnd]	_____
4. [sām]	_____	12. [flī]	_____	20. [flāmə]	_____
5. [wēpə]	_____	13. [fɔ̄]	_____	21. [drɛ̄m]	_____
6. [sūθ]	_____	14. [fīnd]	_____	22. [flɔ̄t]	_____
7. [hū]	_____	15. [bɔ̄θ]	_____	23. [hēr]	_____

B. Give the phonetic symbol for the ME vowel corresponding to the PDE vowels in the following words.

PDE	ME	PDE	ME
0. loud	[l ū d]	5. take	[t___k]
1. child	[c___ld]	6. roast	[r___st]
2. rope	[r___p]	7. moon	[m___n]
3. spoon	[sp___n]	8. mice	[m___s]
4. blame	[bl___m]	9. mouse	[m___s]

7.5   Phonology: Rhymes as Clues to Pronunciation

Rhymes as a source of information about the pronunciation of earlier periods must be used with caution because (1) there were "conventional" rhymes of words that did not actually rhyme in speech, (2) some versifiers were less than fastidious about the accuracy of their rhymes, and (3) rhymes tell us only that the words rhymed, not what the actual sounds were.

Nonetheless, if we find that many authors over a fairly long time span regularly rhymed some words that do not rhyme today, we can assume that at least one of the words in question had a different pronunciation from what it has today. Furthermore, given other sources of information about pronunciation, we can state with some confidence what that pronunciation actually was.

For each of the following groups, indicate what the rhyming vowel probably was.

0. Various seventeenth-century poets rhymed the words *detest, invest, test, beast, best, quest, protest, dressed, feast*. For example,

> Not that we think us worthy such a *guest,*
> But that your worth will dignify our *feast*
> —Ben Jonson, 1616

> Be judge yourself, I'll bring it to the *test,*
> Which is the basest creature, Man or *beast?*
> —Earl of Rochester, 1675

Probable vowel in all the words _[ɛ]_____

1. Throughout the entire EMnE period, (a) *toil, while, beguile, smile, spoil;* (b) *design, nine, join, line, shine, purloin, thine;* (c) *dies, joys, rise.* For example,

> But these were random bolts; not formed *design*
> Nor interest made the factious crowd to *join:*
> —John Dryden, 1681

> Let not Ambition mock their useful *toil,* . . .
> Nor Grandeur hear with a disdainful *smile*
> —Thomas Gray, 1751

Probable vowel in all the words _____

2. Throughout the sixteenth and seventeenth centuries, and into the eighteenth century, *groan, stone, one, moan, sown, alone, none, zone, throne*. For example,

> Of the first nothing the elixir *grown;*
> Were I a man, that I were *one*
> —John Donne, 1633

> Their great Lord's glorious name; to *none*
> Of those whose spacious bosoms spread a *throne*
> —Richard Crashaw, 1652

Probable vowel in all the words _____

3. In the seventeenth and eighteenth centuries, (a) *entreat, beat, wheat, heat, meat, seat, eat, repeat, threat, yet, sweat, get, great;* (b) *speak, weak, neck, break.* For example,

> Though I must go, enture not *yet* . . .
> Like gold to airy thinness *beat*
> > —John Donne, 1633

> But those do hold or *break,*
> As men are strong or *weak.*
> > —Andrew Marvell, 1681

Probable vowel in all the words _____

4. In the seventeenth and eighteenth centuries, (a) *feature, creature, nature;* (b) *sea, tea, away, obey.* For example,

> Bestow this jewel also on my *creature,* . . .
> And rest in Nature, not the God of *Nature;*
> > —George Herbert, 1633

> To cross this narrow *sea,* . . .
> And fear to launch *away.*
> > —Isaac Watts, 1707

Probable vowel in all the words _____

5. Throughout the EMnE period, *lost, ghost, cost, most, crossed, boast, frost, toast, coast, host.* For example,

> Not all the tresses that fair head can *boast,*
> Shall draw such envy as the Lock you *lost.*
> > —Alexander Pope, 1712

Probable vowel _____

6. Primarily in the seventeenth and eighteenth centuries, *doom, come, home, Rome, tomb, bloom, room, become.* For example,

> Souls as thy shining self, shall *come*
> And in her first ranks make thee *room*
> > —Richard Crashaw, 1652

> The soul, uneasy and confined from *home,*
> Rests and expatiates in a life to *come.*
> > —Alexander Pope, 1733

Probable vowel _____

7. Throughout EMnE, *mind, blind, kind, behind, wind* (breeze), *bind, unconfined.* For example,

> She ware no gloves, for neither sun nor *wind*
> Would burn or parch her hands; but to her *mind* . . .
> > —Christopher Marlowe, 1598

Probable vowel _____

8. Throughout EMnE, *sound, mound, wound* (injury), *found, ground*. For example,

> Did rival monarchs give the fatal *wound?*
> Or hostile millions press him to the *ground?*
> —Samuel Johnson, 1749

Probable vowel _____

9. Throughout EMnE, *moan, groan, bemoan, shown, one, gone, unknown, stone*. For example,

> They now to fight are *gone,*
> Armor on armor *shone,*
> Drum now to drum did *groan,*
> —Michael Drayton, 1619

Probable vowel _____

10. In the seventeenth and eighteenth centuries, *pierce, verse, universe*. For example,

> He, who through vast immensity can *pierce,*
> Sees world on worlds compose one *universe,*
> —Alexander Pope, 1733

Probable vowel _____

11. Throughout EMnE, *there, everywhere, forbear, fear, sphere, appear, bear, hair, ear, year*. For example,

> Her captive flames must needs burn *there;* . . .
> She'll shine through all the *sphere.*
> —Henry Vaughan, 1655

Probable vowel _____

12. Primarily in the seventeenth and eighteenth centuries, *James, flames, beams, Thames*. For example,

> And make those flights upon the banks of *Thames*
> That so did take Eliza and our *James*
> —Ben Jonson, 1623

Probable vowel _____

13. Listed are four common words and some of the rhymes for each found in EMnE poetry. Comment.

    (a) good: brood, delude, stood, blood, flood, load

    (b) blood: food, good, stood, underwood, understood, wood, withstood, flood, bud, mud

    (c) flood: good, would, wood, withstood, stood, blood, mud, God

    (d) stood: mood, good, blood, flood, God

_____

_____

_____

7.6   Graphics: A Letter to a New England Town Meeting

Reproduced here is the first page of a letter written by the early American settler, scholar, and political leader Roger Williams, in the year 1650–51. The first few lines have been transliterated for you. Read the letter, complete the transliteration, and answer the questions that follow the facsimile of the letter.

Courtesy of the Rhode Island Historical Society.

Beginning of transliteration:

1 NAR: 22.11.50 (so calld)
2 Well beloved friends: Lo: [ving] respects to each of
3 you presented with heartie desires of yor
4 present & eternall peace. I am sorrie y^t
5 I am occasioned to trouble you in y^e midst
6 of many yor other Troubles. Yet vpon y^e Expe
7 rience of yor wonted Lo: [ving] kindness & Gentle

a. Does WIlliams distinguish *i* and *j?* _____

b. What is the distribution of *u* and *v?* _____

_____

c. What two variants of *e* does Williams use? _____

d. What two variants of *d* does he use? _____

e. How does Williams form an ampersand? _____

f. What words does Williams abbreviate? _____

_____

What are his ways of indicating that a form is abbreviated? _____

_____

g. What marks of punctuation does he use? _____

_____

h. How does his capitalization differ from that of PDE? _____

_____

i. Williams was a highly educated man, so we may assume that his spelling was "correct" for his time. What differences from PDE spelling do you find (apart from capitalization

differences)? _____

_____

_____

j. Williams spells at least one word in two different ways. What is that word? _____

_____

7.7 Grammar: Noun Inflections

A.   By EMnE, noun inflection was in all essentials identical to that of PDE. Still, a few nouns had variant plurals throughout most of the period:

"My *howsys* ther be in decay" (1529)
"The *housen* wherein they dwell" (1557)
"Two busshels of gray *pees*" (1523)
"*Peasyn* are muche in the nature of beanes" (1533)

Similar variation is found for the nouns *hose, shoe,* and *eye*.

1. What three PDE nouns retain plurals in *-en?* _____

_____

2. If you wanted to make an uncomplimentary reference to two large but stupid people, you might call them "a couple of dumb ox _____."

Why did you choose the plural form you did? _____

_____

3. What does this imply? _____

4. Would you refer to your two male siblings as your "two brethren"? _____

5. Why or why not? _____

B.   Like PDE, EMnE had a number of nouns that varied between regular plurals in *-s* and zero plurals (that is, the plural form was identical to the singular form). Consider the following examples:

"command our present *numbers* be muster'd" (c. 1608)
"and those poor *number* saved with you" (c. 1600)
"I knew a man of eightie *winters*" (1612)
"Now I am xix *wynter* olde" (1522)
"The most usual *Kindes* of Apples" (1652)
"Such *kind* of Pamphlets work Wonders" (1681)
"Two miles from an excellent water for *trouts*" (1790)
"The *trout* . . . there have been over praised" (1789)

1. In PDE, we say, "The number of them *is* uncertain," but "A number of them *are* uncertain." Comment. _____

_____

2. Is *kind* ever used as a zero plural in PDE? _____

_____

3. If you were describing a fairly tall person, you would say, "He is six _____ tall."

If you were describing an even taller person, you would say, "He is six _____ four."

What determines the difference between the marked-plural and the zero-plural forms? _

_____

4. Complete the following with the appropriate form of *dozen*. (The same rules apply to *hundred, thousand, million,* etc.)

"We need three _____ folding chairs."

"We need _____ of folding chairs."

5. What determines the difference between the two forms? _____

_____

C.   Consider the following examples of genitive nouns, all from Shakespeare.

for his mercy sake	for duty's sake
for fashion sake	for fame's sake
for god sake	for god's sake
for heaven sake	for wealth's sake
for safety sake	for wisdom's sake
for alliance sake	for your friend's sake

1. Do you think there was a difference in how the genitive ending was pronounced in

these two sets of examples? _____

_____

2. Why was the possessive [s] often omitted in this construction? _____

_____

3. In PDE, how is the expletive "for Christ's sake" sometimes spelled in representing

dialogue? _____

Why? _____

4. Can you suggest a possible origin for the colloquial expression "for Pete's sake"?

_____

7.8 Grammar: Relative Pronouns and Relative Adverbs

Usage of relative pronouns and adverbs was in a state of flux during the EMnE period (as, indeed, it still is today to some extent). For each of the following sentences, indicate in the blank to the left whether the construction with the italicized relative would be acceptable (A) or unacceptable (U) today.

1. ____ "much less then is it lawful for subjects to resist their godly and Christian princes *which* do not abuse their authority" (1547)

2. ____ "And soon after he called his high court of Parliament, *in the which* was demanded by King Henry's friends what should be done with King Richard." (1569)

3. ____ "the Bishop of Carlisle, *which* was a man well learned and of a good courage, stood up . . ." (1569)

4. ____ "There was a lionesse *which* had whelpes in her den, *the which* den was obserued by a Beare, . . ." (1607)

5. ____ "Happy is that city *which* in time of peace thinks of war" (1621)

6. ____ "And now, lastly, will be the time to read with them those organic arts *which* enable men to discourse and write perspicuously, elegantly, and according to the fitted style of lofty, mean, or lowly." (1644)

7. ____ "Coriolanus, who could not attain to that as he wanted, should have forsaken *that which* he had received." (1650)

8. ____ "that man, *which* looks too far before him, in the care of future time, hath his heart all the day, gnawed on by fear of death" (1651)

9. ____ "I had the loose Earth to carry out; and *which* was of more Importance, I had the Cieling to prop up." (1719)

10. ____ "I entreated him to give order that my cabinet should be brought, *of which* I kept the key in my pocket" (1726)

11. ____ That man *that* thy horse hath eten his corne or grasse wyll be greued at the [= thee]." (1523)

12. ____ "I earne *that* I eate: get *that* I weare" (1600)

13. ____ "Be *that* thou know'st thou art, and then thou art As great as *that* thou fear'st" (1601)

14. ____ "they cease not still to search for *that* they have not and know not" (1616)

15. ____ "He *that* hath wife and children hath given hostages to fortune" (1625)

16 ____ "Coriolanus, who could not attain to *that as* he wanted, should have forsaken that which he had received." (1650)

17. ____ "A Tree *that* grew near an old Wall" (1712)

18. ____ "there presented him selfe a tall clownishe younge man, *who* falling before the Queen of Faeries desired a boone" (1589)

19. ____ "*Who* soweth in raine, he shall reape it with teares" (1573–80)

20. ___ "Every man gladly would be neighbour to a quiet person, *as who* . . . doth afford all the pleasure of conversation, without any . . . trouble" (c. 1677)

21. ___ "Sir Roger is one of those *who* is not only at Peace within himself, but beloved and esteemed by all about him" (1711)

22. ___ "I counsel . . . all wise . . . men, that they doo not accompany wyth those *whom* they know are not secret." (1557)

23. ___ "Her cursed tongue . . . Appear'd like Aspis sting, that closely kils, Or cruelly does wound *whom so* she wils." (1596)

24. ___ "For *whom* in the world do you think that I was kept so long kicking my heels?" (1780)

25. ___ "A virgin spoused to a man, *whose* name was Ioseph" (1526)

26. ___ "*Whose* house is of glasse, must not throw stones at another." (1633)

27. ___ "Things, *whose* particular Discussion would . . . exceed the Design of this Book" (1730)

28. ___ "The lawyer saith *what* men have determined; the historian *what* men have done" (1595)

29. ___ "To those *as* have no children" (1603)

30. ___ "Life it self . . . is a burden [*no relative pronoun*] cannot be born under the lasting . . . pressure of such an uneasiness." (1690)

31. ___ "There were of [her Majesty's ships] but six in all, *whereof* two but small ships" (1591)

32, ___ "This night I hold an old accustom'd Feast, *Whereto* I haue inuited many a Guest." (1592)

33. ___ "He lick'd the ground *whereon* she trod." (1667)

Summarize how the usage of each of the following relatives differed in EMnE from what is considered acceptable in PDE. Base your answers only on the sentences listed here.

which _____

that _____

who _____

whom _____

whose _____

what _____

as _____

whereof, whereon, whereto _____

_____

ø (i.e., no relative pronoun used in a relative construction) _____

_____

7.9   Grammar: Pronouns and Pronominal Adjectives

Although few changes in the inflection of pronouns and pronominal adjectives have taken place since ME, pronominal usage during EMnE still differed in many minor ways from that of PDE. For each of the following excerpts, identify the nature of the difference from PDE and rewrite the phrase as necessary to put the phrase into acceptable modern English. The relevant pronouns or pronominal adjectives are italicized; numbers 3 and 5 have two separate constructions to be considered.

0. "For some haue gret plenty . . . and *other some* haue scantly so moche as they nede" (1532) _PDE does not use the two together like this. Rewrite as "others," as "some," or as "some others."_

1. "Doth *any of both* these examples prove that . . . ?" (1540) _____

_____

2. "I feare *me some* will blushe that readeth this, if he be bitten" (c. 1581) _____

_____

3. "sit *thou* by my bedde" (1597) _____

_____

4. "*myself* am Naples, / Who with *mine* eyes, . . . beheld / The King my father wrack'd." (1611) _____

_____

5. "[They] are so proud, so censorious, that *it* is no living with them." (a. 1617) ____

_____

6. "Wee . . . owe him [God] obedience according to *euery* his morall commands" (1626) _

_____

7. "But *whether ever* beginneth, he may be sure the other will follow" (1632) _____

_____

8. "How to renew and make good any sort of Gun-powder that hath lost *his* strength" (1644) _____

_____

9. "The nature of young tulip roots is to runne down deeper into the ground, every year more than *other*" (1660) _____

_____

10. "Presuming on the Queen *her* private practice" (1659) _____

_____

11. "he whispered *me* in the Ear to take notice of a Tabby Cat that sate in the Chimny-Corner" (1711–12) _____

_____

12. "I will relate *somewhat* concerning the Earl of Antrim" (c. 1715) _____

13. "*Every* of the said chirurgeons is to have twelvepence a body searched by them" (1722) _____

14. "We came in full View of a great Island or Continent (for we knew not *whether*)." (1726) _____

15. "We must not let this hour pass, without presenting *us* to him." (1729) _____

16. "Fontenelle and Voltaire were men of unequal merit; yet how different has been the fate of *either*" (1759) _____

17. "A retreat for St. Bridget and *other* nine virgins" (1799) _____

7.10 Grammar: Adjectives

A. In each of the following sentences, the italicized adjectives would be unacceptable in some way in PDE. In the blank following each sentence, indicate the nature of the change that has occurred (morphological, syntactic, or semantic) and rewrite the phrase as it might appear in standard PDE.

0. "For in his books be contained . . . not only the documents *martial* and discipline of arms but also . . ." (1531) *syntactic; "martial documents"*

1. "all appeals made to Rome were clearly void and of *none* effect" (1548) _____

2. "the Percies, affirming them to be their awn [own] *proper* prisoners and their *peculiar* preys, did utterly deny to deliver them" (1569) _____

3. "Sometimes he was sorry and repented, much grieved for that he had done, after his anger had cooled, by & by *outrageous* again." (1621–51) _____

4. "In this Catalogue, Borage and Bugloss [names of plants] may challenge the *chiefest* place" (1621–51) _____

5. "Round about him those fiends danced a *pretty* while, and then came in three more as ugly as the rest" (1624) _____

6. "notwithstanding *what* imputations *soever* shall be laid" (1662) _____

7. "the *more fuller* statement" (1680) _____

8. "some of [the Country People] will needs have it that Sir Roger has brought down a *Cunning* Man with him, to cure the old Woman" (1711) _____

9. "Many of the laws which were in force during the monarchy being *relative* merely to that form of government, . . . the first assembly which met after the establishment of the commonwealth appointed a committee to revise the whole code" (1784) _____

10. "we consider *academical* institutions as preparatory to a settlement in the world" (1791) _____

B. Throughout the entire history of English, past participles of verbs have served as adjectives. In some instances, earlier irregular forms of participles have survived as adjectives although the verb itself has become regular in PDE. One example is *wrought* (from the verb *work*). Add other examples to the types listed below.

1. Participles in *-en* (e.g., "He has *shaved*" vs. "a closely *shaven* man" _____

_____

2. Participles in which the *-ed* of the adjective is pronounced as a separate syllable although it is not as a verb (e.g., "She *dogged* my footsteps" vs. "a *dogged* expression on

her face") _____

_____

7.11   Grammar: Verb Phrases

The grammar of EMnE verb phrases is usually similar enough to that of PDE so that modern readers can understand the general sense even if they often miss the subtleties. Nevertheless, the differences are numerous. For each of the following excerpts, identify the nature of the difference from PDE of the italicized items and rewrite the excerpt as necessary to turn it into acceptable PDE.

0. "Ye *are come* together, fathers and right wise men, to enter council" (c. 1530) ___
In PDE, auxiliary for perfect tense is always "have." Rewrite as "You have come together."

1. "the chief praise of a writer *consisteth* in the enterlacing of pleasure with profit" (1582) _____

2. "With that word his voice *brake* so with sobbing that he could *say* no further" (1590)

3. "You *never saw* her *since* she was deform'd." (c. 1590) _____

4. "Dangerous it *were* for the feeble brain of man to wade far into the doings of the Most High" (1594) _____

5. "Sirrah Jack, thy horse *stands* behind the hedge. When thou need'st him, there thou shalt find him." (c. 1596) _____

6. "The sheeted dead / *Did squeak* and *gibber* in the Roman streets" (1599) _____

7. "*Present not* yourself on the stage . . . until the quaking prologue *hath* (by rubbing) got color into his cheeks" (1609) _____

8. "Wadley in Berkshire is *situate* in a vale" (1621–51) _____

9. "the bell that rings to a sermon *calls not* upon the preacher only" (1623) _____

10. "They *will* on in sinne to their utter ruine" (1647) _____

11. "And he that can tell [count to] ten, if he *recite* them out of order, will lose himself, and not know when he *has done*." (1651) _____

_____

12. "I was formerly a great companion of his, for the which I now *repent me*" (1682)

_____

_____

13. "I *am so used to consider* my self as Creditor and Debtor, that I often state my Accounts after the same manner" (1712) _____

_____

14. "The spoil of the church *was* now *become* the only resource of all their operations in finance" (1790) _____

_____

7.12   Grammar: Adverbs

In each of the following excerpts from EMnE, the italicized adverb (or adverbs) differs in some way from what would be acceptable in PDE. Indicate whether the difference is morphological, syntactic, or lexical/semantic. In some instances, there may be more than one type of difference. Then rewrite as much of the excerpt as is necessary to turn the adverbial portion(s) into acceptable PDE.

0. "albeit he was *sore* enamored upon her, yet he forbare her" (1557) *lexical and morphological. Rewrite: "extremely enamored" or "very enamored."*

1. "He therefore that will be a good scholar . . . must *evermore* set all his diligence to be like his master." (1561) _____

2. "this answer pleased *nothing* the Earl of Worcester, but put him in a great choler" (1569) _____

3. "When the king had well advised upon and considered this matter, he made answer and said that the Earl of March was *not* taken prisoner *neither* for his cause *nor* in his service" (1569) _____

4. "in the company of so many wise and good men together as *hardly* then could have been picked out again out of all England *beside*" (1570) _____

5. "inquire out those taverns . . . whose masters are *oftenest* drunk" (1609) _____

6. "Jack could no sooner get a crown but *straight* he found means to spend it" (1619) _____

7. "Yet that night *betimes* they got down into the bottom of the bay" (1630) _____

8. "His Godhead is in such sort *eachwhere*, that it filleth both heaven and earth" (1649) _____

9. "*What* should I mention beauty; that fading toy?" (1677) _____

10. "I *last night* sat very late in company with this body of friends" (1711) _____

11. "But it is *exceeding* apparent that such ideas have nothing in them which is spiritual and divine" (1746) _____

_____

12. "I pressed him to persevere in his resolution to make *this year* the projected visit to the Hebrides" (1791) _____

_____

7.13 Grammar: Prepositions

Although prepositions are not added or dropped from the language with the ease of nouns or verbs, new ones do enter English and older ones are lost. Further, the meanings change over time. For each of the italicized prepositions in the following sentences from EMnE, indicate what the PDE equivalent would be. Check the *OED* if you are not sure.

0. "All the people of the cyte came *ageynste* hym wyth ioye and praysynge" (a. 1520)
PDE "toward"
_____

1. "They coude not go by it, nether *of* the right honde ner [nor] *of* the left" (1535) ___
_____

2. "It was forbidden vnto them to marie *without* their owne tribe" (1558) _____
_____

3. "to restore their cousin Edmund, Earl of March, *unto* the crown" (1569) _____

4. "[John Winchcomb] . . . being so good a companion, he was called *of* old and young Jack of Newbury (1619) _____
_____

5. *"For* the abundance of milk she [the cow] did give, the owner might eate butter" (1641) _____

6. "And when the endeavour is *fromward* something, it is generally called AVERSION." (1651) _____

7. "He was . . . restored *till* his liberty and archbishoprick" (1655) _____
_____

8. "The Bears and Foxes, who *sans* question / Than we by odds have warmer Vests on" (a. 1687) _____

9. "He . . . spent his time *in* the Solitary Top of a Mountain" (1701) _____
_____

10. "His Cunning is the more odious *from* the resemblance it has to Wisdom" (1710)
_____

11. "The really good are so far less in number *to* the bad" (1771) _____

12. "he talked, as usual, *upon* indifferent subjects" (1791) _____

7.14 Grammar: Conjunctions

In each of the following excerpts from EMnE texts, the italicized conjunction would not be used, at least in this context, in PDE. Give the equivalent conjunction in PDE.

0. "it was concluded that King Richard . . . should have all things honorably minist'red unto him, *as well* for his diet *as also* apparel." (1569) *"for his diet as well as his apparel" or "for both his diet and his apparel"*

1. "Owen Glendower kept [Edmund Mortimer] in filthy prison, shackeled with irons, only *for that* he took the king's part and was to him faithful and true . . ." (1569) _____

2. "and, *for* the time shall not seem tedious, / I'll tell thee what befel me" (a. 1595)

3. "Thou rememberest / *Since* once I sat upon a promontory." (1594–95) _____

4. "Tell me where is fancie bred, / *Or* in the heart, *or* in the head?" (1596) _____

5. "They will set an house on fire *and* it were but to roast their eggs." (1597–1625) _

6. "Baptista Porta . . . will by all means have the front of an house stand to the South, *which how* it may be good in Italy and hotter Climes, I know not, in our Northern Countries I am sure it is best." (1621–51) _____

7. "Henry Percy offered . . . to free the Queene of Scots out of prison *so as* Grange and Carre . . . would receive her at the borders." (1635) _____

8. "No man therefore can conceive anything, *but* he must conceive it in some place." (1651) _____

9. "you have scarce begun to admire the one, *ere* you despise the other" (1672)

10. "Run sweet Babe, *while* thou art weary, and then I will take thee up and carry thee" (1688) _____

11. "he whispered me in the Ear to take notice of a Tabby Cat that sate in the Chimny Corner, which, as the knight told me, lay under as bad a Report as Moll White her self; for *besides that* Moll is said often to accompany her in the same Shape, the Cat is reported to have spoken twice or thrice in her Life" (1711–12) _____

7.15   Syntax

Reproduced here are two English translations of the gospel of St. Mark, 2:13–22, the first from ME and the second from EMnE. For each of the categories listed below, compare the syntax of the ME and the EMnE translations. (See *A Biography of the English Language*, pp. 237–42, for general remarks about EMnE syntax).

ME   [13]And he wente out eftsone to the see,
EMnE   And he went out agayne vnto the see,

ME   and al the cumpanye of peple came to hym;
EMnE   and all the people   resorted vnto hym;

ME   and he tauȝte hem.   [14]And whenne he passide,
EMnE   and he taught them.   And as Jesus passed by,

ME   he say Leui Alfey sittynge at the tolbothe,
EMnE   he sawe Levy the sonne of Alphey sytt att the receyte of custome,

ME   and he seith to hym, Sue thou me.
EMnE   and sayde vnto him, Folowe me.

ME   And he rysynge suede hym.   [15]And it is don,
EMnE   And he arose and folowed hym. And yt cam to passe,

ME   whenne he sat at the mete in his hous,
EMnE   as Jesus sate att meate in his housse,

ME   many puplicanys and synful men saten togidre at the mete
EMnE   many pubplicans and synners sate att meate also

ME   with Jhesu and his disciplis;
EMnE   with Jesus and his disciples;

ME   sothely there weren manye that foleweden hym.
EMnE   for there were many that folowed him.

ME   [16]And scribis and Pharisees seeyinge, for he eet
EMnE   And when the scribes and Pharises sawe him eate

ME   with puplicanys and synful men,
EMnE   with publicans and synners,

ME   seiden to his disciplis,   Whi ȝoure maister
EMnE   they sayde vnto his disciples, Howe is it that he

ME   etith and drinkith with puplicanys and synners?
EMnE   eateth and drynketh with publicans and synners?

ME   [17]This thing herd,   Jhesus seith to hem,
EMnE   When Jesus had herde that, he sayd vnto them,

ME   Hoole men han no nede to a leche,
EMnE   The whole have no neede of the visicion,

ME   but thei that han yuele; forsothe I cam
EMnE   but the sicke;   I cam

ME	not for to clepe iuste men, but synners.
EMnE	to cal the sinners to repentaunce, and not the iuste.
ME	[19]And disciplis of Joon and the Pharisees weren fastynge;
EMnE	And the disciples of Jhon and of the Pharises did faste;
ME	and thei camen, and seien to hym,
EMnE	and they cam, and sayde vnto him,
ME	Whi disciplies of Joon and of Pharisees fasten,
EMnE	Why do the disciples of Jhon and off the Pharises faste,
ME	but thi disciplies fasten nat? [19]And Jhesus seith
EMnE	and thy disciples fast nott? And Jesus sayde
ME	to hem, Whether the sonnys of weddyngis mowin faste
EMnE	vnto them, Can the chyldren of a weddinge faste,
ME	as long as the spouse is with hem?
EMnE	whils the brydgrome is with them?
ME	Hou longe tyme thei han the spouse with hem,
EMnE	As longe as they have the brydgrome with them,
ME	thei mowe nat faste. [20]Forsothe dayes shulen come,
EMnE	they cannot faste. Butt the dayes wyll come,
ME	whenne the spouse shal be taken awey from hem,
EMnE	when the bryde grome shalbe taken from them,
ME	and thanne thei shulen faste in thoo days. [21]No man
EMnE	and then shall they faste in thoose dayes. Also no man
ME	seweth a pacche of rude clothe to an old clothe,
EMnE	soweth a pece of newe cloth vnto an olde garment,
ME	ellis he takith awey the newe supplement,
EMnE	for then taketh he awaye the newe pece from the olde,
ME	and a more brekynge is maad.
EMnE	and so is the rent worsse.
ME	[22]And no man sendith newe wyn in to old botelis,
EMnE	In lyke wyse no man poureth newe wyne in to olde vesselles,
ME	ellis the wyn shal berste the wyn vesselis,
EMnE	for yf he do the newe wyne breaketh the vesselles,
ME	and the wyn shal be held out,
EMnE	and the wyne runneth out,
ME	and the wyne vesselis shulen perishe.
EMnE	and the vessels are marde.
ME	But newe wyn shal be sent in to newe wyn vesselis.
EMnE	Butt newe wyne must be poured in to newe vesselles.

A.   Syntax of Phrases

1. Use of definite article (see especially verses 15, 18) _____

_____

2. Use of *do* as auxiliary (see verses 18, 22) _____

_____

3. Formation of future (what is the auxiliary in ME and EMnE?) _____

_____

B.   Syntax of Clauses

1. Word order of independent clauses (see especially verse 21) _____

_____

2. Syntax of questions (see especially verses 16, 18, 19) _____

_____

3. Syntax of imperatives (see especially verse 14) _____

_____

4. Syntax of negative clauses (see especially verses 17, 18, 19) _____

_____

_____

7.16 Lexicon: Loanwords

I. Borrowing from Romance Languages Other Than French

Spanish, Portuguese, and Italian contributed scores of words to the EMnE lexicon. Identify which of these three languages was the *immediate* source of the following words. (In some cases, the *ultimate* source is different, e.g., an American Indian language.) Because Spanish and Portuguese are so closely related, dictionaries may give both as the origin. When this is the case, list both.

1. buffalo _____	11. negro _____
2. cargo _____	12. picturesque _____
3. cedilla _____	13. port (wine) _____
4. flamingo _____	14. rusk _____
5. launch (boat) _____	15. stevedore _____
6. Madiera _____	16. stucco _____
7. manage _____	17. studio _____
8. mandarin _____	18. torso _____
9. miniature _____	19. umbrella _____
10. mosquito _____	20. vanilla _____

II. Borrowings from Other Germanic Languages

A Biography of the English Language lists numerous EMnE loans from Dutch and German and a few from the Scandinavian languages. From which Germanic language group did the following EMnE loans come?

- A. Low or High German
- B. Dutch
- C. Scandinavian, including Swedish, Norwegian, Danish, and Icelandic

1. brackish _____	12. prattle _____
2. frolic _____	13. rumple _____
3. gabble _____	14. simper _____
4. hamster _____	15. slurp _____
5. hug _____	16. snarl _____
6. hustle _____	17. spanner (wrench) _____
7. minx (hussy) _____	18. sprint _____
8. monkey _____	19. tern _____
9. morass _____	20. vole _____
10. narwhal _____	21. widdershins _____
11. ogle _____	22. wiseacre _____

III. Borrowings from non-Indo-European Languages

In addition to those mentioned in *A Biography of the English Language,* English borrowed numerous words during EMnE from languages in Africa, Asia, and the Americas. Identify the language of origin of the following words.

1. bey _____

2. calico _____

3. catalpa _____

4. chintz _____

5. coati _____

6. cot (bed) _____

7. gopherwood _____

8. jute _____

9. kangaroo _____

10. kayak _____

11. paddy (rice) _____

12. taboo _____

13. tattoo (on skin) _____

14. umiak _____

15. wombat _____

16. yaws _____

7.17 Lexicon: Common Nouns from Proper Nouns

A. The following words entered EMnE from various sources, but all originated as proper nouns, as the names of places, of tribes, of people real, fictional, or mythical. Give the origins of the words and indicate the type of proper noun from which they came.

1. agaric _____
2. amaryllis _____
3. bungalow _____
4. charlatan _____
5. clink _____
6. doily _____
7. fauna _____
8. finnan (haddie) _____
9. frangipani _____
10. gage (plum) _____

11. gardenia _____
12. gavotte _____
13. harlequin _____
14. mausoleum _____
15. merino _____
16. mocha _____
17. morris (dance) _____
18. nankeen _____
19. python _____
20. solecism _____

B. The following words, first appearing in EMnE, originated as short forms of given names or as nicknames. Identify the shortened form or the nickname and the full form of the name.

1. dandy _____
2. davit _____
3. dobbin _____
4. grimalkin _____
5. grog _____
6. hick _____
7. jackanapes _____

8. jenny _____
9. jilt _____
10. jug _____
11. magpie _____
12. tomcat _____
13. zany _____

7.18   Lexicon: New Words by Modification of Old Words

I. Shortened Forms

New words are sometimes formed by abbreviating earlier words. This shortening may take the form of

   A. **Aphesis,** or dropping the unstressed first part of a word, as in *squire* from *esquire*
   B. **Clipping,** or dropping the latter part of a word or phrase, as in *soap* from *soap opera*
   C. **Contraction,** or omitting part of the interior of a word or phrase

All of the following shortened words first appeared in EMnE. Identify which of the processes (A–C) was involved and give the original, unshortened form.

1. char (burn) _____   7. rear (behind) _____

2. fancy _____   8. spinet _____

3. fortnight _____   9. trump _____

4. gaffer _____   10. twit (reproach) _____

5. lunge _____   11. whim _____

6. pester _____

II. Blends

A *blend,* or *portmanteau* word, is a word formed, consciously or unconsciously, by combining parts of two different words, usually by taking the first part of one word and the second part of the other, as in *motel* from *motor + hotel*. All of the following probable blends are first recorded during EMnE. For each, identify the two words that were combined. (Dictionaries vary in their treatment of some of these words. If your dictionary does not list some of these as blends, check other dictionaries for their suggestions. *Random House* is especially willing to hazard guesses about the original components.)

1. blurt _____   10. pennant _____

2. chump _____   11. riffle _____

3. clash _____   12. scrawl _____

4. croup _____   13. smash _____

5. flabbergast _____   14. squirm _____

6. flounder (verb) _____   15. toddle _____

7. fluff _____   16. twiddle _____

8. jolt _____   17. whimsy _____

9. jumble _____

18. In what way are most, though not all, of these words semantically similar? _____

_____

Stylistically similar? _____

_____

III. Back Formations

A back formation is a new word created by removing what is mistakenly assumed to be an inflectional or derivational affix from an existing word. For example, the verb *burgle* was created by removing what looked like an agentive suffix from *burglar*. That is, by analogy with such pairs as *walker : walk, bungler : bungle,* and so on, the relationship *burglar : burgle* was created. The following words all originated as back formations. For each, list the earlier form from which it was created and the apparent suffix that was removed to make the new word.

1. asp _____

2. difficult _____

3. dishevel _____

4. fog _____

5. hero _____

6. laze _____

7. mix _____

8. quip _____

9. truck (noun) _____

10. waft _____

7.19 Lexicon: Doublets

PDE has many *doublets,* words ultimately from the same source but borrowed at different times in different forms. Often, one member of the pair was borrowed, especially from French, during ME and then later borrowed from Latin, Greek, or another language during EMnE. All of the following words were borrowed during ME (or earlier). By checking their etymology in a desk dictionary, you should be able to determine the second member of the doublet that was borrowed in EMnE and the ultimate source of the word.

0. balm _balsam (< L. balsamum)_

1. cipher _____

2. compost _____

3. custom _____

4. desk _____

5. envious _____

6. fashion _____

7. influence _____

8. mean (average) _____

9. memory _____

10. mussel _____

11. native _____

12. poor _____

13. priest _____

14. ray (beam) _____

15. reason _____

16. round _____

17. syrup _____

18. vow _____

19. voyage _____

7.20 Lexicon: Reduplication

A. Pure reduplication has always been rare in English, except for echoic words like *ha-ha* or *tweet-tweet*. Most of the reduplicated words in English dictionaries are loans from other languages, though EMnE saw the first of a very few apparently native formations. Identify the language of origin of the following reduplicative words; three are native to English.

1. aye-aye _____
2. bulbul _____
3. bye-bye _____
4. dodo _____
5. furfur (dandruff) _____
6. gru-gru _____

7. haha (ditch) _____
8. kaka (parrot) _____
9. motmot (bird) _____
10. papa _____
11. pooh-pooh _____
12. so-so _____

B. Much more common than pure reduplication in English is *ablaut reduplication,* or reduplication with a vowel change (e.g., *mishmash* or *dribs and drabs*). The EMnE period seems to have been one in which the process was especially productive, examples include *fiddle-faddle, zig-zag, dilly-dally, flim-flam,* and *whim-wham.* All of these involve the alternation of the high front vowel [ɪ] in the first part with the low front [æ] in the second part. Another fairly common ablaut variation is between [ɪ] and [ɑ] or [ɔ]; EMnE examples include *ding-dong, flip-flop,* and *wishy-washy.*

Ignoring the date of entry into English, what are some other examples of ablaut reduplication in [ɪ] / [æ]? _____

_____

_____

In [ɪ / [ɑ] or [ɔ]? _____

_____

C. Another kind of ablaut reduplication is represented by two different words, varying in their vowels, that share similar or almost identical meanings, such as *rile / roil, sweep / swipe,* and *taffy / toffee.* The vowel differences are of various origins, such as dialectal differences and analogy. For each of the following words, provide another word related in meaning but with a different vowel.

1. sleek _____
2. muss _____
3. poppet _____
4. saucy _____
5. snuffle _____
6. thresh _____

7. flop _____
8. hoist _____
9. blat _____
10. slosh _____
11. skim _____
12. snout _____

D. Still another kind of reduplication, also more common than pure reduplication, is rhyming reduplication, as in *peewee* or *fuddy-duddy*. Again, the EMnE period saw many such formations, including *helterskelter, humpty-dumpty, mumbo-jumbo,* and *roly-poly.*

What are other examples of rhyming reduplication? _____

_____

7.21   Lexicon: Words from Borrowed Phrases or Other Parts of Speech

Most of the loanwords into EMnE retained their original part-of-speech category, but sometimes the part-of-speech category was changed. For each of the following, give the language of origin, the original part of speech (or phrase), and the original meaning.

1. alarm (noun) _____

2. alert (verb) _____

3. atone (verb) _____

4. auto-da-fé (noun) _____

5. caret (noun) _____

6. carouse (verb) _____

7. deficit (noun) _____

8. don (verb) _____

9. fiat (noun) _____

10. habitat (noun) _____

11. handicap (noun) _____

12. malaria (noun) _____

13. quota (noun) _____

14. veto (noun) _____

7.22   Lexicon: Lost Vocabulary

The italicized word in each of the following sentences has been lost from the vocabulary of standard PDE (though some of the words may survive dialectally). By consulting the *OED*, determine the meaning of each word and write it in the blank that follows the quotation.

0. "And if ye will, then leave your *bordes,* / And use your wit and show it so." (early sixteenth c.) *jests* _____

1. "old men may love not only without slander, but *otherwhile* more happily than young men" (1561) _____

2. "that hot love is soon cold, that the *bavin* though it burn bright, is but a blaze" (1579)

_____

3. "Reason, in faith thou act well served, that still / Wouldst *brabbling* be with sense and love in me" (1591) _____

4. "Unto life many implements are necessary; *moe,* if we seek, as all men naturally do, such a life as hath in it joy, comfort, delight and pleasure." (1593) _____

5. "and how zealously our preachers *dehort* men from them [women], only by urging their subtleties and policies and wisdom" (1633) _____

6. "what praise could be then due to well-doing, what *gramercy* to be sober, just, or continent?" (1644) _____

7. "set this house on fire with fevers and *calentures*" (1647) _____

8. "extending along a meadow to a *cripple* or brushwood" (1647) _____

_____

9. "The *Monack,* the Musk-Rat, and several others . . . inhabit here in Mary Land." (1666) _____

10. "Shrink his thin essence like a *riveled* flower" (1714) _____

11. "The Major . . . was so bountiful as frequently to throw me a *tester*" (1722)

_____

12. "He called his *hinds* about him, and asked them . . . whether they had ever seen in the fields any little creature that resembled me" (1735) _____

13. "Sits in yon western tent, whose cloudy skirts, / With *brede* ethereal wove" (1746)

_____

14. "The public reputation is, every moment, in danger of being *compromitted* with him." (1787) _____

7.23   Semantic Change

The italicized word or words in each of the following sentences has undergone a semantic shift since EMnE times. With the help of the *OED*, determine the meaning of the word as used in the sentence and indicate the type of semantic change that has occurred since EMnE: generalization, narrowing, amelioration, pejoration, strengthening, weakening, shift in stylistic level, or shift in denotation. In some instances, more than one type of shift may be involved.

1. "The whiteness of her *leer*" (early sixteenth century) _____

_____

2. "The king . . . kept the day of Sainct George at his manor of Greenwich with great solempnity, and the court was greatly *replenished* with lords, knights, and with ladies and

gentlewomen to a great number with all *solace* and pleasure." (1548) _____

_____

3. "King Richard, perceiving them armed, knew well that they came to his *confusion,* and putting the table from him, valiantly took the bill [battleaxe] out of the first man's hand, and manfully defended himself, and slew four of them in a short space." (1569)

_____

4. "the tricks that in young men be gallantness, courtesy, and preciseness so acceptable to women, in them [old men] are mere follies and *fondness* to be laughed at" (1561)

_____

5. "I doubt not but in this register he may find some to content him, unless he be too

curious" (1573) _____

_____

6. "Or blind *affection,* which doth ne'er advance / The truth" (1623) _____

_____

7. "it will be acknowledged even by those that practise it not that clear and *round* dealing

is the honor of man's nature" (1625) _____

8. "if other things as great in the church, and in the rule of life both *economical* and

political, be not looked into and reformed . . ." (1644) _____

_____

9. "The man therefore read it, and looking upon Evangelist very *carefully,* said Whither

must I fly?" (1678) _____

_____

10. "Where unfledged actors learn to laugh and cry, / Where infant *punks* their tender

voices try" (1682) _____

_____

11. "His manners, it is true, are tinctured with some strange inconsistencies, and he may be justly termed a *humorist*" (1762) _____

12. "little regard is due to that bigotry which sets *candor* higher than truth" (1765) ___

_____

13. "The Indians . . . killed and *captivated* all." (1768) _____

_____

14. "A fine shirt with *chitterlings* on the bosom" (1776) _____

_____

15. "Such a sudden diversion of all its circulating money from trade to land, must be an additional *mischief*." (1790) _____

_____

16. "There was no affectation about him; and he talked, as usual, upon *indifferent* subjects" (1791) _____

_____

7.24   Semantics: Semantic Shift in Borrowed Words

Some of the words borrowed during EMnE had undergone a dramatic shift in meaning by the time they reached English or underwent such a shift after entering English. For each of the following, consult a good desk dictionary to determine the language of origin and the original meaning.

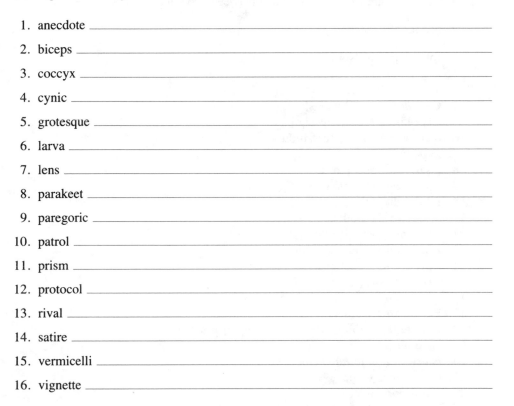

 1. anecdote _____

 2. biceps _____

 3. coccyx _____

 4. cynic _____

 5. grotesque _____

 6. larva _____

 7. lens _____

 8. parakeet _____

 9. paregoric _____

10. patrol _____

11. prism _____

12. protocol _____

13. rival _____

14. satire _____

15. vermicelli _____

16. vignette _____

7.25   Dialects: Eighteenth-Century New England

Used with caution, the writings of literate but poorly educated speakers can be a valuable source of information about earlier stages of the language. James Browne was an eighteenth-century Rhode Island merchant who kept a book of his business letters. The following excerpts are from letters written between 1735 and 1738.

I. Evidence for Phonology

1. for mr *notton* [Norton]
2. take a morgidg *dead* of it
3. a *pritty* good price
4. Capt *hopkings* [Hopkins]
5. Give him a *Resate* [receipt]
6. their best *Rushey* [Russia] duck
7. to *parfection*
8. a safe *Conshius* [conscience]
9. very *Sudently* some go's up
10. I am sadley *disapinted*
11. *instidd* of the holl sum
12. you must *venter* [venture] that
13. I *Bag* you would assiste me
14. a *perticular* freind of mine
15. Give the *Baror* [bearer] a *Resate*
16. you will *obleg* yours to *sarve*
17. Befoar *fardor* orders
18. I muste have him in a *footnit* [fortnight] if *a tall*
19. Give mr mitchl a *Resate*
20. *puaswad* him to *latt* Baror have it
21. to the *naxte* Corte
22. *Consarning* the rum
23. *twantey* two hhds of molasis
24. he did not Receve *tham*
25. I would pray you to *sarch* in to the afair
26. I *sand* you heir [here] *annacounte* of whot . . .
27. sum pots and sum *kittles*
28. the *wather* is so Colde that *orsters* is not to Be Cacht
29. you shall Be no Losar By *sarving* of me
30. *Bagg* of him *anna Counte* not *ondley* of the Rum But of . . .
31. the Coffey that was *Lafte* in his hands
32. *Consarning* mr Jotham
33. I would pray you to *sarch* into the accounte
34. any *purticurler* one
35. this *misfortin*
36. your *whife* is well
37. fail not of *Bringin* of them
38. Geet me sum Beaf Cost whot it *whill*
39. which Being *intarpretid* is patience
40. desire that you *whould* send me
41. your umb[le] *sarvant*

Identify the phonological feature illustrated in the preceding phrases by writing the number of the appropriate phrases in the blank to the right.

A. Omission of preconsonantal or final [r] _____

B. Intrusive [r] _____

C. Final [ŋ] → [n] _____

D. PDE [ð] appears as [d] _____

E. Lack of phonemic /hw/ _____

F. Intrusive consonant _____

G. PDE final [jər] appears as [ər] (and assibilation probably not present) _____

H. PDE assibilation not present _____

I. Earlier [ɛr] → [ɑr] _____

J. Raising of [ɛ] to [ɪ] _____

K. Lowering of [ɛ] to [æ] _____

L. Incomplete GVS; PDE [i] appears as [e] _____

M. PDE [oi] appears as [ɑi] _____

N. Final [ə] → [i] (or [ɪ]) _____

O. False division between words _____

What are possible explanations for the following spellings?

Conshius (No. 8) _____

perticular (No. 14) _____

obleg (No. 16) _____

II. Evidence for Grammar

1. I have thoughts of what you Said to me Concerning *them* fish
2. if you will send them *direct* up here in good Order for Shiping . . .
3. Untill you had *gave* me an account of what you had Cutt
4. he will *Show it you*, if you will *bring it me*, I will give you Twenty Shillings for *so doing of it*
5. I *wonder* you had not *wrote* to me
6. brother Obadiah *is Safe Arrived*, but lost Andrew Harris, *which* died on his passage
7. You are mistaken, *them* Sails *doth* not belong to me
8. I have a Vessell at Nantucket *a whaleing*
9. I am *a going* to send to Boston for Sails
10. you may think that I have *forgott* it . . . but . . . an Article of Eleven pounds Eighteen Shillings & Eight pence is not so soon *forgott*
11. Your wife *remembers* her love to you
12. I would begg the favour of you to send me . . . an Eight inch Cable Sixty *fathom* long
13. tell John Browne that there *is 21 Ox's* left at Sam: Carrs
14. I have According to your desire sent for the Negroe and he *is come*
15. the Charge *in getting of him* is about Seventeen pounds
16. as to your being Concerned in a Sloop with me you write so *Indifferent* about it, gives me Suspition . . .
17. I addmiar you *hath* not sante *them* Cowes and oates you prommosied me

Identify the grammatical feature illustrated in the preceding phrases by writing the number of the appropriate phrases in the blank to the right.

A. Nonstandard plural form _____

B. Singular measure word after number _____

C. Relative pronoun not acceptable in PDE _____

D. Pronoun direct object precedes indirect object _____

E. Nonstandard demonstrative _____

F. Nonstandard strong verb form _____

G. Singular verb with plural subject _____

H. Gerund or present-participle construction not acceptable in PDE _____

I. *To be* as perfect auxiliary _____

J. Plain adverb _____

III. Evidence for Lexicon

In the following selections, the italicized words are used in a way normally unfamiliar in PDE. Check the *OED* to find the meaning intended by James Browne and put it in the blank following the excerpt.

1. Mares will do if they are in good *Case,* they must be between three & *Advantage* & Eight years of Age _____

_____

2. it is *ticklish* times here _____

3. gett me a Jibb Stay—one hundred feet long, and five inches *bigg* _____

_____

4. for a likely *Stone* Horse that you bought of him _____

5. Eight *Tearses* [tierces] of . . . rice _____

_____

6. I will pay them in Rum, hoops, Cydar or some other *truck* _____

_____

7. I hope not to have any more *palavers* before I see the pay _____

_____

8. you write so Indifferent about it, gives me Suspition whether you are *forward* for it or no _____

In the following two sentences, the italicized words are still used in the same meaning, but the phrases are nonetheless not acceptable in PDE. What is the problem?

9. I *wonder* you had not wrote to me _____

_____

10. Your wife *remembers* her love to you _____

_____

7.26   An EMnE Commentator on the Language

During EMnE, for the first time in the history of English, its speakers began to take a serious interest in their language, to describe it, and especially to try to improve it. Most of their works are solemn, plodding, and generally disapproving of the status quo as the authors see it. One exception is Alexander Hume's *Of the Orthographie and Congruitie of the Britan Tongue,* written c. 1617 and dedicated to King James I of England (James VI of Scotland). Its very subtitle, *A Treates, noe shorter than necessarie for the Schooles,* suggests the briskness, clarity, and occasional asperity that characterize this lively little work.

Hume was a Scot; hence his dialect was not that of the standard language in England. But he neither apologizes for his own dialect nor ridicules the language of the south; he seems to accept the two dialects as equally respectable varieties of the same language. There are numerous differences in Hume's northern spelling from that of PDE (and Hume himself is not always consistent), but you should have little difficulty in understanding it.

From the introduction:

May it please your maest excellent Majestie, I, your grace's humble servant, seeing sik uncertentie in our men's wryting, as if a man wald indyte one letter to tuentie of our best wryteres, nae tuae of the tuentie, without conference, wald agree; and that they quhae might perhapes agree, met rather be custom then knawlege, set my-selfe, about a yeer syne, to seek a remedie for that maladie. Quhen I had done, refyning it, I fand in Barret's alvearie, quhilk is a dictionarie Anglico-latinum, that Sir Thomas Smith, a man of nae less worth then learning, Secretarie to Queen Elizabeth, had left a learned and judiciouse monument on the same subject. Heer consydering my aun weaknes, and meannes of my person, began to fear quhat might betyed my sillie boat in the same seas quhaer sik a man's ship was sunck in the gulf of oblivion. For the printeres and wryteres of this age, caring for noe more arte then may win the pennie, wil not paen them-selfes to knau whither it be orthographie or skaiographie that doeth the turne: and schoolmasteres, quhae's sillie braine will reach no farther than the compas of their cap, content them-selfes with ἀυτὸς ἔφη my master said it.

From "Of the Britan Vouales"

1. Of a, in our tongue we have four soundes, al so differing ane from an-other, that they distinguish the verie signification of wordes, as a tal man, a gud tal, a horse tal.

2. Quherfoer in this case I wald commend to our men the imitation of the greek and latin, quho, to mend this crook, devysed diphthonges. Let the simplest of these four soundes, or that quhilk is now in use, stand with the voual, and supplie the rest with diphthonges; as, for exemple, I wald wryte the king's hal with the voual a; a shour of hael, with ae; hail marie, with ai; and a heal head, as we cal it, quhilk as the English cales a whole head, with ea. And so, besydes the voual, we have of this thre diphthonges, tuae with a befoer, ae and ai, and ane with the e befoer, ea. Ad to them au, howbeit of a distinct sound; as, knaulege with us, in the south knowlege.

1. What are the PDE equivalents of the four *a* sounds that Hume discusses here? _____

_____

What is the probable difference between the English and the Scots pronunciation of the vowel in what is today spelled <whole>? _____

_____

7. O, we sound al alyk. But of it we have sundrie diphthonges; oa, as to roar, a boar, a boat, a coat; oi, as coin, join, foil, soil; oo, as food, good, blood; ou, as house, mouse, etc. Thus we commonlie wryt mountan, fountan, quhilk it wer more etymological to wryt montan, fontan, according to the original.

2. What does Hume's statement "oo, as food, good, blood" imply? _____

_____

3. The instrumentes of the mouth, quherbe the vocal soundes be broaken, be in number seven. The nether lip, the upper lip, the outward teeth, the inward teeth, the top of the tongue, the middle tong, and roof of the mouth. Of these, thre be, as it wer, hammeres stryking, and the rest stiddies [anvils], kepping [catching] the strakes of the hammeres.

4. The hammeres are the nether lip, the top of the tongue, and the midle tongue. The stiddies the overlip, the outward teeth, the inward teeth, and the roofe of the mouth.

5. The nether lip stryking on the overlip makes b, m, p, and on the teeth it makes f and v.

6. The top of the tongue stryking on the inward teeth formes d, l, n, r, s, t, and z.

3. Comment on Hume's statement in point 6. Do you think the point of articulation of sounds like [d, l, n, s], and so on, has changed since Hume's time? Or was Hume a poor observer? Or was the articulation of these sounds different in Scots and in southern

English? _____

_____

From "Of Our Abusing Sum Consonantes"

1. Now I am cum to a knot that I have noe wedg to cleave, and wald be glaed if I cold hoep for help. Ther sould be for everie sound that can occur one symbol, and of everie symbol but one onlie sound. This reason and nature craveth; and I can not but trow but that the worthie inventoures of this divyne facultie shot at this mark. . . .

3. First, to begin with c, it appeeres be the greekes, quho ever had occasion to use anie latin word, quharein now we sound c as s, in their tymes it sounded k; for Cicero, thei wryt kikero; for Cæsar, kaisar; and plut., in Galba, symbolizes principia, πρινκίπια.

4. This sound of it we, as the latines, also keepe befoer a, o, and u; as canker, conduit, cumber. But, befoer e and i, sum tymes we sound it, with the latin, lyke an s; as, cellar, certan, cease, citie, circle, etc.

5. Behind the voual, if a consonant kep it, we sound it alwayes as a k; as, occur, accuse, succumb, acquyre. If it end the syllab, we ad e, and sound it as an s; as, peace, vice, solace, temperance; but nether for the idle e, nor the sound of the s, have we anie reason; nether daer I, with al the oares of reason, row against so strang a tyde. I hald it better to erre with al, then to stryve with al and mend none.

4. What is Hume's ultimate position on spelling reform? _____

_____

14. T, the last of these misused souldioures, keepes always it's aun nature, except it be befoer tio; as, oration, declamation, narration; for we pronounce not tia and tiu as it is in latin. Onelie let it be heer observed that if an s preceed tio, the t keepes the awn nature, as in question, suggestion, etc.

5. Has assibilation occurred in Hume's dialect? _____

How did his pronunciation of *question* differ from that of PDE? _____

_____

7. And, be the contrarie, here it is clere that soundes pronunced with this organ can not be written with symboles of that; as, for example, a labiel symbol can not serve a dental nor a guttural sound; not a guttural symbol a dental nor a labiel sound.

8. To clere this point, and alsoe to reform an errour bred in the south, and now usurped be our ignorant printeres, I wil tel quhat befel my-self quhen I was in the south with a special gud frende of myne. Ther rease, upon sum accident, quhither quho, quhen, quhat, etc., sould be symbolized with q or w, a hoat disputation beuene him and me. After manie conflictes (for we oft encountered), we met be chance, in the citie of baeth, with a doctour of divinitie of both our acquentance. He invited us to denner. At table my antagonist, to bring the question on foot amangs his awn condisciples, began that I was becum an heretik, and the doctour spering how, ansuered that I denyed quho to be spelled with a w, but with qu. Be quhat reason? quod the Doctour. Here, I beginning to lay my grundes of labial, dental, and guttural soundes and symboles, he snapped me on this hand and he on that, that the doctour had mikle a doe to win me room for a syllogisme. Then (said I) a labial letter can not symboliz a guttural syllab. But w is a labial letter, quho a guttural sound. And therfoer w can not symboliz quho, nor noe syllab of that nature. Here the doctour staying them again (for al barked at ones), the proposition, said he, I understand; the assumption is Scottish, and the conclusion false. Quherat al laughed, as if I had bene dryven from al replye, and I fretted to see a frivolouse jest goe for a solid ansuer. My proposition is grounded on the 7 sectio of this same cap., quhilk noe man, I trow, can denye that ever suked the paepes of reason. And soe the question must rest on the assumption quhither w be a labial letter and quho a guttural syllab. As for w, let the exemples of wil, wel, wyne, juge quhilk are sounded befoer the voual with a mint [physical movement] of the lippes, . . . As for quho, besydes that it differres from quo onelie be aspiration, and that w, being noe perfect consonant, can not be aspirated, I appele to al judiciouse eares, to quhilk Cicero attributed mikle, quhither the aspiration in quho be not ex imo gutture, and therfoer not labial.

6. In contemporary terminology, what two different pronunciations of the words *who, what, when,* and so on, are at the bottom of this argument? _____

_____

It [the stress] may possesse the last syllab: as supprést, preténce, sincére; The penult: as súbject, cándle, cráftie; The antepenult: as diffícultie, mínister, fínallie; And the fourth also from the end . . . as spéciallie, insátiable, díligentie. In al quhilk, if a man change the accent, he sall spill the sound of the word.

7. Which of the illustrative words here apparently were stressed differently for Hume from the way they are today? _____

_____

CHAPTER **8**

PRESENT-DAY ENGLISH

8.1 Important Terms

1. acronym
2. American Academy of Language
3. American Structuralism
4. Black English
5. Leonard Bloomfield
6. calque (loan translation)
7. Noam Chomsky
8. A. J. Ellis
9. J. R. Firth
10. Benjamin Franklin
11. M. A. K. Halliday
12. hypotaxis
13. James A. H. Murray
14. Lindley Murray
15. *Oxford English Dictionary*
16. parataxis
17. periphrasis
18. Isaac Pitman
19. plain adverb
20. Prague School
21. Received Pronunciation
22. root creation
23. Society for Pure English
24. Noah Webster
25. *Webster's Third New International Dictionary*

8.2   Questions for Review and Discussion

1. Summarize the movement for spelling reform during the nineteenth century.
2. What important developments in English dictionary making have taken place since 1800?
3. Why have efforts to establish a national academy in the United States failed?
4. Distinguish among (a) prescriptive grammar, (b) traditional grammar, and (c) scientific grammar.
5. What changes in the English consonant system have occurred during PDE?
6. What is the chief difference in word stress between American English and British English?
7. What part-of-speech category retains the most inflections in PDE?
8. What verbal inflection that survived into the EMnE period has been lost in PDE?
9. What has happened to plain adverbs in PDE?
10. What type of noun phrase has experienced a great increase between EMnE and PDE?
11. What type of verb phrase first appeared in PDE?
12. Which foreign language(s) has (have) contributed the most loanwords to English during PDE?
13. Why did trade names and acronyms as productive sources of new vocabulary first appear only in PDE?

8.3   Ongoing Changes and Dialectal Variation

Many spelling errors, such as *pray* for *prey* or *vice* for *vise,* result from confusion of two different words normally pronounced the same but spelled differently. Other spelling errors, however, reveal contemporary pronunciation or dialectal variation in some way. Give the probable reason for the deviations from conventional spelling of the following italicized words.

1. "If you have more gears, you won't have to *petal* so hard going uphill." _____

_____

2. "Someone was passing out religious *tracks*." _____

_____

3. "He couldn't move it because it *wheighed* too much." _____

_____

4. "There is no *significant* difference between the two." _____

_____

5. Off-Track *Bedding* (name of a contemporary furniture store; why is the pun possible?)

_____

6. "I was *sought of* tired." _____

_____

7. "Nobody ordered *lamp* chops." _____

_____

8. "The town council passed an *ordnance* against drinking in the park." _____

_____

8.4   Grammatical Trends

What changes in traditional usage do the following suggest?

1. "Michigan Campus Becomes *More Wild* Than the Game" (headline in the *New York Times,* April 5, 1989); "The *most heavy* rainfall will occur in the north" (PBN radio announcer, Orono, Maine) _____

_____

_____

2. Many people object to such sentences as "Drive *slow*" and "Don't feel *bad*." Why? _

_____

3. Why do many people say "for you and *I*" or even "between them and *we*"? _____

_____

_____

4. "*As far as tomorrow,* it should be a beautiful day." (Very common, especially among weather announcers) _____

_____

5. Perhaps nine out of ten people misinterpret the meaning of the second sentence of the Lord's Prayer ("Thy kingdom come. Thy will be done, On earth as it is in heaven.") and read it as a future-tense construction. What does it actually mean and why is it so often misunderstood? _____

_____

6. "I didn't go because I already *saw* the movie." _____

_____

8.5   Lexicon: Loanwords

A.   Although French continues to be the modern language from which English borrows the most heavily, other European languages have also contributed to the PDE lexicon. Because these loanwords have been in the language for a relatively short period of time, their nonnative origin is sometimes obvious in their spelling and even pronunciation (e.g., *putsch* from German or *jai alai* from Spanish). From what European languages have the following words been borrowed?

1. boxer (dog) _____   10. rowan (tree) _____
2. deckle _____   11. rucksack _____
3. dope (substance) _____   12. scrod _____
4. droshky _____   13. slalom _____
5. eisteddfod _____   14. snorkel _____
6. flamenco _____   15. soviet _____
7. hoosegow _____   16. spiel _____
8. mavourneen _____   17. sporran _____
9. poteen _____   18. wanderlust _____

B.   Each of the following words has been borrowed into PDE from a different non-European (though not necessarily non-Indo-European) language. Identify that language.

1. beriberi _____   6. potlatch _____
2. cushy _____   7. safari _____
3. haiku _____   8. swastika _____
4. mukluk _____   9. wapiti _____
5. polo _____

8.6 Lexicon: New Words by Shortening Old Ones

Frequently used words or phrases are often shortened, resulting in a word that may replace the original or at least acquire a separate identity. Shortening may involve any of the following processes.

A. **Clipping** (including **aphesis,** or dropping off the beginning of a word), as in *mike* from *microphone* or *stogy* from *Conestoga*

B. **Contraction,** as in *bos'n* from *boatswain* (the result does not always have an apostrophe)

C. **Back-formation,** as in *self-destruct* from *self-destruction* (rather than the expected *self-destroy*)

D. **Blend,** as in *stagflation* from *stagnation* + *inflation*

E. **Acronym,** as in *OD* from *overdose* or *linac* from *linear accelerator*

For the following items, give the original word or phrase and indicate the process by which it was shortened. In some of the instances, more than one of the processes is involved.

1. aerosol _____
2. amatol _____
3. blimey _____
4. blues _____
5. brash _____
6. bushwhack _____
7. butane _____
8. Conelrad _____
9. coon _____
10. Delmarva _____
11. electrocute _____
12. frazzle _____
13. laddic _____
14. lube _____
15. methadone _____

16. middy _____
17. mum (flower) _____
18. op-ed _____
19. ornery _____
20. ramshackle _____
21. Reaganomics _____
22. recap (summary) _____
23. reminisce _____
24. rev _____
25. Seabee _____
26. sepal _____
27. soccer _____
28. squawk _____
29. sulfa _____
30. telex _____

8.7 Lexicon: Words from Proper Nouns

The process of making new words from proper nouns has continued in PDE. Identify the origin of the following, and indicate whether the proper noun is the name of a place, an animal, a tribe, a real person, or a fictional or mythological person or creature.

1. artesian _____
2. atropine _____
3. bauxite _____
4. bertha (collar) _____
5. bikini _____
6. bowdlerize _____
7. cereal _____
8. cretonne _____
9. dago _____
10. daiquiri _____
11. dobson (fly) _____
12. farad _____
13. fata morgana _____
14. ferris (wheel) _____
15. fez _____
16. gauss _____
17. hansom _____
18. hertz _____
19. julienne _____
20. jumbo _____
21. leghorn _____
22. lesbian _____
23. lima (bean) _____
24. littleneck (clam) _____
25. macabre _____
26. macadamia _____
27. martini _____
28. mazurka _____
29. paisley _____
30. sisal _____
31. stroganoff _____
32. strontium _____
33. tattersall _____
34. thorium _____
35. trudgen _____
36. tulle _____

8.8   Semantics: Recent Semantic Changes

All of the italicized words in the following sentences have been in the language for at least a century (often many centuries). All have undergone semantic changes of some type within the past few years, so recently that none of the new meanings are listed in the first edition of the *OED*, and some of them do not even appear in the second edition. The changes usually involve adding new meanings to words. In some cases, the newer meanings threaten to replace older ones. Some of the new meanings are not yet considered acceptable, but all are frequently encountered. For each word, explain what the newer meaning is and suggest the reason for the semantic change (e.g., technological innovation, euphemism, metaphorical extension, confusion between similar-sounding words).

1. Turn the *antenna* to the right. _____

_____

2. The changes made are only *cosmetic*. _____

_____

3. From this, I *deduct* that he is angry. _____

_____

4. Both of them have *dependency* problems. _____

_____

5. Ellen is totally *disinterested* in tennis. _____

_____

6. We couldn't finish because the computer was *down*. _____

_____

7. Joel has been working with *exceptional* children. _____

_____

8. That rest area has no *facilities*. _____

_____

9. You should have your cat *fixed*. _____

_____

10. It's disgusting the way he *flaunts* the rules. _____

_____

11. The critics all gave *fulsome* praise to our production. (Note: This meaning is listed as obsolete in the first edition of the *OED*.) _____

_____

12. He ran through the *gauntlet* of excuses. _____

_____

13. There's a demonstration for *gay* rights today. _____

_____

14. She's been a *hacker* since she was eight years old. _____

_____

15. Martha was *livid* with anger. _____

_____

16. That hamburger made me *nauseous*. _____

_____

17. They bought a new electric *range*. _____

_____

18. Jobs were scarce during the *recession*. _____

_____

19. His repair service is really a *shoe-string* operation. _____

_____

20. Blutex failed in its *takeover* attempt. _____

_____

CHAPTER **9**

ENGLISH AROUND THE WORLD

9.1 Important Terms

1. accent
2. American Dialect Society
3. American Linguistic Atlas Project
4. Black English
5. Cockney
6. creole
7. dialect
8. English Dialect Society
9. General American
10. Geordie
11. Gullah
12. Krio
13. Hans Kurath
14. William Labov
15. Lallans
16. H. L. Mencken
17. nonrhoticity
18. Pennsylvania Dutch
19. pidgin
20. rhoticity
21. Scots
22. Scouse
23. Sranan
24. Standard British English
25. standard language
26. Strine
27. Tok Pisin

9.2   Questions for Review and Discussion

1. Why are most native speakers of English monolingual?
2. What are some of the factors that have made English the world language?
3. What is the difference between a dialect and an accent?
4. In what ways does standard written English differ from standard spoken English?
5. Summarize the major consonantal differences between Standard British English (SBE) and General American (GA).
6. What is the major prosodic difference between the native English of North America and that of the rest of the world?
7. List some of the differences in morphology and syntax between SBE and GA.
8. Explain why terms relating to transportation differ in Britain and the United States much more than terms in most other semantic fields.
9. Who speaks Cockney?
10. How does the English of England's West Country resemble that of the United States?
11. What historical events have contributed to the difference between Scots English and English English?
12. Summarize some of the major differences between Irish English and SBE.
13. What aspect of Australian phonology is most distinctive?
14. What nonnative influences have contributed heavily to New Zealand English?
15. What are the most important non-English linguistic influences on South African English?
16. Why is it difficult to "map" American dialects back to specific areas in the British Isles?
17. Why are American dialects so similar (compared to British dialects)?
18. What are the major distinguishing features of General American?
19. Which of the major dialectal areas in the United States have the most distinctive (not necessarily distinguished) accents?
20. What are some of the reasons why "r-lessness" seems to be declining in its traditional strongholds in the United States?
21. Is Black English a regional dialect? Explain.
22. In what aspects of the language does Black English differ most strikingly from General American?
23. Why is Canadian English so similar to the English of the United States?
24. What is unique about Newfoundland English?
25. What is unique about Western Atlantic English?
26. Summarize the characteristics that most varieties of nonnative English share.
27. Why is English still at least the second most important language of India?
28. Upon what native variety of English is the (nonnative) English of the Philippines based? Why?
29. Why is English the official language of Nigeria when it has very few native speakers of English?
30. What is unique about English in Liberia?
31. What is the difference between a pidgin and a creole?

9.3   The Dissemination of English

On the accompanying map, use one color to identify those countries in which English is the first language of the majority of the people. Use another color to identify countries in which English is not the primary native language but in which English is either the official state language or a significant second language. (See Chapter 9 of *A Biography of the English Language* for the names of these nations.)

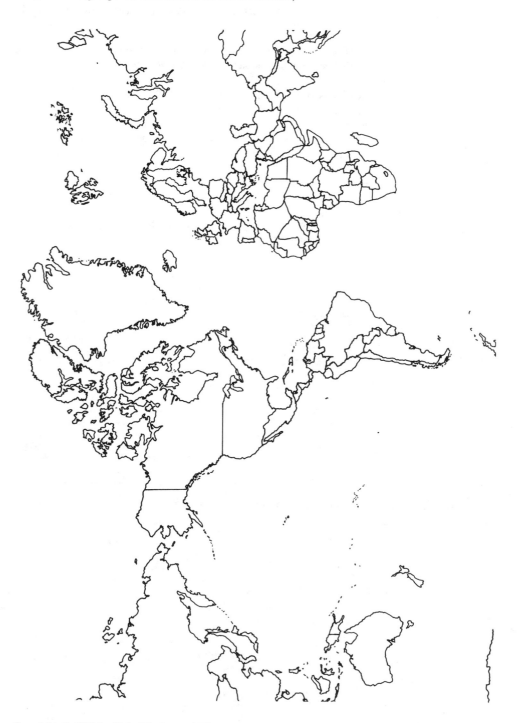

9.4   British English

A. The following is an actual, although abridged, letter received by an American from a friend in Britain. It contains at least nine examples of minor differences between British and American English. Identify these nine differences and state what the equivalent American usage would be for each. Do not count the lack of the possessive form in "Andrew having to have extra time" because Americans do this too. Do not count "headmaster" because many American schools have a headmaster instead of a principal.

> Dear Janet,
>
> How about Easter? That would mean Andrew having to have extra time off school and we would have to clear that with the headmaster. He gets his holidays from 28th March to 15th April.
>
> I have to admit that I was in the States myself last May and I didn't even phone you as I meant to do. But I was only there for seven days and it was all such a rush. Richard went over to sit the professional exam so that he could work in the U.S. We even went down to Williamsburg for a day. This had been highly recommended to us and we thought it was all so pleasant and relaxed though we didn't realise before we went that it was all a tourist trap.
>
> Thank you for the snaps. We thought they were very good ones. It was nice to be reminded of them together again. Andrew has several times started a letter to Jim but he is so lazy he never goes back and finishes them and posts them.
>
> This is election day here. I've just been along and voted Liberal, but Labour seem likely to get in and I don't think that will solve any of our problems.
>
>   Anne

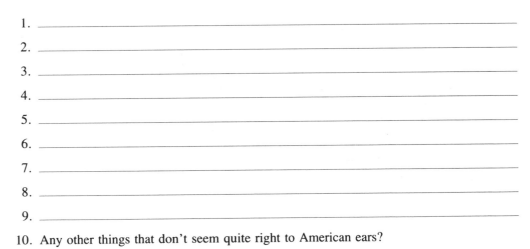

1. _____

2. _____

3. _____

4. _____

5. _____

6. _____

7. _____

8. _____

9. _____

10. Any other things that don't seem quite right to American ears?

_____

_____

B. Although British and American speakers normally have no difficulty in communicating with each other, the natives of each region frequently accuse those on the other side of the Atlantic of having a "strange" sense of humor, of telling pointless jokes, or even of having no sense of humor at all. This misapprehension sometimes results from a difference in vocabulary, as is the case with the following joke told to me by a Scottish child.

> When the woman of the house answered the doorbell, her dog came to the door with her. The man at the door said, "That's a nice dog. What's his name?"
> "Joiner."
> "Joiner? That's a funny name for a dog. Why do you call him Joiner?"
> "Because he does odd jobs around the house."
> "Maybe you should teach him to make a bolt for the door."

Most Americans will see that there are puns involved in *does odd jobs around the house* and *make a bolt for the door*. But if they do not know the British, and especially Scottish usage of the term *joiner,* they will miss the real point of the joke. Look up the word *joiner* in the *OED* or, if available, *The Concise Scots Dictionary*. What does it mean and how does it explain the joke? _____

_____

_____

C. British children sing a ditty to the tune of *Frère Jacques,* to which the only words are "Life is but a melancholy flower." It is broken up for singing as follows:

Life is but a, life is but a
Melancholy flower, melancholy flower
Life is but a melan-, life is but a melan-
Choly flower, choly flower.

What are the puns involved in the first, third, and fourth lines? _____

_____

_____

Why are these not good puns for most American speakers? _____

_____

_____

9.5   Nineteenth-Century Black English

Following is a facsimile of a letter written in 1851 by a young black man named Benewell Kemler to an acquaintance in Pennsylvania; Kemler himself lived somewhere in the American South. Following the facsimile are transcriptions of three other letters that Kemler wrote to his friend Eliza. In the originals of the three transcribed letters, Kemler continues his practice of writing in all or nearly all capitals and of separating all words with periods. In the transcriptions, minimal conventional capitalization and punctuation have been provided.

MACH 1S 1851

ELIZA. MY. DEAR. FREIND. I. AM

WELL. PLEST. THAT YOU. SEND. THAT

BACK. TO MAKE. IF RITHE YOU. HAVE

DONE WELL. I. MADE. IT. FOR SAMUEL

MORAS DAUGHTER. AND. I. AM

VERY. SANKFUL. TO. YOU. DEAR. MASAR

FOR THE. NISC. PRESENT. WICH. YOU

SEND. TO. ME. AND. I. ALSO. SANK. THE. LORD. FOR

HIS. GOODNESS. AND KINDNESS. WICH. I. HAVE

RECEVED. FROM. HIM. BY. MY. DEAR.

FRIENDES. AND. I. AM. GLARDE. TO SEND

LEDERS. TO. YOU. IF. YOU. CAN. REDE. THEM

AND. MY. FRIENS. SEND. ME. LETTES

ANEY. TIME. I. AM. WILLENS TO. PAY

THE. MALE. FOR. THEM. AND. I. HOPE

TO. SEE. YOU. BEFORE. LONG

July the 30 day 1851

My dear friende Eliza. I am more unwell wis a pain in my head and tees and I recevd your wellcom letter the 18 of July I am wery sankfull to my dear friendes for dhar kindness to me. I hope that our Lord will remember my friends for the greate mercy wich they showed to me. My dear friends we had a wery blesen sommer and I was most all the time out doors in the shade. Bud the winder is drawing on now and I must stay in the house. And my friends if you ples send me a coppy book to print in. My dear friend Eliza dis littel book mark I sent for you. Farewell.

The 16 day of October 10.M. 1851

My dear beloved frinde Eliza. I am well as userl and wery glate to hear that you are goen to see my fare distn friends. I hobe they are all well. We are in a wery unwell time. The children are dien wery fast in our nabrerhoot, somtimes too sree in one famely and too of my sisters are sick and too of her children. We ough allways try to doo the will of our Lord while we are well. My friend I receved your kind letter and note the 10 day of October and are wery sankfull for it. Fare ye well my friends. . . .
Benewell H. Kemler

[undated]

My dear friend Eliza. I am as well as comon and I received the kind present of Beulah Moras the 29 of May and I thank her very much for it. I will sent a letter along for Beulah Moras. And I am wery glad to hear of Thomas Wisper and I thank him wery much for his tracs and my dear friends I hobe you will come to see me.

1. Did Benewell Kemler probably speak an "*r*- full" or an "*r*-less" dialect? _____

What words provide evidence to support your answer? _____

_____

2. How did Kemler pronounce /θ/ and /ð/? _____

What is the evidence for your answer? _____

_____

3. What was the probable status of voiced and voiceless stops in his speech? _____

_____

Your evidence? _____

Does the spelling *leders* indicate a voicing of poststress intervocalic /t/ as in modern American English? _____ Why or why not? _____

_____

4. How did he pronounce the suffix *-ing?* _____

How do you know? _____

5. Did Kemler distinguish the words *where* and *wear?* (That is, was /hw/ phonemic for him?) _____ How do you know? _____

_____

6. Do you find any evidence for simplification of consonant clusters (a common feature of Black English today)? _____

_____

7. How did he probably pronounce the word *very?* _____

8. What is the significance of the misspellings *freind, nisc, receved, comon, wellcom, greate, coppy?* _____

_____

9. Does the fact that Kemler usually spells the word *thank* as <sank> but occasionally as <thank> indicate that he similarly varied the pronunciation in his speech? Explain. _

_____

9.6   Literary Representations of Dialect

I. British Regional Dialect

The uniform spelling system of modern written English normally conceals the many phonological differences among English dialects. Some authors, however, use "phonetic" spellings that reflect, to some extent at least, deviations from the standard, whatever version of English the standard itself may be. One such writer is Alan Garner, a British author of supernatural tales for young people. His two young heroes, Colin and Susan, speak Standard British English; standard spellings are used for their dialogue. The farmer Gowther Mossock and his wife Bess, with whom the children spend their holidays, are natives of the West Country of England, and various adjustments to standard spelling are used to represent their speech.

'Well,' said Colin, 'if it's all right with you, we thought we'd like to go in the woods and see what there is there."

'Good idea! Sam and I are going to mend the pig-cote wall, and it inner a big job. You go and enjoy yourselves. But when you're up th'Edge sees as you dunner venture down ony caves you might find, and keep an eye open for holes in the ground. Yon place is riddled with tunnels and shafts from the owd copper-mines. If you went down theer and got lost that'd be the end of you, for even if you missed falling down a hole you'd wander about in the dark until you upped and died.'

'Thanks for telling us,' said Colin. 'We'll be careful.' . . .

'And think on you keep away from them mine-holes!' Gowther called after them as they went out of the gate. . . .*

'The funny thing is,' said Gowther when the children had finished reading, 'as long as I con remember it's always been said there's a tunnel from the copper mines comes out in the cellars of the Trafford. And now theer's this. I wonder what the answer is.'

'I dunner see as it matters,' said Bess Mossock. 'Yon's nobbut a wet hole, choose how you look at it. And it can stay theer, for me.'

Gowther laughed. 'Nay, lass, wheer's your curiosity?' 'When you're my age,' said Bess, 'and getting as fat as Pig Ellen, theer's other things to bother your head with, besides holes with water in them.

'Now come on, let's be having you. I've my shopping to do, and you've not finished yet, either.'

'Could we have a look at the hole before we start?' said Susan.

'That's what I was going to suggest,' said Gowther. 'It's only round the corner. It wunner take but a couple of minutes.'

'Well, I'll leave you to it,' said Bess. 'I hope you enjoy yourselves. But dunner take all day, will you?' . . .

'I suppose you'll be wanting to walk home through the wood again,' said Gowther.

'Yes, please,' said Colin.

'Ay, well, I think you'd do best to leave it alone, myself,' said Gowther. 'But if you're set on going, you mun go—though I doubt you'll find much. And think on you come straight home; it'll be dark in an hour, and them woods are treacherous at neet. You could be down a mine hole as soon as wink' . . .†

*Alan Garner, *The Weirdstone of Brisingamen* (London: Williams Collins Sons & Co. Ltd, 1960), p. 19.
†Alan Garner, *The Moon of Gomrath* (London: William Collins Sons & Co. Ltd, 1963), pp. 11, 12, 13.

A.   1. What do the spellings *inner, dunner,* and *wunner* suggest about the pronunciation of contracted negative auxiliaries? Use phonetic transcription in your answer. _____

_____

2. How do Gowther and Bess pronounce *there* and *where?* _____

_____

3. What do the spellings *any* and *can* suggest about the pronunciation of these words? _

_____

4. What does *nobbut* mean? If you don't know, look it up in the *OED.* _____
From what two words is it formed? _____

5. How does Gowther pronounce the world *old?* _____

6. How does Gowther pronounce *night?* _____ What does this suggest about the
status of the Great Vowel Shift in the West Country? _____

_____

7. Comment on the spelling *th'Edge.* _____

_____

B.   The preceding sample also illustrates several deviations from standard English grammar, some familiar to Americans, others perhaps unfamiliar. Supply a standard English equivalent for the following phrases.

1. *sees as you dunner* _____

2. *Yon place* _____

3. *think on you keep away; think on you come straight home* _____

_____

4. *them mine-holes; them woods* _____

5. *there's a tunnel from the copper mines comes out* _____

_____

6. *I dunner see as it matters* _____

7. *Yon's nobbut a wet hole* _____

8. *choose how you look at it* _____

9. *(it can stay theer), for me* _____

10. *let's be having you* (Hint: You can find the appropriate meaning in the *OED*, where
it is labeled "obsolete.") _____

_____

11. *as soon as wink* _____

II. American Regional Dialect

Because of the limitations of the alphabet, most dialect writers can do little more than hint at phonological features. It is much easier to represent in writing the grammatical and lexical deviations of social and regional dialects. In the following excerpt from Andrew Lytle's "Mister McGregor," the author scarcely hints at phonological features (use of [n] instead of [ŋ] in -*ing* endings is one exception). On the other hand, this relatively brief passage contains at least a score of grammatical and lexical items that deviate from standard written English today. Examine the passage and list these items on the lines below.

> "I wants to speak to Mister McGregor."
>
> Yes, sir, that's what he said. Not marster, but MISTER McGREGOR. If I live to be a hundred, and I don't think I will, account of my kidneys, I'll never forget the feelen that come over the room when he said them two words: Mister McGregor. The air shivered into a cold jelly; and all of us, me, ma, and pa, sort of froze in it. I remember thinken how much we favored one of them waxwork figures Sis Lou had learnt to make at Doctor Price's Female Academy. There I was, a little shaver of eight, standen by the window a-blowen my breath on it so's I could draw my name, like chillun'll do when they're kept to the house with a cold. The knock come sudden and sharp, I remember, as I was crossen a T. My heart flopped down in my belly and commenced to flutter around in my breakfast; then popped up to my ears and drawed all the blood out'n my nose except a little sack that got left in the point to swell and tingle. It's a singular thing, but the first time that nigger's fist hit the door I knowed it was the knock of death. I can smell death. It's a gift, I reckon, one of them no-count gifts like good conversation that don't do you no good no more. Once Cousin John Mebane come to see us, and as he leaned over to pat me on the head— he was polite and hog-friendly to everybody, chillun and poverty-wropped kin especial—I said, Cousin John, what makes you smell so funny? . . . Then I didn't know what it was I'd smelled, but by this time I'd got better acquainted with the meanen.

1. Grammatical Features

_____   _____

_____   _____

_____   _____

_____   _____

_____   _____

_____   _____

_____   _____

_____   _____

_____   _____

2. Lexical Features

_____   _____

_____   _____

_____   _____

_____   _____

3. The context makes it clear that the "speaker" here is white and young. Make a guess as to the geographical location and approximate date when this story supposedly took place. _____

9.7   Regional Variations in Meaning

Despite the extraordinary homogeneity of American speech, there are still extensive differences in lexicon in the various areas of the United States, especially at the colloquial level. Communication is less likely to break down if a word is totally unfamiliar to one of the speakers; he or she can simply ask what the word means. More confusing is the situation where the term means one thing to the speaker and something else to the listener. Give the usual meaning *for you* of each of the following terms. Then, by checking the *Dictionary of American Regional English* or a good general dictionary, find another, different meaning that could lead to confusion to speakers from another area of the country.

1. *bug*, as in "He's always trying to bug me." _____

_____

2. *mango*, as in "Order me a pizza with mangoes." _____

_____

3. *gumption*, as in "He needs a little more gumption." _____

_____

4. *afoul of*, as in "Guess who I ran afoul of this morning!" _____

_____

5. *alley*, as in "You must have dropped it in the alley." _____

_____

6. *wait on*, as in "I'm sick and tired of waiting on him all the time." _____

_____

7. *ambitious*, as in "The trouble with him is that he's too ambitious." _____

_____

8. *cabinet*, as in "That pig had a cabinet for breakfast!" _____

_____

9. *boulevard*, as in "You can't park on the boulevard." _____

_____

10. *cleanser*, as in "I'm looking for a better cleanser." _____

_____

9.8   Written Indian English

The following selections are from the April 1, 1989, edition of *The Hindu* (International Edition), published in Madras, India. The English is fluent and sophisticated and uses an extensive vocabulary. It is clearly not a creole, let alone a pidgin. Nevertheless, there are numerous differences from what one would find in an equivalent American or British newspaper. Read the passages carefully, then identify the differences between American and Indian English in the grammatical and stylistic categories listed after the passages. In some instances the *OED* will provide clues to puzzling constructions (e.g., *berth* in "missed the berth"). *Pan masala* is a popular addictive mixture for chewing, consisting of betel and other ingredients such as spices and tobacco.

I. Political news story

Sailing smooth on troubled waters

Nothing disturbs the equanimity of the Karnataka Chief Minister, Mr. S. R. Bommai, who is already set to earn his partymen's sobriquet, "Sthitapragna", in the midst of the jams that he has been caught in from time to time.

Right now, his partymen are cross with him. It is over the manner of the expansion of his Ministry. He has added 10 more Ministers to his existing team of 11. The exercise has misfired, say his partymen who want him to make amends, sooner than later.

Mr. Bommai's latest pursuit falls into a pattern as a thankless job evoking long faces from those who have missed the berth. His party critics have however missed a point. The striking aspect of Mr. Bommai's Ministry-making is that the exercise materialised, after all. In the process, he had brought his aspirant flock to the verge of desperation and breakdown, either by design or by default.

Lucky number

Seven long months the Chief Minister took to keep his promise, exact to the day, since he constituted his first team of Cabinet Ministers on August 14, 1988, a day after he himself was sworn in. He has a weakness for the numeral 13. He got into the "gaddi" vacated by his illustrious predecessor, Mr. Ramakrishna Hegde, on August 13 last year, with a team of 13, including himself. On March 13, 1989, he expanded his Ministry. Number 13, so it seems, is his mascot.

However he seems to have displeased more people than he has pleased. Instead of a war cabinet that the election year demanded, the Chief Minister has given himself a 'lacklustre' outfit. It need not have taken him that long to form the team that he has is the snide remark one hears in the party.

The Chief Minister has, however, promised a second expansion, within the next one month. He has dangled the carrot, understandably. The Budget session, though a short one, began on March 17, when he presented his first Budget, as Chief Minister, for 1989–90.

II. Letter to the editor

Sir,—Whatever be the merits of the Budget presented by the Union Finance Minister, Mr. S. B. Chavan, the salaried man has been badly let down again. The salaried class has been bracketed with cigarette and pan masala. As Mr. Chavan has put it "a spoonful of sugar makes the medicine go down". The IT cut on the first slab is nothing but a spoonful of sugar. The surcharge on income above Rs. 50,000 is a cruel joke on the already over-burdened tax-payer. This indirectly makes a salaried man feel that it is no use asking for an increase in pay, for an increase in pay will only mean a disproportionate increase in the tax burden.

The Budget therefore is a poor man's Budget in the sense that it makes a middle income earner a poor man.

The concession under section 80C will be only a pittance unless the scheme of deduction is changed to benefit the tax payer. The exemption limit of income could have been raised to atleast [sic] Rs. 25,000 or under Section 80C the deduction could have been raised to 100 per cent of the first Rs. 15,000 and 50 per cent of the balance. The salaried man, the most honest tax payer, now feels that he has been let down. Truly, this should not be the price for honesty.

However, the Finance Minister deserves kudos for making cigarettes, pan masala and the idiot box costlier. It is hoped against hope that this will discourage people from falling a prey to any one of these. This will contribute to the social and moral health of the economy and not to the economic health of the economy as desired by Mr. Chavan.

III. Stock market report

Smart recovery in stock markets

A spurt in values at the fag end of the week was the highlight of trading on the Bombay Stock Exchange for the week upto [sic] March 25.

Share prices began lower and dropped further in the absence of support and offerings. Speculative support was not emerging in the initial stages due to end of account considerations. Most of the bull operators preferred to reduce their overall commitments by unloading. The decline was not heavy as bears were covering their earlier short sales. The sellers were, however, more than the buyers.

However, the downward march proved shortlived and equities staged a smart recovery on Thursday on shortcovering. Bull operators also turned aggressive buyers because of first day of new account trading. The final list showed a mixed trend.

There were only three sessions due to closure of market for two days.

IV. Book review

Love story

THE LAST WORDS: By Sukumar Chatterjee, Sangeeta Chatterjee, 50, Protapaditya Place, Calcutta–700 026; Rs. 50/.–

A highly independent and religious Shubhamoy, on a wandering adventure, reaches Bombay penniless and chance-meets a fabulously rich Sindhi woman. Already married, young Eva shows extraordinary interest in the well-groomed Bengali youth; but, the upright Shubho discovers the trap in time and gives the slip.

In his next phase of adventure, Shubho takes up a job in Madras and develops acquaintance with an innocent local belle, Damini. Soon their friendship blossoms into a deep love. Shubho, however, meets his villain in Damini's father who is bent on exploiting his daughter's dancing skill to grow rich. Becoming aware of her father's plot to murder her lover, a shocked Damini falls seriously ill. Forced to leave Madras, Shubho moves to Aurobindo Ashram at Pondicherry with memories of Damini and hopes of getting united with her in wedlock some day.

V. Film Review

'Pattukku Oru Thalaivan'   Tamil

A familiar plot of an innocent rustic youth going through the vicissitudes of life to face the challenges of society is retold with some humour in the first half in Tamil Annai Creations' "Pattukku Oru Thalaivan." The title has little to do with the hero but Vijayakanth, as the uneducated youth in love with the MLA's daughter, steals most of the frames here where director Liyakath Ali Khan provides him his script, with veiled vulgarity, to keep the proceedings going.

The hero is considered a bungler by his parents because of his over enthusiasm to help others and not being wordly-wise. The director brings in enough scenes to show this weakness of the hero which Vijayakanth seizes avidly. The sequence where hero Arivu's father Veluchamy (M. N. Nambiar does a neat job) taking out the cow for breeding with Arivu's questions providing a few guffaws is to show the hero's poor knowledge of breeding, which even children in villages are aware of, then thank god, he knows the difference between a cow and bull as he sings along with his friends "how can one milk a bull!"

Vijayakanth is all fire and brimstone in the second-half where the plot takes the familiar lines crashing and burning cars highlighting the climax where Rajarajan's camera makes the best use of the action. So also his lens beautifully picturising the fountain background of Brindavan for the song sequence.

Shobana is the heroine Shanti, unable to give her consent to marry Arivu because of her father's (Vijajayakumar) cunning tactics. Her gazelle like features add to the elegance of her work. Senior artist K. R. Vijaya as the mother of the hero shows the younger elements what an understanding portrayal means. There is nothing much in the S. S. Chandran—Senthil comedy.

"Ninaithathu yaaro" (lyrics: Gangai Amaran) is a beautiful number tuned in by Ilayaraja.

VI. Cassette review

Penchant for speed   **MADRAS**

Carnatic music lends plenty of scope for innovation but it does not imply the rendering being converted into jazz or choir types of presentation. Also, respect for tradition provides an unwritten injunction that the form of the songs should be in the tempos usually adopted. The young Ganesh-Kumaresh have a penchant for speed and almost all the songs in the two volumes of their violin recital, released by AVM audio, are in the fast pace. The swaras too are so fast that the beauty of the various combinations is beyond the pale of an ordinary listener.

No doubt, their technical skill is superior, the sruti absolutely pure and such a rendering requires remarkable practice and precision. They combine perfectly and bow in a masterly manner but these plus points alone cannot be ennobling. They can be termed Mod-music. The opening Kamalamanohari of Thyagaraja itself reveals their racing style. Such a small piece does not require elaborate swaras but perhaps the youngsters expect the listeners to admire their virtuosity. The familiar Nalinakanti piece resembles an English tune. The Hindolam piece of Papanasam Sivan has an overdose of swaras, though pure, yet with a variety of unfamiliar combinations. Listening to the Sindhu Mandhari, one feels he is inside a church where western instruments are played. Both have however excelled in the Kalyani raga elaboration.

VII. Personal advertisement

Matrimonial

Straightforward, simple, openminded lifepartner wanted for an Indian girl, 26. Preferably with profound interest in cosmology, metaphysics, psychology, philosophy and Rajayoga. With a liking for nature and adventure. With a strong belief in good and virtue. Preferably interested in the elimination of evil. Preferably below 33. Compatible person with other interests acceptable. Absolutely no bars. Write to . . .

1. Native (non-English) vocabulary items _____

_____

2. Unexpected meanings of English words or phrases _____

_____

3. Unfamiliar compounds or phrases, including hyphenation differences _____

_____

_____

4. Unexpected use or omission of definite or indefinite articles _____

_____

5. Differences in verb tenses or moods _____

_____

_____

6. Differences in punctuation _____

_____

_____

7. Unexpected incomplete sentences _____

_____

_____

8. Unfamiliar treatment of idioms or colloquialisms _____

_____

_____

9. Stylistic differences, especially mixing of stylistic levels _____

_____

_____

_____

10. Other differences _____

_____

_____

_____

9.9   Melanesian Pidgin

Melanesian Pidgin, or Tok Pisin, originated during the nineteenth century in the northern part of Papua New Guinea and has spread throughout the country and to neighboring islands. It is an important *lingua franca* in an area that has scores of indigenous, mutually unintelligible languages. Tok Pisin is sufficiently well established to have developed dialectal differences. However, because English is the language of most education, commerce, and diplomacy in the country, Tok Pisin is under constant influence from the standard language.

The following excerpt is from a Melanesian culture-contact myth. A relatively free translation follows the passage.

Orait. Em tufela man, hir—wanfela manki, na wanfela pusi. Em

_____

manki tru hir, i-gat longfela tel. I-no pikinini, i-manki tru. Orait.

_____

Em tufela i-go long bush. Tufela go wokim bigfela hol long graun.

_____

Gisim spaten, na wokim bigfela hol i-go dawn tumas. Orait.

_____

Wokim finis, tufela i-go gisim bigfela ston. Baimbai ston i-fas long

_____

ai bilong hol. Baimbai olsem dor hir. Na tufela i-go long ples

_____

bilong waitman. Tufela wetim tudark, na tufela wokabaut long

_____

nait i-go. Tufela i-go kamap long ples bilong waitman. Orait. Na

_____

tufela stilim plenti samting bilong waitman—plenti nadarkain

_____

samting. Tufela stilim machis, stilim laplap, stilim masket, stilim

_____

katlas, stilim shu, stilim tinbulmakau, stilim cher, stilim tebal,

_____

blanket oltageder sumting bilong waitman. I-no gat wanfela

---

samting tufela i-no stilim.*

Translation

Very well, [There were] these two men—one monkey and one cat. It was a real monkey, which had a long tail. It wasn't a boy, it was a real monkey. Very well. The two of them went to the bush. They went and made a big hole in the ground. They took a shovel and made a big, deep hole. Very well. When they had made it, they went and got a big stone, to fasten it at the mouth of the hole. Then it was like a door. Very well. Then they went to the European's village. They waited until dark, and then walked along in the night. They went and arrived at the European's village. Then they stole many of the European's things—many things of all kinds. They stole matches, stole loincloths, stole muskets, stole cutlasses, stole shoes, stole tinned beef, stole chairs, stole tables, blankets, all of the European's things. There wasn't a single thing they didn't steal."

With the help of the translation, you should be able to identify most of the underlying English words or phrases. Fill in as many of the rest as you can. *Na* means "and"; *-fela* (<*fellow*) is an adjective suffix for single-syllable adjectivals. *Em* is an all-purpose third-person pronoun (= *he, she, it, him,* etc.).

1. What is the verb suffix? _____

2. What is the possessive marker? _____

3. What does *i-* signify? _____

4. Is a distinction made between singular and plural of nouns? _____

*From Robert A. Hall, Jr., *Hands off Pidgin English* (Sydney: Pacific Publications Pty. Ltd, 1955), p. 139.

9.10 Surinam Creole

Surinam Creole, also called Taki-Taki or Sranan, is an English-based creole that is the language of coastal Surinam and a *lingua franca* for the entire country (which has two other English-based creoles). Surinam was first settled by the English, but was then ceded to the Dutch in 1667 in exchange for New York. It became independent of the Netherlands in 1975. Because of this political history, Sranan has been without significant influence from standard English for over three centuries. Hence, unlike the pidgin Tok Pisin, it is virtually unintelligible to an English speaker.

In addition to its English base, Sranan has had influence from Dutch and Portuguese. For example, in the following passage, the words *tanta* 'aunt,' *omu* 'uncle,' and *erken* 'recognize' are from Dutch (*tante, oom, herkennen,* respectively). The word *sabi* 'know' is from Portuguese *saber; pikin* 'children' is ultimately from Portuguese *pequeninho* 'very small,' but it is widespread in English pidgins around the world (cf. English *pickaninny* from West Indian pidgin). *Fesa* 'feast' could be from Portuguese *festa,* but could equally well be from English *feast* or Dutch *feest.*

This Sranan excerpt is much more difficult to read as an "English" text than the Tok Pisin passage. However, with the aid of the translation, you should be able to identify a number of the underlying English words, especially in the first three sentences. Fill in as many as you can.

Mi papa no lobi mi moro. A no lobi mi mama tu. A no lobi mi

_____

mama pikin tu. Me tanta dati, fu mi mamasey, a no lobi srefsrefi.

_____

Famari fu papasey di e seni suku pikin gebroke a e yagi. "Meki

_____

den suku masra efu go na lansigron! Mi no ben opo fraga seni

_____

kari no wan sma!" Wan leysi wan famiri seni kari en fu kon na

_____

wan fesa. Ma di na wan omu fu Nelis ben erken na lutu fu na

_____

famiri dati, sobu fu di den no ben de trutru famiri, en ati teki faya.

_____

"Mi dati no bay famiri! Mi no sabi fu san ede den piki ebi poti na

_____

wi tapu!" Nanga dati a tori kaba.*

_____

Translation

My father doesn't love me anymore. He doesn't love my mother either, nor does he love her children. My aunt on my mother's side, he can't stand her at all. He sends away his

*From Jan Voorhoeve and Ursy M. Lichtveld, eds., *Creole Drum: An Anthology of Creole Literature in Surinam,* trans. Vernie A. February (New Haven: Yale Univ. Press, 1975), pp. 260, 261, 262, 263.

own relations when they come to ask for something. "Let them look for a man or go to the almshouse. I have no flag at the mast inviting people to come and fetch something." Once a member of the family invited him to a feast. But because one of Nelis's uncles had recognized this branch of the family, so that, as far as he was concerned, they were not really family, he became angry. "I did not buy family. I don't understand why they cause us this trouble." And that was that.

1. What is the negative marker? _____

2. What is the undeclinable first-person singular pronoun? _____

3. What does the word *a* mean? _____

4. Many pidgins and creoles include reduplicated words; the Tok Pisin passage had *laplap* 'loincloth.' One example in this Sranan passage is *srefsrefi*. The root of a second

reduplication is an English adjective. What is it? _____

Acknowledgments

Excerpt from *A Bowl of Bishop* by Morris Bishop, copyright © 1954 by Morris Bishop. Used by permission of Doubleday, a division of Bantam, Doubleday, Dell Publishing Group, Inc.

Photographs of handwriting from AElfric, Abbot of Eynsham; Reginald Peacock; and Edward Gibbon from Verlyn Klinkenborg, Herbert Cahoon and Charles Ryskamp, *British Literary Manuscripts, Series 1, from 800 to 1800* (New York, 1981): pp. 2, 9, and 115. Copyright The Morgan Pierpont Library.

Photograph of the Beowulf manuscript, folio 190r of BM MS. Cotton Vitellius A.xv, courtesy The British Library.

Excerpts from Cecily Clark, ed., *The Peterborough Chronicle, 1070-1154* (Oxford: Clarendon Press, 2nd ed. 1970): pp. 8-9, 60.

Excerpts from Kenneth Sisam, ed., *Fourteenth Century Verse & Prose* (Oxford: Clarendon Press, 1921): p. 14, 1. 25-p. 16, 1. 95; p. 41, 1. 1-p. 42, 1. 32; p. 117, 11. 1-9.5; and pp. 118-119, 11. 49-65.

Excerpt from Henry Sweet, ed., *The Oldest English Texts*; Early English Text Society O.S. 83 (1885; repr. 1966), pp. 447-49.

Excerpt from Henry B. Wheatley, ed., *Alexander Hume: Of the Orthographie and Congruitie of the Britan Tongue*; Early English Text Society O.S. 5 (1870; repr. 1965), pp. 1, 2, 9-10, 11, 12, 13-14, 16, 18, and 22.

Photograph of *Mandeville's Travels* from top portion of Bodley Rawlinson manuscript D.99, f. 8v, courtesy of the Bodleian Library, Oxford.

Excerpt from N.F. Blake, ed., *Middle English Religious Prose* (York Medieval texts [Edward Arnold], 1972), pp. 53-54.

Excerpts from Rolf Kaiser, *Medieval English: An Old English and Middle English Anthology* (1961 impression), Proclamation of Henry III, pp. 347-48; William Caxton's Prologue to Chaucer's *Canterbury Tales*, p. 566.

Excerpts from *The Works of Geoffrey Chaucer, Second Edition.* Copyright © 1957 by F.N. Robinson, Editor. Used with permission of Houghton Mifflin Company.

Photograph of Roger Williams' letter to the Providence Town Meeting courtesy of the Rhode Island Historical Society.

Excerpts from April 1, 1989 issue of *The Hindu* (International Edition).